MW00440305

"Memories swirl by: hope, joy, sorrow—a jumble of thoughts and feelings, music and song, interlaced with teasing glimpses into the unknown, as made manifest by a remarkable series of synchronicities ..."

The Doves
of Synchronicity

A true story

Bryan Flamig

Desert Skies Publishing
Phoenix, Arizona

Published by Desert Skies Publishing
PO Box 22140, Phoenix, AZ 85028
www.desertskiespublishing.com

Printed in the United States of America.

Paperback: ISBN 978-0-9832534-0-2

Book and cover design by Bryan Flamig.
Cover photo and author photo by Leslie Nelson.
Catherin illustration by Bryan Flamig.
Digital photo manipulations by Bryan Flamig.

Typeset in Whitman and Avenir fonts.

---

[1]Catherin's songs are published under a pseudonym.

Contents

Lyrics

Acknowledgements

Thanks to my wife Leslie for allowing me the many hours it took to finish this manuscript, and for providing valuable critique and help with copy-editing. I know it must have been awkward for her, given the subject matter.

Thanks to Barb Atwell, Barbara Shock, and Tansy Mattingly for their review of early drafts of this work, and for the valuable feedback they provided. Thanks also to my brother Chris, for his review and for serving as a springboard to bounce off ideas and to help make sure the metaphysical topics were presented consistently and coherently. And thanks to my brother Marlen for his input, and for catching a stray word or two.

Special thanks go to Laurie Lewis and Judy Sanders, for graciously allowing me to incorporate lyrics of their songs in such an integral way. This story would have suffered greatly without these lyrics.

In Memory of
Catherin

Prologue

A summer's eve, 1987

Though exhausted and emotionally spent, I toss and turn in bed, memories of Catherin haunting me. *It's not possible she's gone,* I say to myself, tears streaming down. *It's just not.*

And maybe she isn't gone, really. For what to make of the day's events—this, the day of her memorial? The events replay in my mind: Sitting with eyes closed in reverie that morning, feeling her presence nearby; a friend coincidentally touching my shoulder, sending shivers down my back when she says, "You know Catherin is here with you, don't you?" And later, under darkening skies, having torches flare unexpectedly as we carry them down an old irrigation canal and plant them to stand as guard and witness to the *Magic Farm*—her secret place of solace.

Maybe tonight her spirit roams the green fields and cottonwood trees of the Magic Farm. Or maybe she's beside me now, trying to communicate.

"Catherin, if you are still here, show me a sign. Give me some proof."

I speak the words out loud and close my eyes to wait for sleep, hoping she'll appear in my dreams.

The next morning I rise and prepare for work, disappointed that no dreams of her have come in the night, and disappointed that no signs have presented themselves either. I grab a clean pair of pants from my dresser. Something falls out with them. It's a small, fuzzy wad of paper—like something you might find in the pocket of laundered jeans. Printed on the paper's surface is one word:

"Proof."

Chapter 1.
The Dark-Haired, White Mountain Bike Woman

Late summer, 1986

M y heart races as the banjo player nears the end of his solo. Soon it will be my turn. *Key of C,* I tell myself while testing notes on the fiddle, *that's what we're playing in … I think.* A bass player named Dwight interrupts my concentration.

"You're next, Bry," he says. "Are you ready?"

Dwight keeps a steady beat on his stand-up bass, while sounds of fiddles, guitars, mandolins, and banjos bounce off the saguaro-covered slopes of Squaw Peak Park. Crammed under the shade of a ramada are twenty or thirty musicians—the less fortunate ones spilling onto an adjacent patio under full assault of the Phoenix sun.

The monthly picnic and jam session is in full swing. It's a typical bluegrass session: First the musicians establish a tune by playing in unison, and then each player takes a turn in the spotlight, improvising on the melody and chords. It's an opportunity for players to polish their chops, and for the more experienced, a chance to show off a little.

With the frantic banjo licks of the last break fading away, all eyes turn to me. I have to think of something quick. In a panic, my mind goes blank and I forget which key we're playing in. The sour notes of my first few guesses leave me wincing.

In my dreams, I fire off an impressive set of riffs, each note following with perfection the fast changing chords. Everyone is amazed by my fiddling talents. I'm popular in the local bluegrass and folk music circles. I fit in. No longer am I that introverted, socially awkward computer programmer. No longer are my girlfriends few and far between.

In reality, my bowing is tentative, my tone thin and scratchy, and my fingers fumble through a series of disjointed arpeggios while

I struggle to find the right key. Eventually I recover and succeed in patching together the semblance of a solo, even managing to include a few well-chosen blues notes at the end.

"Nice job!" says Dwight. "I liked that last riff."

"Thanks," I say. "Even if it *was* pure luck."

I just wish my luck extended to meeting members of the opposite sex. Out of a lonely habit, I scan the crowd. There are a few women present—a guitar player or two, and another fiddler, but all appear spoken for.

The ongoing music attracts a number of onlookers who are mostly hikers and bikers threading their way along the interconnected trails of the park basin. Softly playing backup fiddle while a mandolin player picks his way through a turn in the spotlight, I lift my gaze out across the roadway leading to the ramada.

That's when I see her.

Riding up the roadway is a woman on a white mountain bike. A blue T-shirt and brown shorts reveal an attractive, earthy gal of medium height and weight. She stops at the end of the parking lot and leans on the handlebars of her bike to watch us play. Her dark, slightly curly hair, which reaches down to her shoulders, frames an expression of loneliness written on an otherwise pleasant face. This woman of fair complexion looks to be in her thirties, and I sense hidden qualities waiting to be discovered.

Here's someone for me, I say to myself. *She's perfect.*

With a wistful gaze, I saw back and forth on the strings of my fiddle. The woman doesn't seem to notice me, but she does seem interested in the music, watching intently as she sips a water bottle. Maybe she'll ride closer to the ramada. Maybe I'll find a way to talk to her, and maybe …

Fat chance. The dark-haired, white mountain bike woman rides away, taking opportunity with her.

~ ~ ~

After returning to my apartment, I don't give the dark-haired, white mountain bike woman a second thought. There isn't time. The phone rings as I walk through the door. I pick up and say hello.

"Mr. Flamig," says the person on the other end, in a deep, robotic voice. "Your presence is requested at the Interdisciplinary Intelligence Perspectives meeting tomorrow night."

I laugh. It's a colleague from the university, calling to remind me about the monthly meeting of a study group we had both joined earlier in the year.

"Dr. Thomason, I presume," I say to that robotic voice, paraphrasing a famous quote about a certain Dr. Livingston. It was an inside joke to greet Dr. Thomason this way.

Not really a PhD, we tagged Dr. Thomason with that title because of his aspirations in the doctoral program at Arizona State, and with his light-brown, professorial beard, he played the part perfectly, especially when he pontificated at length on the topic of the day.

Usually those topics centered on computers and artificial intelligence, or AI as it's called. AI is a field of study that endeavors to impart intelligence onto computers. It's a tricky field, for no one knows what intelligence is, let alone how to create it. That challenge drew me to AI, and I once worked in a robotics lab at the university, where I met Dr. Thomason.

Old-time fiddling and robotics. What could they possibly have in common? One is warm, creative, alive; the other, just the opposite. So why the attraction to both? It's a mystery, even to me. But whatever the reason, it's in my nature to live in these separate, very different worlds. I definitely have the interdisciplinary inclinations of our study group.

"So what's the meeting about tomorrow?" I ask Dr. Thomason.

"Um, you should know," he replies. "You're the main speaker."

"I am? ... I am!" I slap myself on the forehead. "I completely spaced it."

"That's what I figured," says Dr. Thomason. "You do remember what you were going to talk about, don't you? Programming in Prolog? The best computer language for AI, you keep saying?"

"Ah, yes," I reply. "I was going to show how Prolog is just as general as the language Lisp. You Lisp'ers are always telling me otherwise."

"Not for me to judge," says Dr. Thomason. "I'm curious, though, what your arguments will be."

Lisp is an older rival language to Prolog, and many consider Lisp the gold standard for writing AI applications. But Prolog feels more natural to me.

Prolog stands for 'Programming in Logic.' The language is designed to follow chains of logical inferences—mimicking, however crudely, the way humans think when problem solving. There is controversy whether we think that way, and I agree with much of the criticism. We humans are anything but logical.

"Both languages are complete," I tell Dr. Thomason. "Meaning anything you can do in one, you can do in the other. But it's how they go about it that counts."

"And what is Prolog's claim to fame?" asks Dr. Thomason. "Besides implementing logic."

"It's all about symbolic processing," I say. "Taking symbols and building them into structures, and then tearing them apart and rearranging them in new ways. It's about matching patterns of symbols."

"And that's important because?"

"Recognizing patterns is central to intelligence, and to perception—to the way we see and hear. It's fascinating how completely different fields of endeavor can have things in common—patterns that keep appearing."

I hadn't always been interested in such matters. I started my career in mechanical engineering. That led to work in control systems—in a group that designed space-based telescope pointing mechanisms—and that led to robotics, which led to artificial intelligence, which led to the study of intelligence in general, which led to philosophy, and finally to a branch of philosophy known as metaphysics: the study of the nature of reality itself, including the relationship between mind and matter.

During this time I had read many books on these subjects, books like Douglas Hofstadter's *Gödel, Escher, Bach*; and *Metamagical Themas: Questing for the Essence of Mind and Pattern*. And unlike many of my colleagues I wasn't averse to delving into more esoteric, non-scientific topics like New Age spirituality—anything that challenged my notions of how it is we are alive and self-aware.

The Interdisciplinary Intelligence Perspectives group was comprised of individuals who weren't just computer science majors. Some had engineering backgrounds—Dr. Thomason was into hard-core electronics; others came from liberal arts backgrounds, like philosophy and psychology. But few had a more diverse background than me: old-time fiddling, mechanical engineering, and computer science. Over the years I've tried to unify these seemingly disparate interests. And the key word here is *unify*, a subject I planned on talking about at the meeting: something at the heart of Prolog called *unification*.

Prolog unification is concerned with pattern matching. A pattern might have *holes*—missing items that other matching, compatible patterns can fill. The patterns are *unified* together to create new patterns with no holes. These completed patterns serve as answers. A Prolog program is basically a list of facts—or relationships—and a set of rules to follow when consulting these facts. A goal is declared—essentially a pattern with missing items, and it's these items that are filled in by discovery when the program runs, using pattern matching. The missing items are unified with known facts, using a chain of logical inferences, thus solving the goal.

I summarize this to Dr. Thomason. "Somehow," I tell him, "I'm going to illustrate how unification works at the meeting tomorrow. I want to use simple examples."

"I'm looking forward to seeing what you come up with," says Dr. Thomason.

And just what *am* I going to come up with? After the phone call I worry about this the rest of the evening. I get out my fiddle and play for a while, hoping the movement of bow and fingers will trigger something in my mind. My thoughts drift to the jam session earlier in the day, and to the attractive, dark-haired, white mountain bike woman that happened by. What a match she would be …

That's it. That's my cue! I lay my fiddle down to find pen and paper, quickly jotting down a few notes. Problem solved.

~ ~ ~

The next day I arrive on campus and find the room in the engineering center where the meeting is being held. I'm nervous. I don't like speaking in front of people, because my mind doesn't function well in such settings. I'm more a deep thinker in the back room, not an off-the-cuff, out front guy.

No matter, I have my talk well-prepared. To illustrate unification, I use an example I came up with the previous evening: Suppose you wish to find a woman to go out with, someone who has dark hair and likes bluegrass. The missing item: the woman. A program to find her might contain a list of single women and their associated hair color and interests. The program would then match this goal against the database of women, and the result would be a candidate list of those having the desired attributes.

After giving this example I move on to more abstract ones, trying to show, with much technical and theoretical hand-waving, that through the use of pattern-matching and unification, Prolog is as powerful and general purpose as any computer language.

I don't know whether I succeed in convincing anyone in the group, but you'd think, given my familiarity with pattern matching and general curiosity about the workings of perception, that I'd have better skills in recognizing and responding to what was coming next in my life.

Well, you'd think.

~ ~ ~

Late summer turns into early fall. I'm back at Squaw Peak for another bluegrass picnic, something I'd been attending regularly since the spring, back when my former fiddle teacher, Jessie, had encouraged me to meet other musicians and start playing in public.

And who do I see when I drive up to the ramada? Jessie, her long, black hair swishing in the breeze while she plays a bluegrass tune—on her cello. Her boyfriend is there too, playing banjo. Fiddle in hand, I join the crowd and watch.

Jessie often furrows her brow in an endearing way that's unique to her. But she would stand out in a crowd anyway, for who else plays fast fiddle tunes on a cello. And who else also plays fiddle—but like a cello? I've seen her do this while standing, propping the fiddle on her knee.

Jessie sees me and smiles, lifting her head in acknowledgement. When the tune ends I go over to say hello.

"It's good to see you," says Jessie, giving me a hug. "I'm glad you took my suggestion and started coming to these jams."

"Oh, I've been coming for months," I say. "But where have you been? I haven't seen you in ages."

"That's the life of us professionals," Jessie says, light-heartedly. "We don't usually have time for any fun."

Jessie plays in a local country band, along with her boyfriend. She also teaches lessons on cello and fiddle, and is enrolled at Arizona State in the music program.

On Jessie's right a woman leans on her stand-up bass. She looks familiar. Jessie nods in her direction.

"Do you know Sherry?" Jessie asks me.

I say hi and shake hands with Sherry. She has blonde, shoulder-length hair and a friendly demeanor that makes me think she must be from the Midwest, like me.

"A bass player, huh?" I say to Sherry. "Do you know Dwight? He plays bass too."

"I do," says Sherry. "We often trade bass duties at these jams."

"I thought I'd seen you before," I say.

As we're talking, Jessie and her boyfriend begin packing their instruments away.

"You guys aren't leaving are you?" I ask Jessie.

"We hate to," she says, "but we've got a gig tonight." She then adds with a chuckle, "Say Sherry, be sure to keep Bryan in line."

Jessie and her boyfriend soon drive away, and the group takes a break. People migrate over to the ramada, where food awaits.

"Come sit with me and my husband," says Sherry.

Sherry's husband isn't a musician but had come to the picnic. We find him sitting at one of the tables and go over to join him, shooting the breeze while munching on chicken wings, watermelon, and other picnic fare.

"So, Jessie's your fiddle teacher?" asks Sherry at one point.

"*Was* my fiddle teacher," I reply. "I stopped taking lessons from her last spring."

"I see. How long have you been playing, anyway?"

I pause to calculate. "Three years."

"Three years? … I wouldn't have guessed it. I've heard you play, and for not having much experience, I'd say you're doing fine."

"Thanks!" I say, head bowing down out of humbleness—which I try to mask by reaching down to tie a loose shoe string.

"It seems many fiddlers come from a classical background," says Sherry. "Did you play classical violin before?"

"No," I say, shaking my head and sitting up again. "I was originally a drummer. Learned that as a kid. And I dabble on guitar."

"So ... fiddle, drums, and guitar. You're a complete band!"

"I guess so," I say, laughing. "It's funny, even though I listened to country music growing up, I never paid attention to the fiddle. It never occurred to me to try playing one until a few years ago. Who knew I had any talent for it."

"So what made you start?"

I shrug. "One day an ad in the paper caught my eye. It was for fiddle lessons at the *Phoenix School of Country Music*, and on a whim, I signed up."

"I don't think I've heard of that school," Sherry says.

"I think it went out of business," I say. "I took group lessons there, and then private lessons later on."

"So Jessie taught there?"

"No, my first instructor was a classical violinist, but she enjoyed country fiddle as well. After a year of private lessons, she thought Jessie would be better suited to teach me."

It was Jessie who helped me gain an appreciation for bluegrass and old-time fiddling. She did her best to inspire me, often inviting me to come hear her band in the local country bars, sometimes waving me up on stage for a fiddle tune or two. Occasionally the drummer would let me play his drums. It was a thrill to be on stage. My normally introverted disposition would disappear when I let the fiddle or drums do the talking.

I should have joined a band years ago, but shyness always got the best of me. I had a hard time getting to know other musicians. Heck, I had a hard time getting to know people in general. This was especially true with members of the opposite sex. Not always, though—Sherry being a case in point. Since she was married, I had no difficulty talking to her. But had she been unattached, it would have taken me months to say more than "hello." Even so, I'd been working on this flaw. My social skills were slowly improving.

After we finish eating, the group begins another round of tunes. I wipe greasy remnants of chicken wing from my fingers as best I can and grab my fiddle to join the circle of musicians. But I'm not familiar with the tunes being played and stay near the back.

Stray thunderheads roam the valley skies, holdovers from the waning monsoon season. Though lacking its former mid-summer intensity, the heat and glare from the blazing sun make it worthwhile to seek relief in the shade. I head in that direction.

That's when I notice a dark-haired woman talking to others over in one corner, a guitar slung over her shoulders. She is wearing a folksy green blouse and long, black skirt. A plain silver bracelet circling her left wrist completes the outfit. An enchanting quality surrounds her—a mysteriousness that instantly intrigues me. She looks familiar too: shoulder-length hair, fair complexion, and a pleasant face tinged with loneliness. Recognition dawns. This is the same woman I had seen a month earlier, riding up to the ramada on her mountain bike. I may have thought of her as perfect before, but now knowing she's also a musician really sparks my interest.

At one point, I find myself standing next to her as she discusses favorite bluegrass bands with another musician. I'm only half listening to the conversation, my head turned partially away. It's simply not in my realm of possibilities to interact with someone who entrances me so. Holding the fiddle as though playing a guitar or mandolin, bow dangling from my first finger, I absent-mindedly pluck fiddle strings, and simultaneously pluck thoughts from the thunderclouds roiling off in the distance—until I hear a question being asked.

"What about you?" asks the dark-haired woman. "What bands do you like listening to?"

I don't hear any response to this question, and then realize, as I turn towards her, that I'm the one being asked.

"I'm sorry," I say, stopping my absent-minded plucking. "Were you talking to me?"

She smiles, her brown eyes shining.

"I was just asking who your favorite musicians were," she replies.

I think for a moment, and finally shrug. "Oh, I don't know. Nobody in particular."

Fool! rumble the distant thunderheads. *Can't you come up with anything better than that?*

Apparently not, I silently answer. *But I'll try.*

I tap the bow on my right leg, and hold the fiddle precariously, grasping its neck lightly in my left hand, letting the instrument dangle—a somewhat dangerous and curious habit of many a fiddler. I stare down at my scruffy tennis shoes, once again not able to look directly at the woman who has just spoken to me.

"I guess I don't pay much attention to the names of artists—or the names of songs for that matter," I manage to say, looking up into her eyes. Her shining, smiling eyes. "I just like playing the tunes."

"I see," says the dark-haired woman.

She hesitates a moment, as though thinking of a way to extract more usefulness out of our conversation, and finding little promise, she begins to turn those shining eyes and clear, pure voice away.

"You play guitar?" I ask, immediately regretting the foolishness of that question. Of course she plays guitar—she has one slung over her shoulder, doesn't she?

"Yes, but I've only played bluegrass a few months," she says. "That's why I'm looking for tips on bands to check out."

My feeble attempt to strike up further conversation is cut short, for at that moment another guitar player appears, and the two of them soon walk off together, already deep into a private discussion. *Probably her boyfriend*, I tell the thunderheads, *or soon to be, since that's the way things usually go.*

~ ~ ~

Unbeknownst to me, the appearance of this dark-haired woman is really life conjuring up a 'cosmic two-by-four,' whose purpose is to 'gently' tap me in the direction I'm supposed to go. Apparently, I'm a bit stuck. So another tap is prepared, ready to strike later that fall at a bluegrass festival held on a large outdoor patio in the back of *Gila Joe's*, a country bar located in the charming, rural community of Cave Creek, twenty miles north of Phoenix.

I find bass player Sherry relaxing at a picnic table under the shade of mesquite trees lining the enclosed patio. It's mid-afternoon, and a pleasant fall breeze ruffles my shirt as I sit down across from her. A band plays on stage, with the usual bluegrass combination of stand-up bass, banjo, mandolin, guitar, and fiddle. The music is loud, but we are far enough away from the speakers to make it tolerable.

"Where were you?" asks Sherry, brushing back her long blonde hair as she sips an iced tea. "You missed my band play a while ago."

"I'm such a space case," I say, slowly shaking my head. "I forgot about the festival until a few hours ago, so I scrambled to get up here. It figures I missed you play."

A waitress comes by and I follow Sherry's lead and order an iced tea. I notice no other left-over drinks at the table. "Your husband didn't make it today?"

"He had to work," says Sherry.

As the band plays a few numbers, I compare notes with Sherry about the band members, judging their respective talents.

"So when are *you* going to join a band?" asks Sherry at one point.

"Who, me?"

"Yes, you. I've heard you get in a few good licks at the Squaw Peak jams."

"Oh, I don't know," I say, looking down at my feet, my right leg bouncing on its toes in a perpetual fidget, a lifelong habit. "I doubt I'm good enough."

"Hogwash," says Sherry.

The band starts a fast and furious fiddle tune, and I tap my hands on the table to the 2/4 rhythm most common in bluegrass, adding syncopation in the process—a fidgety habit that any drummer would instantly identify with. I catch Sherry watching me, a look of amusement on her face.

"Sorry," I say, halting my antics. "I guess that's the drummer in me."

"Do you still play the drums?"

I shake my head no. "They spend most of their time boxed up in the closet," I say. "They're too loud to play in the apartment, and too bulky to haul around. Fiddles are much more portable."

"Except for big fiddles like my stand-up bass," Sherry says, laughing.

After the band finishes their set, Sherry tells me the activities are moving indoors. She says there's a group dinner planned.

"Are you going to stay for that?" she asks.

"Might as well," I reply.

We make our way inside as people pour into the bar. Long rows of tables had been set up, adorned with red and white plaid tablecloths. Dimly lit lamps hang from old wagon wheels raised to the ceiling.

The bar fills quickly, and just as we hurriedly claim seats, I see the other bass player Dwight come in. I motion him over to one of the few remaining seats at our table and he climbs onto the bench across from Sherry and me.

Dwight wears a mustache and is about my height and weight: six feet, a hundred and seventy-five pounds. His hair is the same shade of brown and we are sometimes seen wearing the same color and style jacket. We often joke about being twins.

"What have you been up to?" I ask Dwight. "I didn't see you last month at Squaw Peak."

Dwight sighs. "I really should get out and play more. But I've been working a lot lately."

"I know how that goes," I say.

"Where do you work, anyway?" asks Dwight.

"At a small company in Mesa. They do computer-aided design for window manufacturers. I'm one of the main programmers."

"I see," says Dwight, nodding his head and taking in what I'm saying. "So you play fiddle *and* work on computers? Now that's a curious combination."

"They have more in common than you might think," I say. "Cranking out notes on the fiddle, and tracking the chord progressions in the process—it's not unlike typing on the keyboard, and managing all the variables and logic of a program."

"That's interesting," says Dwight, further nodding his head up and down and then sideways. "Although I have no idea what you're talking about. Computers are way beyond me."

"Well, I've had lots of practice with them," I say. "I've been programming computers since the mid-seventies."

My computer career began in a roundabout way. I became fascinated with programming while taking engineering courses in college. But I had to be dragged kicking and screaming to reach that point. During my senior year of high school, I was mulling over the idea of going into engineering, and learned I would have to take computer classes as part of the curriculum.

"No way!" I said at the time. "I'll *never* work on computers!"

Dancing through my head were visions of IBM employees in white shirts and black ties, pouring over cryptic chicken scratches printed on sheets of paper colored with alternating bars of green and white. That vision almost made me drop the whole idea of engineering right then and there. But I did sign up as an engineering major, and within weeks of starting my first computer course, I knew I had found my calling. Much to my surprise, programming was natural to me. I liked making mathematical equations and logical pathways come alive on the computer.

My close friends know that the word *never* as used by me is often coupled with irony. Usually when I say I will *never* do something, it doesn't take long before that is exactly what I am doing. Since I had said that I would *never* work with computers, of course I would take up programming as a career.

I summarize this history for Dwight, and he asks where I went to college.

"I went to graduate school at ASU," I say, "in computer science. But my undergraduate degree is in mechanical engineering, from the University of Nebraska."

I immediately regret that last reference. I have a feeling what's coming next, and pre-empt the expected question with a reply. "Yes, that's where the Cornhuskers play."

Dwight laughs. "I take it people always ask about the football team when you say you're from Nebraska?"

"It seems to be all they know about the state. But it isn't that different from anywhere else. Things happen at a slower pace, that's all."

Having lived away from Nebraska for a number of years, I find people who grow up there tend to have an air of innocence that takes life a while longer to erode, compared to those living in the more populated areas of the country.

A waitress comes by as the evening performances begin, and we order meals of barbecued chicken and steak. Just before our meals arrive, Dwight happens to lean to the side, only to reveal an unexpected sight, for there is the dark-haired, white mountain bike woman, sitting a few tables down.

The cosmic two-by-four readies its swing.

I stare past Dwight towards this woman. She is wearing the same green blouse and black skirt she wore at Squaw Peak. An older woman with graying blonde hair sits with her—forcing the appearance of being interested in the activities, but not quite succeeding. In contrast, the dark-haired woman seems totally absorbed. Perhaps her companion had been dragged along. Perhaps the dark-haired woman is unattached after all.

Halfway through the meal, I rise from the table and sidle up to the bar to order a drink, pretending to be the drinker I am not. I don't touch alcohol these days. A year before, Jessie had bought me a ceremonial 'last beer' at a lounge in Scottsdale where she was playing. I was never a big drinker anyway; alcohol made me queasy long before I got any buzz from it. I had also stopped drinking most soft drinks, cutting out the extra sugar in the name of health. That leaves few choices at the bar.

My choice this time: a club soda. I take a sip, pretending the slightly bitter drink to be that last ceremonial beer.

I lean against the counter and survey the crowd. Sherry is talking to the two women at the other table. I should head over there. It *would* be the perfect opportunity to be introduced to the dark-haired woman. But no, I head back to our table instead.

I regret my lack of courage the moment I sit down. But before I can do anything about it, Sherry returns. Oh well, maybe I can at least find out who the two women are.

"The blonde's name is Irene," says Sherry, after I ask. "And the dark-haired woman is Catherin."

Catherin. So that's her name.

Stealing further glances towards her, I can't help notice that this Catherin seems older and more experienced than me. But any age comparison is difficult. I have always looked young for my age, and a relatively sheltered upbringing in small town Nebraska leaves me feeling younger too.

There's no chance with her, I surmise. She surely wouldn't be interested in the likes of me.

I finish dinner and turn part of my attention to the band on stage. The music is good, but annoying cigarette smoke soon has me entertaining thoughts of leaving. I don't, though. I can't help staying to watch Catherin. Although I see her smiling from time to time, her face cannot mask a dark undercurrent of sadness that I interpret as loneliness. What is she like, this attractive, yet lonely looking woman? I never make the attempt to find out—for that is too far removed from the definition of 'things I can do.'

Even so, the cosmic two-by-four is not about to strike out.

~ ~ ~

In fading twilight I peer inside the brightly lit windows of a recreation center, where the bluegrass club is having their Christmas party. I don't recognize anyone. Holding back, I choose not to go in, yet at the same time, I feel left out. It's a foolish quandary, self-imposed.

I had been in that quandary all day, pacing back and forth in my apartment, asking myself, *Should I go to the party, or not?* Of course I should go; for why had I answered that classified ad a few years back—the one that advertised, "Learn to play fiddle at the *Phoenix School of Country Music.*" Wasn't it to meet people with mutual interests in music? To break out of this shell of my own making?

Yet it wasn't until the very last moment that I decided to attend the party, and even now, having arrived, I need several trips around a small lake nearby before gathering enough courage to venture inside.

Once indoors, I find party-goers clustered at tables in small, private circles, finishing the last of a supper I evidently missed. The atmosphere is subdued. There's no music, either.

That's it? I say to myself. *This is what I fretted and worried about all day?* I head for the exit to go home—only to encounter Sherry on the way out.

"Oh, hi Sherry," I say, after she sees me and says hello. "I didn't know you were here."

"You're not leaving already, are you?" asks Sherry.

"I … I was just going outside for some fresh air," I say.

I don't think Sherry believes me. She probably sees the jacket and truck keys I'm carrying.

"I saw Dwight come in a little bit ago," she says, "and the performances are starting soon. Why don't you come sit with us?"

I follow Sherry into a big room where a stage has been set up and a band is preparing to play. Chairs are lined up against the walls on opposite sides, with the middle of the room cleared for dancing. We find Dwight and join him to watch the performances.

At one point I look across the dance floor, and there she is, that enigmatic woman named Catherin. When did she show up? She's sitting with Irene, the same woman I had seen her with at *Gila Joe's.* I note with interest that no male companions are in sight.

The last band finishes, and I hear talk of a jam session. I hurry out to the parking lot to fetch my fiddle. There it is, lying on the front seat of the truck, all alone. Like me, it needs a companion— perhaps the guitar belonging to the enticing dark-haired woman. Wouldn't that be nice? I grab my fiddle case and sling it over my shoulder, barely remembering to shut the door before rushing back to join the music.

Inside, I'm lost in the crowd. But then Sherry finds me.

"Hey, Bryan. I was just talking to someone who is thinking of starting a band. I thought you might be interested."

"Gosh, I don't know."

Sherry's eyes widen, and she shakes her head in disbelief. "Why not? What have you got to lose?"

"Well, nothing I guess. But ..."

What *is* my problem? Why is it so hard for me to act on my dream of being in a band—a dream that spans back to my childhood, listening to my mom's collection of country-western albums on her large, cherry wood stereo console, with me banging away on a pair of bongos she bought for my seventh birthday? (What bongos have to do with country music I never did figure out.)

"So who is starting the band?" I ask Sherry.

"I'll go find her."

Sherry leaves to find this other person, as I ponder over the word *her.*

I soon revert to a silent wall-flower mode that is my habit, isolating myself from all the people milling about. Before long, someone taps me on the shoulder, breaking that isolation. I whirl around and see Sherry.

"Bryan, I would like you to meet somebody," says Sherry, gesturing to her right. At first, it doesn't register who the woman is that holds out her hand in greeting.

"Hi, I'm Catherin," says the dark-haired, white mountain bike woman.

The cosmic two-by-four makes a solid hit, leaving me dumbstruck.

We shake hands, Catherin's melting into mine. I find her pleasant to the touch—a soft feel that complements her shining brown eyes and warm, inviting face. She is wearing another black outfit, this time with a more country-western motif that goes well with her figure and matches her light complexion perfectly. I am struck by Catherin's friendly, outgoing nature, and by her smooth, clear voice that has just the right timbre—like someone you might hear on the radio. She projects poise and confidence. I wasn't expecting that.

"Sherry tells me you play the fiddle," says Catherin.

"I play some."

"Well, as Sherry told you, I'm forming a band. Why don't you join?"

Try as I might to block my own hopes and aspirations in my usual, self-defeating way, this time, I manage not to. I manage instead to say yes to her offer, without hesitation.

My pulse quickens, and not just because I'm about to fulfill a long-held dream of being in a band. But suppose Catherin has a husband or boyfriend lurking around the corner?

"How many others have you lined up for your band?" I ask.

"Oh, it's just you and me for now," she says.

Before that has time to sink in, Catherin adds, "Come, let's join the jam session."

In the next room musicians have gathered and are playing hot and fast fiddle tunes. Catherin unpacks her guitar while I get out my fiddle, and we join the circle. Catherin carefully watches me, no doubt evaluating this new joint venture as much as I am. I can scarcely believe this sudden and fortunate turn of events. Here is this attractive woman, who seems talented and intelligent to boot. And now that I'm in her band, I figure she has no choice but to discover those same qualities in me. At least, that's my hope.

Alas, a guitar player from North Carolina joins the circle, and boy, can he pick a mean guitar. He certainly puts my playing to shame. The worst of it is that Catherin seems to know him well—he's the same person I had seen her with at Squaw Peak.

When the party ends, the two leave together. That figures. I follow them out to the parking lot, walking behind like a lost puppy, watching with envy as they drive away. I climb into my pickup and head home, both excited and discouraged.

Chapter 2.
A New Year, A New Beginning

Desert canyons drift slowly by, huge earthen cracks shaped in maple leaf patterns. Out the front window, past the instrument panel and whirling prop of the Beechcraft Sierra, mountains loom on the horizon, their lonely snow-capped reaches telling tales of high adventure. I take in a breath, which turns into a half sleepy, half nervous yawn. It's risky for me to be flying in a small plane, as prone to motion sickness as I am. Encountering the turbulent air of the mountains, the aircraft pitches and tosses, and my stomach bottoms out as the plane bounces and lurches over invisible bumps and unexpected dips. My hands and arms tingle. My breath is shallow. I instinctively rub my tightly clasped hands together to take attention away from a jostled stomach.

Jeff, my friend and pilot of the Beechcraft taking us across the Rockies, seems to sense my discomfort.

"You doing okay?" he asks over the drone of engine and propeller.

"I'm a bit queasy," I say. "But the Dramamine has taken the edge off. At least, I don't *think* I'm going to barf all over your front seat."

Jeff laughs. "Let's hope not. If it's any consolation, we'll be landing in Pueblo soon, and it should be smooth sailing from there. I doubt we'll see much turbulence over eastern Colorado or western Kansas."

Jeff had called me a few days after the bluegrass Christmas party, wanting to know if I'd be interested in taking a plane trip to Nebraska for the holidays. We were once roommates and had worked at the same aerospace company in Phoenix. He too was a mechanical engineer, having graduated from Nebraska a year ahead of me. He was from a small town in the western part of the state, as was I—but it's a big state.

"I'd love to fly up to Nebraska with you," I had said when he called, "but do you realize my hometown is at least a hundred miles out of your way?"

Jeff hadn't thought of that, but later in the conversation I had suggested he drop me off to see my two sisters in Colby, Kansas, which was right on the way to his hometown.

Since our plane trip would take most of the day, I had plenty of time to think about things while enjoying the high altitude view out the window. And first and foremost on my mind? Catherin. She had called right after I talked with Jeff. I had half expected not to hear from her, figuring the band was just a pipe dream on her part, and wishful thinking on mine. And I sure wasn't expecting her to suggest practicing the week of Christmas, but that's what she did. The surprise didn't end there, however.

"What would you say about practicing Christmas day?" she had asked. "It's the only day I have free."

Didn't she have family or friends to celebrate the holidays with? Apparently not. For a moment I had entertained thoughts of accepting her offer until I realized I couldn't. I informed her of the scheduling conflict with my upcoming trip.

"I see," she had said, sounding more disappointed than a postponed practice called for. "Why don't you get in touch with me when you get back?"

I hadn't wanted that phone call to end. I was afraid I'd never talk to her again. Though excited about the plane trip with Jeff, the last thing I wanted to do was leave Phoenix and miss an opportunity to be with Catherin. What if she changed her mind about the band?

~ ~ ~

We land in Pueblo, Colorado, top off the fuel tanks, and then resume our flight east towards the Kansas flatlands, across miles and miles of alternating, rectangular fields of wheat and summer fallow, broken occasionally by the signature green circles of center pivot irrigation, the vast blue skyline providing the only other relief. Not long after crossing the invisible border into Kansas, I see a small clump of trees and weathered farm buildings, arranged in a vaguely familiar pattern. A sudden realization hits me.

"Well, would you look at that!" I say to Jeff, pointing out the window. "See that clump of trees? And those buildings? That's a farm where I once lived."

Over the roar of the engine Jeff asks, "Are you sure? How can you tell?" He can see, as well as I, that there are many such clumps of trees and buildings dotting the landscape, all looking rather alike.

"Well, I guess I've never seen the place from the air," I say. "And we only lived there two years, but as sure as I'm sitting here, that's my family's old place. I was seven at the time."

A bend in an otherwise ruler-straight ribbon of asphalt triggers long forgotten memories and confirms the location of the farm. I motion to Jeff. "See that road down there? That's the highway between Goodland and Sharon Springs. I remember our farm being just north of that bend."

"I didn't realize you once lived in Kansas," says Jeff.

"For a few years," I say, "both in the country and in town. My mom raised the eight of us kids by herself."

"I'd forgotten you came from such a large family."

"And what a place to grow up, out here in the middle of nowhere. My family didn't farm the place, though. My mom rented the house and an old farmer tended the fields. He sometimes slept in a shack by the barn. Could we drop down and take a look?"

Jeff nods yes and points the nose of the plane downward and banks into a fairly tight 360-degree turn, the right wing tipping to provide a convenient rotating line of sight to the old farmstead. Nauseating G-forces press into my stomach.

"You sure you can handle this?" asks an amused Jeff. "I seem to recall a time when you practically passed out while flying with me. And if I recall correctly, I made no hard turns that particular day, and the weather was smooth and clear."

I do an internal survey of my stomach and hands. No knots, no tingling. Nope, I'm not hyperventilating. That was known to happen to me while flying. I would get nervous about getting motion sickness, only to bring on the very symptoms I was trying to avoid.

"I guess the Dramamine is still doing its job," I finally say.

The farm scene grows closer as the plane drops in altitude. The dwelling that once housed my family is sadly in ruins: the barn in near collapse, the once-gravel driveway now mostly weeds, and the house looks like it hasn't been painted since the day we left, over twenty years ago. No kids are around to make tunneling paths through the tall weeds, or fight imaginary wars in the fields, or daringly hack rattlesnakes to death with shovels and hoes. (The dangers we never appreciated as kids!)

I blink my eyes, which brings back memories of a game I had started on that Kansas farm. In this game, I blink and say, "I promise to remember this time." The eye blinks are like the shutter of a camera, and whenever I add the accompanying promise, I remember the other times I have blinked my eyes with that same promise, triggering a recursive chain of memories, similar in feel to *déjà vu*.

Looking down from the circling plane with these recursive memories is like seeing a slowly rotating picture review of my early childhood. Some of my most formative memories are centered around that farm in western Kansas, and like the farm, those memories have long been neglected.

Jeff levels the wings and steers the plane east towards Colby, a small town along Interstate 70. We soon touch down and are met by my oldest sister and her husband. Jeff refuels and takes off for his hometown in Nebraska.

During my stay in Colby, my sister's husband tries to set me up with a neighbor's daughter—a young lady who works at the local drugstore. She's pretty enough, with black, slightly curly hair, but all that does is remind me of Catherin.

Will I be more than just another member of Catherin's band? I try not to get my hopes up, and by the time Jeff returns to Colby and we're in the plane and on the runway waiting for takeoff, I have convinced myself that nothing romantic is going to happen back in Phoenix. I doubt the band will get off the ground either.

Fortunately, Jeff's plane does. The Beechcraft Sierra climbs off the runway, turning west towards the mountains of Colorado and the deserts of the Southwest. We pass Goodland along Interstate 70—this time too far north to see the old farmstead. But memories of that place and time seep into the present.

One Christmas long ago my family took a dream-like trip to the bright lights and snowy mountains of Denver. The Rockies have always brought a sense of wonder and excitement in me, and that trip was not soon forgotten. I was haunted for years by bittersweet memories of shimmering white peaks receding through the rear window of our car, as we headed back to the uninspiring flatlands of western Kansas. Throughout my childhood I had recurring dreams of sitting on the roof of our farmhouse, looking towards the west, where I swore I could see those shimmering white peaks. In reality, they were much too far away.

But not now, for we are flying swiftly westward at ten thousand feet, soon well into eastern Colorado. The first of the snow-capped peaks pops onto the horizon. Among these, Pikes Peak is the most prominent. Jeff uses it as a guidepost and steers the plane just to the left, towards the city of Pueblo.

We land in Pueblo, fuel up, and resume our flight back to Arizona. High mountain vistas greet us as Jeff pilots the Beechcraft directly west, up and over the Front Range. I've explored much of Colorado and the Southwest in my adult life, and can call many of the peaks by name. During the entire trip back to Phoenix, I know at all times where we are, stringing imaginary lines between the high-lonesome mountain ranges of Colorado, New Mexico and Arizona. I'm so caught up in the sight-seeing that for a while, Catherin is gone from my mind.

~ ~ ~

Dr. Thomason calls me not long after I get back from Kansas. "Any interest in going hiking on New Year's Day?" he asks. "Out in the Superstition Wilderness?"

"Sure," I say. "What time? … Don't make it too early, seeing as how we both might be up late on New Year's Eve."

"How about I come by your place around noon?"

"Sounds like a plan."

"Oh, I almost forgot to mention," says Dr. Thomason. "Alden wants me to tell you he's having a party on New Year's Eve, and you're invited. I won't be there. I've already been invited somewhere else."

Alden was another colleague from the robotics lab, and his roommate was also in our AI classes. So I imagined Alden's party would be your typical geek party. But I called him anyway and told him I'd come.

~ ~ ~

As the days go by, I start wondering why I haven't heard from Catherin, until it dawns on me that *I'm* supposed to call her. I give her a ring and ask if she still wants to start a band.

"I sure do," she says. "Some friends of mine are having a party on New Year's Eve. Why don't you come with me? We can have our first practice there."

The possibility of going to a party with Catherin causes flickers of excitement to course through me. A knot forms in my stomach, and it's not from motion sickness or hyperventilation.

"Have you found other musicians for the band?" I ask.

"No, not yet," she says. "It's just you and me."

I catch my breath. How curious it is that for the second holiday in a row, Catherin has invited me to be with her. That guitar player she left the Christmas party with must have been only an acquaintance. After the phone call ends, I whistle tunes while doing chores around the apartment. Things are looking up.

On New Year's Eve, I drive to Catherin's house in Gilbert, ten miles east of my Tempe apartment. "Past the ugly pink apartments," Catherin had said—a description that helps me find her house easily. I park on the street and walk up the sidewalk. Out front is an eclectic mix of blue clay pots, rocks, yucca plants, prickly pear cactus, palm trees, and a green lawn.

The houses in Catherin's neighborhood are fashioned in a pseudo-Spanish style popular in the Phoenix area, with white or adobe-colored stucco, and red, concrete-tiled roofs. Like most things in the valley, the neighborhood is fairly new. Not long ago, the area had been farm land, mostly cotton fields and citrus groves. Before that, it had been raw Sonoran desert. But now palm trees and lush Bermuda lawns incongruously cover the dry desert valley.

I knock on the front door and an older woman with graying blonde hair answers. I have seen her somewhere before. She invites me in and I step inside.

"You must be Bryan," she says. "I'm Irene, Catherin's roommate. She'll be out in a bit. Why don't you have a seat?" Irene guides me to the table in the dining room and I pull up a chair.

Irene goes back into the kitchen, which adjoins the dining room, and finishes fixing herself sizzling stir-fried vegetables. Although my sense of smell is virtually non-existent, (has been as far back as I can remember), I can taste soy sauce and garlic in the air.

Irene comes back with dishes and sets herself a place for dinner. "Catherin tells me you are going to play in a band with her."

"I'll be playing fiddle."

"Well, I'm impressed. The fiddle seems like a hard instrument to play. I don't know how you do it."

"Do you play anything?" I ask.

"Who, me?" she replies with a surprised look. "Heavens no."

"Did you happen to go with Catherin to the festival at *Gila Joe's* last month? And the bluegrass Christmas party?"

"Yes," says Irene. "Catherin often drags me to these events. I don't mind. It gets me out of the house."

"I thought you looked familiar," I say.

After Irene goes back into the kitchen, I casually thumb through magazines lying on the table, even though my heart is pounding. I never was good at meeting new people, particularly when one of them is an attractive female who, for all practical purposes, I'm going on a date with.

On the table are issues of *Smithsonian* and *Sky and Telescope*.

"So which one of you is the astronomer?" I ask, holding up the magazines, *Sky and Telescope* being prominent.

Irene pokes her head through the doorway with a questioning look, until she sees the magazines. "Those are Catherin's," she says.

I try to envision what kind of woman would read *Smithsonian* and *Sky and Telescope*, and play bluegrass to boot. Certainly not your ordinary woman.

I scan the surroundings. Overall, the house has a pleasant, airy feel, with skylights cut into the roof. A high ledge supports numerous house plants, their tendrils dangling towards the floor. Only a smattering of furniture covers the handsome wood floors and abundant, white ceramic tiling. It's as though the tenants never quite moved in, or planned to leave soon. Two doves flit about in an aviary custom-built into the wall separating the living room and a smaller sitting room.

Hanging on the wall behind me is a picture of a white dove flying through the clouds.

Catherin soon appears, ravishingly dressed in black, ready for the party. Knowing that she plays bluegrass, reads *Smithsonian* and *Sky and Telescope*, and has such tantalizing dark hair and shining brown eyes; well, I fall in love with her right then and there. She motions me into the living room and opens the door to the aviary, introducing her birds. They are small and cream-colored, with black rings around their necks.

"Meet Bubba and Mrs. Bubba," she says, lifting the birds onto her fingers and taking them out of the aviary.

I stroke Bubba's feathers and say, "You sure have a funny name, Bubba. Are you from Arkansas? Texas? Tennessee?"

Bubba answers by bouncing up and down on Catherin's finger, then cooing.

I laugh and ask Catherin, "Why do your birds with black-ringed necks have redneck names?"

Catherin chuckles. "No reason."

"What kind of birds are they?"

"They're ring-necked turtle doves," she says. "Do you want to hold one?"

I tentatively extend a finger and Catherin transfers Mrs. Bubba over to me. She coos softly as I pet her smooth, creamy-white head. After a few moments, Catherin plants the birds back on their perches in the aviary, and Bubba starts bobbing his head up and down, edging his way over to Mrs. Bubba, cooing all the while.

"Oot-oooo-weee-hooo! Oot-oooo-weee-hooo!"

"That's his mating call," Catherin remarks with a chuckle.

Mrs. Bubba flits to the other side, presumably trying to get away. She makes a cooing sound of her own and Bubba joins in.

"Heh-heh-heh. Oot-oooo-weee-hooo! Oot-oooo-weee-hooo!"

Catherin closes the door to the aviary and goes to retrieve a jacket from the hallway closet.

"Let's head for the party," she says. "We can walk, by the way. It's only a few blocks."

As we leave the house, I offer to carry Catherin's guitar, and grab my fiddle from the front of my truck before heading down the sidewalk. To help balance the load, I carry Catherin's guitar in one hand, and my fiddle in the other. Catherin takes the lead.

Just a few weeks ago at the bluegrass Christmas party, I had wished my fiddle could have a companion, thinking Catherin's guitar would be just the ticket. It seems that wish is now coming true. And what about the wish for my own companionship?

A block down the street, Catherin turns to me and says, "I'm glad you were able to come tonight."

"So whose party *are* we going to anyway?" I ask.

"Larry and Amy's," Catherin says. "People I work with."

"What kind of work do you do?"

"I'm a leasing agent at a shopping center in Tempe. Larry's older brother, Vincent, is the developer of the center. He'll be at the party with his girlfriend Arielle."

We arrive at Larry and Amy's, and I'm introduced to Catherin's friends, including a woman named Cecilia. She lives across the street. I find out Cecilia used to work in the same office as Catherin and the others. This adds up to an unusual arrangement.

"How is it that all your co-workers live in the same neighborhood?" I ask.

"It was Vincent's doing," Catherin says. "He found all these houses, and arranged loans for us."

We choose a corner of the living room to set up and play, underneath stairs leading to the second floor. It's as though neither of us wants to be too exposed. Catherin tunes her guitar while I rosin my bow and try to settle my nerves. It's one thing to play in a crowd, where my scratchy fiddle is masked by more experienced players, but now with just the two of us, Catherin will discover my true fiddle abilities. Not that they are *that* bad, but I so want to impress her.

"What tune do you want to play first?" she asks.

"I don't know … how about *Billy in the Low Ground*? It's my current favorite."

Catherin doesn't know the tune, but she finds the minor chords easily, needing little prompting on my part.

"That was good!" says Catherin. "I like that tune."

"Thanks," I say. "I once came up with words for it—well, one verse anyway."

"Really?" replies Catherin. "Why don't you sing it for me?"

I laugh silently. It's hard enough to keep my nerves at bay while playing, but singing too? Oh well, I *did* bring this upon myself …

"My voice isn't that great," I say to her, "but here goes ..."

I clear my throat and begin singing a capella:

There was a Billy in the Low Ground, he's looking mighty fine
But he ain't got a ladder, so that he can climb
Out of the hole that he fell in, while fiddling away
Oh, Billy in the Low Ground, right here he's going to stay

"How fun," says Catherin, looking on admiringly. "I see this band has possibilities."

And just what *are* those possibilities, I wonder ...

"Any other tunes you want to do?" she asks.

"How about one of *your* favorites?"

"Okay," she says. "Do you know *Nashville Blues?*"

I shake my head no. "But play it anyway. I'll see if I can fake it."

Catherin plays the chords and hums the melody while I follow along best I can, playing by ear.

It's soon apparent we don't have many songs in common. That doesn't matter, for the rest of the crowd knows little about bluegrass. Their frequent calls for *Orange Blossom Special* and *Dueling Banjos* provide evidence of that.

We trade a few more songs. All the while I have a dryness in my throat that isn't cured by frequent gulps of water from a glass placed precariously at my feet, the latter which are often tapping, both to the beat of the music, and out of nervous anticipation. Catherin seems to answer a longing that until now had appeared impossible to fill.

We eventually run out of tunes and pack our instruments away. Catherin moves to the couch in the living room, where the rest of the party-goers are absorbed in a game of Trivial Pursuit. I have no interest in participating—the game is too much like the computer programming I do every day. I remain glued to my stool underneath the stairway, reverting to my usual wall-flower mode: watching and listening, but pretending not to.

I'm quiet like this at most parties. I have never liked competing for attention in a social setting. Though I can be as talkative as any-one when it's just me and someone else, in a crowd of three or more I tend to clam up.

Catherin sees me sitting away from everyone and motions me over with a puzzled but inviting look. I move to the couch and sit beside her, rubbing shoulders with her in the process. Electricity shoots between us—and I'm not talking the static kind. To my delight she makes no attempt to move away.

Midnight approaches. Someone turns on the TV to the familiar scenes of Times Square and the strains of *Auld Lang Syne*. Our hosts graciously offer everyone a traditional glass of champagne, but I politely refuse, and interestingly enough, so does Catherin. She asks Amy if they have any apple cider or plain sparkling water. Amy says there might be some in the fridge.

I go into the kitchen with Catherin and we find a bottle of sparkling water, bringing our filled glasses back into the living room. We perch on tall chairs that someone moved in from the kitchen bar.

The countdown begins on TV. We click our glasses together in a toast for the New Year. Impulsively—and quite uncharacteristically for me—I reach over and give Catherin a 'New Year's Kiss,' lightly pecking her on the cheek.

This does not go unnoticed by others in the room. But nobody has more disbelief about what just happened than me. Someone laughs and gives us a warning: "Better watch out … for whatever you do tonight, you'll be doing the rest of the year."

I sure hope so, I say to myself.

The party winds down and goodbyes are said. I escort Catherin back to her house along the dimly lit sidewalk, carrying her guitar in one hand, and my fiddle in the other. A chill in the air adds to the trembling I feel, now that we are alone. The tension builds as we reach her house and turn up the sidewalk. What's going to happen next?

At her doorstep, I set the instruments down as Catherin unlocks the door ahead of me. She turns around and hesitates.

Don't you want to come in? her eyes seem to ask.

Yes, I do, my heart says back.

But I don't.

I hug her goodnight and pick up the guitar and hand it back to her. With a fleeting look of disappointment, the dark-haired, white mountain bike woman quietly slips away behind the door.

Chapter 3.
"What are you doing way over there?"

January 1, 1987

M y first thoughts on New Year's morning are of Catherin. So are my next thoughts. And next. These sprout as little tendrils of hope. Did she really invite me to the party last night just to practice music? Did I really give her a kiss to start the new year? What have I done?

Excited yet tired, I stumble out of bed and have a quick shower. While eating breakfast I get the idea to go over to my friend Alden's and see what's up in his world. Maybe that will provide a distraction from all these romantic daydreams.

I climb the stairs to Alden's apartment and knock. The door soon opens and we exchange hellos.

"Where were you last night?" asks Alden, rubbing his ruffled black hair and trimmed beard. "I thought you were going to stop by. We were having a party, remember?"

"Oh … sorry about that! I got invited to another party. Guess I forgot about yours."

I move into the living room and plop down in a chair. My crossed feet are soon wiggling. Alden sits by his computer desk.

"I'm such a space cadet," I say, shaking my head.

"So whose party did you go to?" asks Alden.

"No one you would know. I was with someone I just met. We were at her friend's house in Gilbert."

"Her? Did you just say *her*?" Alden asks. "You went to a New Year's Eve party with a woman, on a date? That's big news!"

Alden's roommate, also a computer science major, was lying on the couch watching TV, half listening to the conversation. He perks up at the mention of females.

"So!" he says, rising from the couch to grab a soda from the refrigerator. "You were with some babe, huh?" He pulls back the tab on the soda can, letting out a hiss of escaping gas.

"Oh, it wasn't a date or anything," I say. "I joined a bluegrass band with her, and we were just practicing."

"Sure, sure," Alden's roommate says, taking a gulp from his can of soda. "I'll bet you were practicing!"

I laugh, but not without some embarrassment. I've never liked being teased about girls. On my seventh birthday, I was chased around a neighbor's farm by their daughter, the same age as me. She eventually caught me and planted a big birthday kiss on my cheek, much to my acute embarrassment. My brothers witnessed the whole affair and taunted me for days. That embarrassment still lingers. Even so, I did privately enjoy that kiss, though I would never have let my brothers know it at the time.

The conversation soon drifts to other topics. Alden and I had shared office space in the robotics lab at ASU. He was often found roaming the hallways of the engineering center with Wacky the Robot—an electric powered cart with a video camera and an IBM PC for brains. Since I had graduated before Alden the past spring, I don't know the details of his ongoing research. I ask him about it.

Alden discusses his latest efforts with Wacky. He's having trouble getting the robot to process all the data from the video camera. The robot can't keep up. It takes too much time to recognize the objects in a room, and that leaves little time for Wacky to decide on a course of action and coordinate the control of its motor drive. I struggle to pay attention as Alden drones on with technical details—something about programming Wacky to recognize the empty space of the floor instead of objects like tables and chairs—but it is mostly a one-way conversation on Alden's part. Preoccupied with my own thoughts, I don't contribute much. I begin to stifle yawns.

"I'm sorry, Alden. I can barely keep my eyes open. I think I'll call it a morning."

"Okay, but give some thought on how I can program Wacky to recognize empty space."

I tell Alden I will, and leave for home. Once there, I search for empty space in my own cluttered apartment, and finding the couch in the living room, I lie down and conk out immediately.

The next thing I know someone is knocking on the door. I drag myself off the couch to open said door, trying to focus my eyes on the person standing there. He looks familiar.

"Dr. Thomason, I presume," I say to the man wearing a T-shirt, shorts, and hiking boots.

"We *were* going hiking today, weren't we?" he asks, with a quizzical look on his face. "In the Superstitions?"

"Jeesh, you're right," I say, rubbing sleep from my eyes. "I forgot. And I forgot Alden's party last night too."

"Well, no excuses, Mr. Flamig. You're going hiking whether you want to or not."

With hasty preparation, I put on hiking shoes, fill a water bottle, and stuff the bottle into a small backpack, along with an orange and a package of trail mix. I meet Dr. Thomason at the door.

"Okay, I'm ready."

"What about your shoelaces?" he asks, pointing at my feet. "Don't you want to tie them first?"

I look down and laugh. "I once had a roommate who called me 'Space,'" I say as I reach to tie my shoes. "I guess there was a reason for that."

Soon we're out the door and into Dr. Thomason's car, heading east on the Superstition Freeway towards the city of Mesa, beyond which lies the Superstition Wilderness. Along the way we pass through Gilbert. Catherin's house is a few tantalizing miles to the south. I look in that direction. Her house *is* down there, isn't it? I hope I haven't just been dreaming ...

At the eastern edge of Mesa, we turn off the freeway and drive up Highway 88, otherwise known as the Apache Trail. The drive takes us through some of the prettiest Sonoran Desert to be found. Interspersed between the pinkish-gray boulders and green cactus are a few patches of blazing yellow poppies, growing incongruously in the harsh environment. The ever-present, deep blue Arizona sky provides a colorful contrast. The poppies are early this year. Usually, they come out in force in late February or early March.

In seventeen miles we reach Canyon Lake on the northern side of the Superstition Wilderness, and park by the Boulder Canyon trailhead. We crunch up the trail of rocks and gravel, climbing southeast over a hill covered with saguaros and teddy bear chollas—the latter being a particularly prickly form of cactus having a mockingly false resemblance to cuddly teddy bears. Sunbathing lizards poise stealthily on boulders along the trail, scattering for cover when we approach too close. Between breaths, which become more pronounced the higher we climb, we discuss a mutually favorite subject: artificial intelligence.

"Has Alden had much success with Wacky the Robot lately?" asks Dr. Thomason.

"A little," I say. "Right now he's struggling with the main approach to the robot's vision—whether it should concentrate on recognizing objects, or empty space instead. Alden realizes the robot doesn't need to recognize furniture in order to move around. Just finding the floor will do."

Dr. Thomason strokes his beard in thought, almost stepping on a lizard in his distraction. "That reminds me of those figure-ground illusions, like the black and white drawing of a vase, where you either see a vase, or the head profiles of two people facing each other. I guess in the case of Wacky, the couches and chairs are the figure, and the empty space—the floor of the room—the ground."

"It's the other way around," I say, "at least for Alden's robot navigating through empty space. The furniture is the ground, and the floor is the figure—the main point of interest. It's a curious reversal, which leads to some interesting thoughts. What the robot perceives depends on what it pays attention to, and what it pays attention to is what we tell it—that is, the rules we program into it. By changing the rules, we change the robot's perception."

We huff further up the trail before stopping to take a drink of water. I continue my thought. "It makes me wonder what's going to happen when robots get powerful and intelligent enough to see for real. What exactly are they going to see? They might see things we don't."

"You mean like radio waves, or ultraviolet or infrared?"

"No," I say. "It's not that we couldn't make robots see these other wavelengths, but I'm talking about the rules of perception."

"Rules of perception?" asks Dr. Thomason.

"The rules that determine how we interpret what's in front of us. Our perception is influenced by our upbringing and culture. For example, in the figure-ground vase illusion, people are able to see face profiles, because faces are important to us as humans. But for a robot? Depends on the rules we program into it. If the robot is programmed to handle inanimate things, like vases, and not necessarily to interact with people, what would it see in the black and white vase drawing?"

"Most likely a vase," says Dr. Thomason.

"Right," I reply. "And in the case of a robot moving about in a room full of furniture, it might behave differently than we would, being held up by things we don't think are important, and completely missing the things we think are."

"True," says Dr. Thomason. "That robot might be fascinated by the texture of the couch—and completely ignore the beautiful woman lying on it."

The bouts of laughter that follow make it hard for either of us to catch our breath. This gives us an excuse to rest a while longer. We find a shady spot underneath a large Palo Verde tree and sit down, trying to avoid all the prickly spines of the desert. We rummage through our small backpacks for snacks. I pull out an orange. Dr. Thomason pulls out crackers and cheese.

"Seriously, though," I continue, chewing on an orange slice, "perhaps the robot would see something else entirely—although probably not in the case of the vase, but in more complex surroundings, like a room, or out here on the trail."

"What do you mean, something else?" asks Dr. Thomason. With his knife he cuts off a hunk of cheese and hands it to me.

"We are conditioned to only see things our experiences—our life rules—say should or could be there. Anything else is filtered out. Suppose we goofed when programming the rules of perception for our robot, or suppose the rules had unintended consequences. The robot might see something we ourselves would miss. For example, how do you know there isn't a gargoyle standing next to that cactus over there?"

I point to a tall saguaro with the classic one-armed bandit shape, just off the trail. Dr. Thomason looks to where I'm pointing. Any normal person would see only boulders, sage brush, and cholla cactus around that saguaro, and nothing but blue sky beyond.

"You don't see any gargoyle there, right? ... Right?" I laugh at my own implied joke. "But suppose a gargoyle really is there. Since we're not expecting to see a living, breathing gargoyle, our mind would explain it away into nothingness, filtering it out with rules we have built over the years. But with a different set of rules, who knows? Maybe that gargoyle would pop into existence—that is, into our awareness."

"Well, maybe," Dr. Thomason says. "It seems a little far-fetched to me."

"Yeah, I know. But I really do think there are more kinds of perception than the ordinary, everyday kind."

"I don't see how changing a few rules can make things that aren't there come into existence."

"How do you *know* they aren't there? What if the rules we have aren't the right ones to see them with?"

"Well, I don't know," Dr. Thomason says, sounding exasperated. He strokes his beard as though to soothe his mind—or perhaps to coax more thoughts from it. "It seems to me there is only one set of rules. You know, like the fact that the laws of physics work the same everywhere in the universe—"

"Or so we think," I interject. "Even so, I'm not talking about physical laws, but rules of perception, of awareness. There may be a large world outside the ordinary one we experience. The rules we ordinarily employ help filter out that world."

By its very nature, whenever the topic of AI is discussed, the conversation often leads to one of philosophy, and for me, that often leads to questions of metaphysics and spirituality. That's a big reason I was drawn to the field of AI. Ordinarily, I didn't discuss these other topics with my engineering friends, but I thought I'd test the waters.

"Our perception is the lens we see the world through," I tell him, after we finish our lunches and continue our hike. "Perhaps by changing our perception, we can change our reality."

Dr. Thomason looks at me with raised eyebrows, eyes beginning to roll …

He probably thinks I've gone off my rocker. Maybe I have, but there came a time in my life when my views were altered significantly. Having been good at math and science, and having majored in engineering and computer science in college, I always thought of myself as a rational, logical guy. But one day a co-worker gave me a book he thought I might enjoy. It was the first in a series of books by Carlos Castaneda about a Yaqui warrior-sorcerer named Don Juan. I was surprised how much I enjoyed the first book, and subsequently went on to read the rest.

While many dismissed these books, saying they were only drug-induced fantasies, or even worse, works of fiction that pretended to be otherwise—none of that bothered me, and seemed beside the point. They may have been fantasy, and most likely were, but I enjoyed the bizarre descriptions of non-ordinary reality and the idea that we might be 'luminous eggs' consisting of fibers of perception. It seemed just as plausible as any other explanation of awareness. In the modern world, we know all about invisible radio waves, so why not invisible fibers of perception? Why should that be any more far-fetched?

Also described in the Castaneda books was the notion of shifting our 'assemblage point' and changing the world we perceive. This notion of a slippery, elusive world—as opposed to the supposedly solid world we ordinarily experience—was something up until that time I had given little thought.

Many questions arose when I first encountered these ideas. Are we merely observers of reality, or do our minds play a part in its creation? What is reality anyway? Is my reality the same as yours? Or do we share a mutually agreed upon portion of it, in order to interact with one another?

Science has revealed that matter at the scale of sub-atomic particles is affected by the very act of observation. Some seize on this as evidence that we can affect reality at the macroscopic scale too. This extrapolation is not necessarily justified—it's a big leap. Still, the link is possible, and that leads to further questions. How are mind, matter, and reality related? Can matter or reality exist without observation? Without mind?

I suspect these topics are too esoteric for Dr. Thomason, so I try to couch them in a more mundane fashion. "I believe there is more to our world than what our rational mind thinks," I say.

"What do you mean, *rational mind?*" he asks.

"I mean the way our intellect views the world. The way we organize and rationalize what we observe."

"So what is this other way?"

"Well, for want of a better description, it's a non-rational, non-thinking way. Perhaps some of the inexplicable mysteries of life can be accessed in this manner, but we have to shift from our ordinary rational point of view in order to fully experience these mysteries. We have to change our perception."

"You sure have strange notions," he says, laughing.

"I can get stranger if you want," I say, eyebrows moving up and down. "But seriously, this idea of a non-rational way to experience the world seems perfectly rational to me, as ironic as that sounds."

"How so?"

"If it is impossible for anything to have just one side, then if rationality is on one side, there has to be a non-rational side as well, and this non-rational side is just as real and valid as the rational one."

This leaves Dr. Thomason speechless, but I know he will take my exposition and chew on it a while. That's his forte. And being a master pontificator—much better than myself—I know he will soon begin an exposition of his own. But I've grown tired of the conversation. I'm not ready to argue his points. Something else is clamoring for attention. I'm bursting to talk to anyone I know about Catherin, wanting to speak her name out loud—feeling this will make her existence more real, more solid, less slippery.

"Well, Dr. Thomason," I say, stopping to tie my shoes and then proceeding on. "You'll never guess what I've done."

"You've built a gargoyle detector?"

"No!" I say, laughing and almost tripping over a rock. I have to stop and re-tie my shoes. "I've joined a bluegrass band."

"Oh? That's quite a ways from making robots see gargoyles! But you do play the fiddle, don't you? … So who's in the band?"

"Just two of us so far. Me and a woman named Catherin. We had our first practice last night."

"How intriguing … you join a band with a woman, and it's just the two of you, eh?" Dr. Thomason brushes his beard as if to coax out the full consequences of my revelation. "And how did you manage to get a date with her on New Year's Eve, may I ask?"

"Oh, it wasn't a date or anything," I say, repeating what I had told my other friends. "We were just practicing tunes. I met her by pure chance, at a Christmas party a few weeks ago."

Well, it wasn't exactly pure chance—seems like a certain cosmic two-by-four had something to do with it.

"So tell me more about this … what was her name?" asks Dr. Thomason.

"Catherin."

"Tell me more about this Catherin."

"I don't really know much," I say. "She's a leasing agent at a shopping center. Plays guitar. She's older than me, I think."

"Aha! An older lady! This is getting more interesting all the time. Is she single? Good looking?"

"I'm just playing in a band with her, that's all," I say, not believing for one second my own projected nonchalance. I'm not sure my friend believes me either, what with his look of amused skepticism.

"Okay, so she *is* nice," I admit. "Smart too. And you know, I've always had a hankering for women with dark hair."

"So what are you waiting for?" asks Dr. Thomason. "Here's your chance."

"Pffft," I answer, waving off the possibility with my hands. "I can't see anything happening, given my track record. I'm sure that to her, I'm just another guy to play tunes with."

"Well, you never know," says Dr. Thomason. "All you have to do is change a few rules."

I have to admit, he does have a point.

We reach the top of the hill and discover a valley off to the south, with a bluff sitting smack square in the middle. The steep, downward trail looks imposing. Even more imposing is a thrusting, spindly rock formation off in the distance known as Weaver's Needle, a famous landmark in the area supposedly near the site of the mythical Lost Dutchman Gold Mine. But going even partway that direction would mean having to climb uphill on the return, and I have no desire for that. At my suggestion we turn around and clomp back to the car, scattering sunbathing lizards in our wake.

On the drive home we stop at a restaurant for a bite to eat. You'd think I'd be famished from all the hiking, but I'm not able to eat much of the large sausage and mushroom pizza we order. I already feel stuffed, filled as I am with the hopeful anticipation of meeting Catherin again. No doubt about it, I'm infatuated with her, and have no less than a teenage-like crush. I sleep very little that night, despite being exhausted from the day's activities.

~ ~ ~

I spend the day after New Year's listening to music on the stereo. Someone had recently loaned me two albums recorded by the same group of musicians, but with completely different musical styles and band persona. Spear-headed by Tim O'Brien, *Hot Rize* is a straight-up bluegrass band. The band's alter ego, *Red Knuckles and the Trail-blazers*, plays old-style honky-tonk music with pedal steel, electric guitar, and drums. The contrast in styles is striking and amusing. The albums are quickly becoming my favorites.

I also practice fiddle tunes out of a book by Mark O'Conner, probably the finest fiddler alive. In this book are variations of *Black-berry Blossom*, a standard bluegrass fiddle tune. I spend several hours trying to play these variations, finally giving up in frustration. They are beyond my abilities.

In the late afternoon I leave to go grocery shopping, and when I return and open the door, I hear a familiar voice that makes my heart skip a beat.

"… and we could practice tomorrow if you'd like."

It's Catherin's voice on the answering machine. Flustered at first, I pause and subsequently don't make it to the phone before she hangs up. I wait for the answering machine to finish its recording cycle and then play back all the messages, encountering one from a friend about a new folk music coffeehouse having its debut that evening. After mentally noting this fact, I listen to Catherin's message and call her back. From the sound of her voice, Catherin seems very pleased that I returned her call so soon.

"How about we practice tomorrow evening?" she asks.

"Okay."

There is silence on both ends. I think she is expecting me to say more—which I would, if I could think of anything.

Catherin speaks first. "I'm staying in Tempe this evening, house-sitting for a friend. I might go out later to a poetry reading down-town, at *Changing Hands Bookstore*."

"That's my favorite bookstore," I say.

More silence. You can almost hear the proverbial crickets chirp-ing over the phone. A normal guy would have offered to go with her to the poetry reading, but the life rules I had built over the years said that I didn't get to go out with attractive women, so the thought never surfaces. What does surface are the other phone messages I had listened to previously.

"I was thinking of going to hear some folk music," I say. "There's a new place having its inaugural night. The *Desert Sky Coffeehouse,* or something like that."

"I hadn't heard about it," she says. "Worth checking out."

Still more silence. The seconds tick slowly by until eventually, an idea courageously makes itself known to me.

"I guess we could go together—"

"—I'd like that," she promptly replies.

I'm momentarily disoriented by the realization I have just asked—if you can call it that—an attractive woman out. Catherin may have been momentarily disoriented as well.

"But did you mean the coffeehouse or the poetry reading?" she asks.

"Whichever you'd like," I say. "On second thought, I just remembered, tonight is the Fiesta Bowl. Downtown Tempe is likely to be a real zoo. Parking close to the bookstore would be difficult."

"I didn't realize there was a football game tonight," she says. "Let's just go to the coffeehouse."

We make arrangements for me to pick her up in a few hours, and then Catherin says, "If you don't mind, I wonder if you could tell me when your birthday is."

"My birthday? Why do you want to know?"

"I want to see what sign you are. I'm just curious."

"My sign? Oh, you mean my astrological sign."

"Yes."

I give her the particulars, pointing out my birthday in late August. In a few moments Catherin replies, "I just knew you were a Leo. You have such warm and sunny looks—which is a common trait of Leos, by the way. I'd like to be more accurate though. Do you mind telling me your time and place of birth?"

"You seem to have more than a passing acquaintance with astrology," I say.

"I've been studying it for the past few years."

I'm not sure how I feel about this, but what's the harm? Besides, the 'warm and sunny' compliment is nice, so I give Catherin the information she wants.

"Give me a moment to do some calculations," she says.

The pause gives me time to reflect on this new revelation about Catherin. How do I feel about astrology? Well, it has its flaws: carefully worded yet vague descriptions of personalities, traits, and events, and a reliance on star positions that have changed over the millennia. But then again, most systems have flaws of one kind or another. To me, astrology seems mostly harmless.

Many people dismiss astrology outright. Personally, I'm inclined to not completely dismiss anything. I'd rather keep an open mind. Our understanding of how the universe works is ever-changing—and woefully limited. Experiments keep proving the universe to be far stranger than we ever imagined. Take modern particle physics, with its notions of virtual particles flitting into and out of existence. How are these notions any less bizzare than those you might find in the realm of metaphysics?

Our supposedly solid world is anything but. Matter is elusive when you inspect it up close, and interestingly, elusiveness is also found in the study of intelligence. Trying to sort out the puzzle of what it means to be intelligent and aware is fraught with paradox and self-referential loops. The common thread of elusiveness found in matter and mind suggests they are related. Who knows what connections between them might someday be revealed by science?

And what about the scientific method: observe, hypothesize, and test? It's a fine system, but if you don't have a belief in something going in—such as astrology—you aren't likely to conduct serious, authentic experiments about it. Even if you do conduct experiments, you may miss patterns in the experimental data, because your rules, your belief systems, might filter them out, and you could be totally unaware of this—just like being unaware of the gargoyle standing by the saguaro.

How should I respond to Catherin's interest in astrology? My views are too jumbled to summarize over the phone, and I don't want to give the wrong impression. Then I remember the *Sky and Telescope* magazine I had seen on Catherin's dining room table.

"I guess I've never paid much attention to astrology," I tell her. "But I do like looking at the stars."

"I'm sorry," she replies. "I missed what you said. I was concentrating on calculating your chart."

I repeat my comment about looking at the stars.

"I like star-gazing too," she says. "In fact, I belong to an astronomy club in town."

"Is-that-right?" I ask, using a popular Nebraska idiom, where the three words are spoken in a slow, sing-song cadence. "Are you doing your calculations by hand?"

"Yes, I am," she says. "It's a bit time consuming."

"I once took a solar energy class in college. I learned all about the equations used to track the sun. Similar equations would work for the planets as well. That solar energy class was my all-time favorite. I got an A-plus in it."

"That figures," she says, laughing. "You being Leo and all." She explains that since my zodiac sign is Leo, my central influence is the sun.

"Perhaps I could write a program for you to help with your calculations. It shouldn't be too hard."

"You mean on a computer?" she asks. "So you're a programmer too?"

I've never liked telling people I work on computers. There's all the nerdy connotations that come with the profession. But the cat, or should I say, nerd, is out of the bag.

"Yes, I am a programmer. But I like to think of myself as a musician first. Too bad that doesn't pay as well. You know, I've always been torn between these two interests."

"I wonder if your chart illustrates this," Catherin remarks.

~ ~ ~

Later that evening I take Catherin to the *Desert Sky Coffeehouse*. On this inaugural night, the place is jammed with people. Tight rows of chairs had been set up, interspersed with small tables used to hold drinks. Having arrived late, we are forced to stand in the back of this dark, cramped venue.

As we watch the performances, I glance over to Catherin from time to time, wondering how it can be that she is here with me, the quintessential loner. Tonight is probably no big deal to her. I'm just someone to go out on the town with, just another person to play tunes with, and nothing more. Still …

Catherin is wearing a pinkish-purple dress with matching earrings—the color of which I honestly don't care for. Even so, that has little effect on my attraction towards her. She is wearing little makeup, and that coupled with her plain silver bracelet lends her an air of simplicity and wholesomeness. Well, almost—for she has a certain manner that suggests these traits are something recently rediscovered, trying to reassert themselves through difficult times. Despair and anguish may have once ruled her life—and still might.

The performances end, and we mill around the crowded hall afterwards. I want to introduce Catherin to musicians I know, and see two of them across the way.

"There's Tom and Lisa," I say to Catherin, pointing to the couple. "They sponsor folk-music concerts, and are part of the local contra dance scene."

"Contra dance?" asks Catherin. "What's that?"

"It's a form of folk dancing, similar to square dancing."

"I've never heard of it," says Catherin. "Why is it called contra dancing?"

"The dancing is done in pairs of long lines, where the dancers in each pair face each other. Contra means *against*, or *in opposition*. In this case it's the long opposing lines."

"I see," says Catherin. "I remember learning a dance like that back in high school."

"Probably the Virginia Reel."

I try to maneuver over to Tom and Lisa, but there are too many people in between. We stay put momentarily.

"So you say there are contra dances here in Phoenix?" asks Catherin.

I nod yes. "And in Tucson. Contra dancing is more popular on the East Coast, especially in the New England area, and on the West Coast as well. Here in Arizona, it's just getting off the ground."

"Are these like the square dances at senior centers, where the music is often recorded?" asks Catherin. "Do people dress up?"

I shake my head no. "Contra dancing tends to be more casual, with less formal dress. And there is usually live music."

"Sounds interesting," says Catherin. "So what bands play at these events? Maybe our band should."

"Well, we *could*, but bluegrass isn't what's usually played, though there is some overlap in the tunes."

"Such as?"

"In contra dancing, the music is mostly old-time Irish, Scottish, English, and French Canadian tunes—jigs and reels, that is. And these days, a lot of new tunes have been written to sound old-timey, in both New England and Southern Appalachia styles. The tunes of bluegrass are from the same roots, but they are played in a different style."

"How do you mean?" asks Catherin.

"For contra dances, the emphasis is on danceability, as opposed to the improvisation and hot licks of bluegrass. Also, contra dance tunes usually follow a regular A-A-B-B structure."

"We should go to one of these dances," says Catherin.

"By all means," I say. "The Phoenix dances are held once a month at a school auditorium near downtown. There is usually an open band. You could bring your guitar and sit in."

As we finish talking I spot someone else I know.

"There's Cody," I tell Catherin, pointing to a guy who bears a remarkable resemblance to Buffalo Bill, with long, curly hair and mustache. "He's a friend of Tom and Lisa's. I met them all a year ago at a party that my former fiddle teacher, Jessie, invited me to."

There is a clear path to Cody through the crowd. I guide Catherin over and make introductions.

"Bryan says you're a musician," says Catherin to Cody.

"Yeah, I play guitar," replies Cody, sounding modest but trying to be cool, too.

"Well, I've started a bluegrass band," says Catherin. "I play guitar. Bryan's going to play fiddle. You wouldn't happen to know any available banjo players, would you?"

"Actually, I play banjo as well as guitar," replies Cody.

Without a moment's hesitation, Catherin asks, "You do? Well how about joining our band?"

Cody shrugs and thinks for a moment. "Banjo isn't my main instrument, but sure, why not?"

"Really? That'd be great," she says.

Turning to Catherin I comment, "Well, *that* was quick!"

She laughs. "I don't like to waste time."

I couldn't believe what just happened. I hadn't given much thought to who we might ask to join our band, but it never dawned on me to consider Cody. He already played in a band with Tom and Lisa, doing mostly Irish tunes, and they played at the contra dances. I didn't know Cody was interested in bluegrass.

"We're thinking of practicing tomorrow evening at seven," Catherin tells Cody. "Could you make it then?"

"Yeah, I guess so," he says, a look of amazement on his face. I'm not sure he believes the rapid turn of events either.

"Say, if you guys are interested, Tom and Lisa are having a party tonight," says Cody. "Maybe you would like to come."

Catherin looks to me, questioning.

"There's likely to be a lot of musicians," I say to her.

"Then let's go," says Catherin. "And Cody, we'll see you over there. Maybe we can figure out which tunes we have in common."

We leave the coffeehouse to round up our instruments for the party. Our first stop is back to where Catherin is house-sitting so we can fetch her guitar. I carry it for her as we leave the house. Since it's not good to have instruments in the uncovered, unprotected back of the truck, I place her guitar in the middle of the front seat. Catherin quickly changes that as she gets in, strategically rearranging the guitar to her right side, by the door.

"I would much rather sit next to you than my guitar," she remarks.

The only trouble is, seat belts jut out from the middle, making for uncomfortable sitting. It's funny how I'd never noticed that before. I guess it's a sad commentary on my recent dating history …

"I'm sorry about these seat belts," I say, reaching over to help move them out of the way. In doing so, I brush against Catherin's hips, practically embracing her. She doesn't seem to mind. I'm delighted by her warm reaction, but in my usual, bashful, self-defeating way, I show no outward sign of this.

We make a quick trip to my place where I fetch my fiddle, and we reach Tom and Lisa's house around midnight. There doesn't seem to be many cars parked on the cul-de-sac. The front of the house is dark.

"Maybe they decided not to have a party," Catherin says. "They're probably already asleep."

"Oh, they'll be playing," I say. "Tom and Lisa are not known to renege on party plans."

I knock on the door, which Lisa soon opens to a houseful of guests. Music of all styles fills the air until the wee hours of the morning, and by three o'clock, things are getting silly, the tunes regressing into parodies and 'dead dog songs'—popular songs from the past that are so overplayed they have become musical clichés. Later, a certain sleepy seriousness settles in, and we sit in a circle and start singing original songs. Catherin sings one of hers:

My Lover, My Friend

Bring me a smile, I'll give to you laughter
Bring me a ray, I'll give you the sun
Bring me a poem, I'll give you a poet
With sonnets for you, my lover and friend.

Bring me a flower, I'll give you a meadow
Bring me a twig, I'll give you a tree
Bring me a stream, I'll give you a river
Of love overflowing, my lover, my friend.

Bring me a heartache, I'll give you compassion
Bring me a teardrop, I'll cry with you then
Bring me a sign, I'll give you my kisses
To soothe your pain, my lover, my friend.

Bring me a day, I'll give you a lifetime
Bring me a story, I'll write you a song
Bring me some warmth, I will love you forever
These things I give you, my lover, my friend.

— *Catherin Delaney, 1980*

I watch Catherin from across the circle, impressed. Those are nice lyrics, and what a clear, pleasant voice she has.

Soon, it's my turn. Borrowing Catherin's guitar, I play a song about the Superstition Mountains I had written a few years back. I'm not the best singer in the world, and rarely sing in public, but this night I sing better than usual:

The Superstitions

City streets and freeways make me cry
Along with all the smog that's in my eye
I've got to get away
And go where I can find peace of mind.

The desert sure is green this time of year
The yellow poppies blooming everywhere
And the Palo Verde trees
'Neath the blue skies, it just brings me to my knees.

This city life has really got me down
It seems that all you do is run around
How can you find yourself
Lost in the maze, of other people's ways?

You know I really like it way out here
Away from all the noise and crowds and fears
You can see the stars at night
And shadows from the moon in the desert sky.

Sit down beside me, smell the dew
And we'll share a memory or two
You'll never be the same
When you find out you don't have to play their game.

City streets and freeways make me blue
Circle K's and shopping centers too
Where has the desert gone?
I don't know, but all I see are Bermuda lawns.

You know I'd really like to settle down
And get a place that's far away from town
Goodbye, suburbia
And hello to all the things that wait for me
Out in the country.

— Bryan Flamig, 1982

The party ends around four, and we leave Tom and Lisa's for the place Catherin is house-sitting. Since we're both hungry, Catherin suggests buying food for breakfast. We find the nearest 24-hour grocery store and search the aisles for appropriate breakfast fare. I also search my memories for other times as fortunate as this early morning is shaping up to be. Those times were few and far between.

Catherin fixes a breakfast of eggs and toast, and puts on a pot of tea. Sitting at the kitchen table, my body is as alert as ever, but my mind is beginning to fade like the darkness of early morning. I struggle to find interesting things to say.

"I liked the song you sang over at Tom and Lisa's," I say to Catherin, as she pours tea for both of us. "It's hard to believe it isn't a traditional folk song. It sure sounded like one."

"Thanks," Catherin replies, modestly. She returns to the table and sits across from me. "I liked your song too—very much so."

Sipping her tea, Catherin looks at me with admiration. I blush. I'm not used to this kind of attention and it must have shown. Catherin props an elbow on the table and cradles her jaw in the palm of her hand. She searches my baby blue eyes with a gaze I'm not able to reciprocate for long. My gaze drops to my fidgety feet.

"Let's see, if you were born when you say you were, that would make you twenty-nine," says Catherin. "But if I didn't know better, I'd guess you to be twenty-two ... twenty-three at the most."

"Well, I truly am twenty-nine," I reply between bites of toast and sips of tea. "I've always looked young for my age. When I graduated from college at twenty-two, I looked no older than sixteen, and hated every minute of it. I had to start wearing braces my senior year of college, which didn't help matters."

"I'll bet all the girls were madly in love with you anyway, braces or not," Catherin remarks.

I almost sputter into my tea cup and feel my face flush again at the implication of what she is saying.

And what is she saying? Is she just teasing, or is she projecting her own feelings? Usually, I find such teasing discomforting—but that's when it comes from my peers. Coming from her, I can handle the teasing. Relish it, even. Besides, there may be some truth in what she's saying.

"Come to think of it," I say, "I *was* voted king at my senior Prom in high school."

"Really?" says Catherin, slowly. "I'm impressed."

Her admiring eyes make my heart race. Once again, I am unable to hold her gaze and have to look away.

"It was a total shock when I was chosen," I say, staring into the kitchen, avoiding eye contact. "I had only been going to that school for a year and a half, and really didn't know my classmates. I was shy and kept to myself. I never saw it coming."

I finish my tea and look back towards Catherin. She still looks on with admiration.

"So how about you?" I inquire. "May I ask your age?"

"Oh, I'm thirty."

Catherin abruptly gets up and turns away, going over to pour herself another cup of tea from the stove.

She's thirty? I would have figured her older than that. But I'll go with thirty. That way, I don't feel quite so young, in comparison.

After breakfast we move to the couch in the living room, where an awkward silence develops. It's all my doing—my shyness taking hold. Catherin gets up to turn on the TV, and we half heartedly watch an old Andy Griffith rerun, not paying much attention to the show—at least I know I'm not. Acutely aware of Catherin's presence, I'm sitting at the opposite end of the couch, arms in lap, too shy to make a move that would reveal any overt interest in the attractive woman sitting at the other end. And there she is, probably wondering just what is going on. After all, hadn't I kissed her a few nights before? So why am I ignoring her now?

Finally, out of seeming frustration, the dark-haired, white mountain bike woman motions me to her side of the couch, asking, "What are you doing way over there? Why don't you come over here?"

Chapter 4.
"Don't waste time!"

At her invitation, I move over to Catherin's side of the couch, slipping her hands into mine. She feels warm and pleasant to the touch. My whole body begins to tingle.

"Hi," I say to the dark-haired, white mountain bike woman.

"Hello."

Catherin leans over and rubs shoulders with me, sending sparks flying. I run my fingers through her tantalizing, dark curls.

"So, you're Catherin."

"That's my name."

She gazes back with her shining brown eyes. I just have to kiss those eyes. She returns my actions with a passionate kiss of her own, this time on the lips, turning to wrap her arms around me in a full embrace. This triggers an indescribable feeling of being home. At that moment, electrical circuits close, opposite charges counterbalance, and the promise of the previous night is fulfilled. It feels so natural holding Catherin in my arms.

We lie down on the couch—and I immediately fall asleep. At least I must have, for the Andy Griffith show on TV ends, followed by a loud, blaring commercial. Startled awake, my eyes open to find brown eyes staring back at me, questioning me with amusement. I feel my face flush. This is how I repay her interest in me, by falling asleep?

"Sorry, I must have drifted off," I say, taking a deep breath and pushing myself upright.

"Well, I guess I'll let you off the hook," she says laughing, and sitting up with me. "After all, we *have* been up all night."

"Did you fall asleep too?" I ask. "Or were you watching the whole time?"

"You'll never know," she says, giving me another passionate kiss.

Catherin gets up and turns off the TV. "Come on," she says, motioning amorously down the hallway. "It's time for bed."

~ ~ ~

I wake, finding Catherin curled luxuriously on my chest like a contented kitten. She stirs from time to time and repositions herself, murmuring. I have the feeling that, in her dreams, she is already planning our life together. She stirs one more time, and the early morning sunlight shines on her face, causing her to wake fully. She reaches over to kiss me and we snuggle momentarily—until she sees the alarm clock and jumps out of bed.

"I've got to get to the shopping center," she says. "I promised a leasing customer I'd meet him there at ten-thirty, and I've got rental documents to prepare." The alarm clock reads eight-thirty.

She hurries into the master bathroom, but not before turning her bare, well-developed figure in my direction to ask, "Do you want to take a quick shower with me?"

Of course I do. I follow right behind. In the cramped and intimate shower stall I turn the water knob the wrong direction, shocking us both with cold water, and we fumble around looking for soap and shampoo, kissing every chance we get. I feel like an intruder. Not only is this not my shower, it's not Catherin's either. I wonder about her friend, whose place Catherin is supposedly 'house-sitting.'

While dressing, I notice Catherin rubbing something greasy onto her face in front of the bathroom mirror.

"What's that you're putting on?" I ask.

"It's Vitamin E," she says, squeezing the contents of a yellowish gelatin capsule into her hands. "It helps keep your face youthful."

More pills emerge as Catherin rummages through bottles in her overnight bag. She pops numerous vitamins into her mouth, and then gathers a multi-colored handful for me.

"You should take these," she says, handing me the vitamins and a glass of water. "They will help your strength and vitality."

"If you say so," I reply, taking inventory. There must be a dozen pills, some rather large.

Catherin must have seen my furrowed brow. "I perhaps go overboard on the vitamins."

"Hey, whatever works," I say, gulping down the whole lot.

After we finish dressing, Catherin suggests we go out for a quick and early brunch. Using separate vehicles, we drive to a restaurant on the way to Catherin's shopping center, and climb into a booth to order a shared chef salad. Catherin is dressed in a professional-looking outfit—a dark blue pantsuit and matching shoes. I look down at my clothes: wrinkly cotton shirt, faded blue jeans, scruffy tennis shoes. I make sure the latter are well-hidden under the booth.

"What are you going to do the rest of the day?" asks Catherin, finishing the last of the chef salad. A waitress comes by to refill our glasses with ice water.

"I thought I'd go over to Squaw Peak for the monthly jam."

"Oh, that's right. I'd forgotten it was today." Catherin sighs. "I sure wish I could go with you. I really don't feel like dealing with leasing customers this morning."

The waitress comes by again with our bill. Catherin looks at her watch—a cheap, plastic, discount store special that clashes with the rest of her outfit. Oily traces of Vitamin E still glisten on her face. "I've got to run," she says.

We pay the bill and leave the restaurant hand in hand. At her car, Catherin gives me a hurried but affectionate kiss and says, "Remember, we have band practice this evening at seven. I'll call Cody to remind him."

I watch Catherin drive away. It's funny the way people weave in and out of the lives of others. One minute Catherin was there, the next minute, she wasn't.

~ ~ ~

Back home I change clothes and leave early for the jam session. I want to go hiking beforehand to help clear my head. It's an invigorating thousand foot climb to the top of Squaw Peak, something I used to do all the time. Lack of sleep should have left me exhausted, but warm thoughts of Catherin propel me easily to the top.

Propping my back against sharply cut boulders at the summit, I survey the sprawling metropolis of Phoenix that lies below, the sun glittering on numerous swimming pools dotting the valley floor like a sparkling multitude of iridescent turquoise jewels. Phoenix has grown considerably the past few years, and the street grid-pattern is a constant buzz of activity. All those people, all those chances to meet someone special. How many years had we lived our separate, lonely lives in the Phoenix valley, unaware of each other, yet so close by?

By the time I climb down from the peak, musicians have gathered under the usual ramada. I grab my fiddle out of the truck and join the fun.

I play with an unusual amount of energy, but it's short-lived. Lack of sleep finally catches up with me and I head home to rest a few hours, only to toss and turn in bed. Usually, when I have trouble sleeping, I work on my computer. Decision made, I climb out of bed and go into the living room where the computer sits on a wobbly table. It's the perfect time to start working on that astrology program I promised Catherin.

I fire up the computer and after what seems like a short time, I glance at the clock. Jeesh, it's almost seven. Computers can get you into such a time warp, and this one just made me late for band practice. The computer's hard drive has not finished winding down before I'm out the door, fiddle in tow, on my way to Catherin's.

After a short drive down the freeway and onto a few side streets, the ugly pink apartments come into view. I park my truck and walk up the sidewalk to knock on the door, only to find it ajar.

"Come on in!" says a male voice. "And take off your shoes—house rules."

It's Cody, busy tuning his banjo in the living room. I leave my shoes by the door. Catherin comes out of the kitchen, a large bowl of popcorn in her hand.

"Do you want some?" she asks, offering the bowl.

This is it? This is my welcome? No kiss, no hug? My heart sinks. Perhaps what had transpired just hours before was nothing but a dream, or perhaps Catherin doesn't want to expose our new relationship yet. That must be it.

I grab a handful of popcorn—actually, several handfuls, for popcorn *is* my favorite snack—and then get out my fiddle. After playing a few test notes while tuning up, I immediately regret the popcorn when I feel my greasy fingers on the strings. Unclean hands lead to sticky strings, and for a fiddler, that spells disaster. Your fingers need to glide smoothly over the strings so you can press down on exactly the right spot and hit the right note. Having good intonation is perhaps the hardest part of playing fiddle. My intonation needs all the help it can get. I wipe my hands on my jeans as best I can.

Catherin brings her guitar from another room, along with a calendar and a couple of typewritten sheets. She also pulls a small yellow notepad out of her guitar case, presumably to write down ideas.

"Here's a list of songs I'd like us to learn," she says, handing the typewritten sheets to us. "I'm sure you guys can think of others."

"Boy, you don't waste any time, do you?" says Cody, scanning the selection of songs, and seeing Catherin poised with notepad and pen, ready for action.

Catherin laughs. "I figure if we practice real hard, we can be ready for our first public performance in six weeks."

"Six weeks?" I ask. "Do you really think we'll be good enough by then? I can't imagine people paying *us* to perform!"

"I was thinking more along the lines of playing for free at the *Desert Sky Coffeehouse*," she replies. "It would be good experience for us. I've already talked to the owner about it. But I need a commitment that you'uns guys will practice diligently."

"You'uns guys?" Cody replies, chuckling. "Now where have I heard that phrase before?"

Catherin laughs. "I hadn't realized I was saying that. 'You'uns guys' is Pittsburgh talk for y'all."

"So I take it you're from Pittsburgh?" asks Cody.

"Yes, but I've also lived in other parts of the northeast."

"I'm from Ohio myself," says Cody.

"Ohio?" Catherin replies. "Why, we were practically neighbors!"

As I watch the camaraderie develop between the two of them, old insecurities reappear. So far, Catherin has given no outward sign that anything transpired between us the night before. Was I just another band member, after all?

Catherin continues shuffling papers, looking over the list of songs she wants us to play. The list is rather long for a band just starting out.

"We've got a lot of tunes to learn," she says. "I want you'uns guys to practice hard—you'uns guys!"

This makes us all laugh, and throughout the rest of the evening, we try to intersperse as many y'alls and you'uns guys as we can into the conversation.

We attempt some of the tunes from Catherin's list. On one occasion, I hit a particularly sour note on the fiddle—I'll blame it on the greasy popcorn—and hear another type of laughter from across the room:

"Heh-heh-heh. Oot-oooo-weee-hooo! Oot-oooo-weee-hooo!"

It is Bubba and Mrs. Bubba, Catherin's turtle doves. "So you think you can play music!" they seem to say.

"Boy I don't know, we have a ways to go before we'uns guys are any good," I say, laughing. "At least that's what the birds think. Good thing Irene's not here to listen to our noise. Where is she, anyway?"

"She's out with her friend Guthrie," Catherin says. "And I'm not worried about our band. We'll get there. But we sure could use a bass player. Do either of you know anyone we could ask?"

"Well, there's Sherry," I offer. "But no, she's already in a band ... I know, how about Dwight? He might want to join. I know he's been wishing to play more."

"Dwight?" inquires Catherin.

"He looks kind of like me," I say, "maybe a little taller, has a mustache. He was at the Christmas party."

I realize then that Catherin doesn't know who I'm talking about. She probably hadn't noticed me sitting with Sherry and Dwight that night, staring in her direction across the dance floor. And what about the festival at *Gila Joe's* in Cave Creek? I was with Sherry and Dwight there too.

"I still can't place him," says Catherin. "Why don't you call him first chance you get?"

"I guess I could," I say, shrugging with little conviction.

I've always been afraid of approaching people about anything. Catherin seems to sense that.

"Tell you what," she says. "I don't mind calling if you'll give me his number. The sooner we find a bass player the better."

As I search my billfold for Dwight's number, I start thinking. I'm the quiet and passive type. Catherin seems to be the outgoing and aggressive type. Is this going to work?

Cody interrupts my thoughts. "You know guys—I don't pretend to be any wizard on the banjo. I'd feel better playing guitar or mandolin."

"We could have you play mandolin instead," says Catherin. "And come to think of it, I know someone who might be interested in playing banjo. He can play Dobro too. Do you'uns guys know Pete?"

Neither of us do.

"He's actually the person who introduced me to bluegrass," said Catherin. "Turns out he's from the same small town in Pennsylvania as I am. He was in the same grade as my sister."

"That's amazing," I say.

"I'll call tomorrow to see if he's interested."

Catherin jots down a reminder to herself on her yellow note pad. "We need to talk about practice schedules. I was thinking twice a week."

"Fine with me," I say.

"I can handle that," says Cody.

"Okay, we'll practice Sundays and Thursdays, if that's all right with you'uns guys," says Catherin. "That'll leave Friday nights and Saturdays open for performances."

"You've got this all planned out, don't you?" I say to Catherin. "But better you than me. I'm terrible at planning."

"I'd rather not do the organizing either," says Cody.

It soon became clear that this was to be Catherin's band, and it wasn't long before we were calling her the 'boss lady.'

When practice is over, Cody puts on his shoes and prepares to leave. I also put on my shoes, tying my shoestrings slowly, trying to arrange it so that Cody is out the door before me. Cody seems to notice this, and gives a knowing look. He must have figured out that something *is* going on between me and Catherin. With good grace, he says goodbye and leaves.

Now the onus is on me—and I fail miserably.

"I guess I'd better be going too," I say to Catherin at the doorway, awkwardly fidgeting with my fiddle case.

Catherin looks confused and disappointed. A moment passes as we both stand there, me not wanting to leave but too unsure of the situation. Catherin finally breaks the stalemate.

"Don't you want to stay even for a little while?" she asks, moving closer and wrapping her arms around me. Her kisses resolve all doubts.

~ ~ ~

The next morning I wake, and like the previous morning, it takes me a while to get my bearings. This isn't my bed, and it isn't my apartment. Then I hear what's becoming a familiar sound.

"Heh-heh-heh. Oot-oooo-weee-hooo! Oot-oooo-weee-hooo!"

It's Catherin's turtle doves, waking us with their morning repertoire. Catherin stirs.

"I'm sure glad it's Sunday," she says, nuzzling up to me. "It'll be nice to just snuggle here with you."

"I can't argue with that," I say, returning her tender caresses.

We fool around and doze on and off all morning, at one point being awakened by the sound of doors opening and closing. That must be Irene getting up and about. Around noon, we finally manage to get up and about ourselves. We drink orange juice at the dining room table—underneath the picture of a white dove, flying through the clouds. Irene left us a note saying she and her friend Guthrie were going to a party later that afternoon and that we could come if we wanted. She left directions and a phone number.

"Maybe we could walk downtown and have lunch," says Catherin. "There's an old café that has a decent menu. Later, if we feel like it, we can go to the party."

"You know, I've never been to downtown Gilbert."

"I kind of like it," says Catherin. "It still has a small town feel, with many older shops and businesses. Can't say much about the surrounding area, though."

"I know what you mean," I say. "I'm not enamored with all the growth in the valley. I realize people need places to live, but I'd rather see farms and fields. That's the Nebraska in me, I guess."

We walk the mile to downtown and eat old-fashioned hamburgers at the café Catherin had mentioned, and then browse through the old shops. Later we stroll hand in hand through the town park, play like kids on the swings, and sit on a bench kissing like teenagers. Eventually we make our way back to her place.

"What do you want to do the rest of the day?" I ask Catherin as she opens the door to her house. "Do you want to go to the party?"

"I can think of better things," she says with conspiratorial eyebrows, motioning me down the hallway.

~ ~ ~

The following morning is a repeat of the day before. I wake to the sound of Catherin's turtle doves.

"Heh-heh-heh. Oot-oooo-weee-hooo! Oot-oooo-weee-hooo!"

Catherin nestles in my arms. I'm sure glad it's—Monday? The cruel reality of the work week comes crashing down. I glance at the alarm clock, which says six-thirty.

"Did you set your alarm last night?" I ask Catherin.

"Yes, for a quarter-to-seven, but the birds usually wake me first," she says, reaching over to turn off the alarm. She stretches her arms overhead and rises out of bed.

I follow her lead, swinging my legs over the side and noticing my rumpled clothes littering the floor.

"Oh-oh," I say. "I should have gone home yesterday to get clothes for work. I don't have anything to wear."

"I'm sorry. It's my fault," says Catherin. "I suspect I caused you to have other things on your mind."

Catherin giggles, and we fall back into bed and steal a few more moments of those 'other things.'

"Are you going to stay here tonight?" asks Catherin.

It has been three nights since I last slept in my apartment. I feel drained. I'm not used to interacting with someone else for such an extended period of time. I need my time alone.

"Do you mind if I stay home?" I reply. "This is all going too fast for me."

"I understand," she says. "But if you'd like, you can come stay tomorrow night. We can practice fiddle tunes."

Catherin gives me a passionate kiss as further incentive.

I put on my dirty, rumpled clothes and start the drive back home to shower and get ready for work. Catherin's house is halfway between my apartment and office. It's mostly freeway, but that's rush-hour freeway. I'll have to drive to Tempe, and then turn around and drive all the way back to northeast Mesa.

As expected, I arrive late for work. I say hello to the secretary, trying to act like my normal reserved and quiet self. Apparently that doesn't work.

"Did you have a good holiday weekend?" asks the secretary, with suspicion raising her eyebrows as soon as she sees me.

"Yes, I did."

"Is that all you've got to say?"

"I joined a band."

"Well that's news! You play fiddle don't you? So what kind of band?"

"A bluegrass band," I say. "A friend of mine is going to play mandolin, and then a woman I just met is playing guitar. She's the one who started the band."

A look of revelation sweeps over the secretary's face. She tilts her head and says, "Is that *all* she started?"

I feel my face flush. "Why do you ask?"

"It's that big grin on your face."

I quickly avert my eyes. "I'm late for a meeting," I lie, hurrying down the hallway.

That dang Nebraska grin, giving me away. I've been told by other friends that we Nebraskans always seem to possess these big grins. I guess they get even bigger when things go our way.

The company workplace is actually a converted residential house, my office being in one of the bedrooms. There is open desert to the north, and out my office window I can daydream as I watch jackrabbits scampering between the saguaros and chollas. It's a fine way to spend the day.

~ ~ ~

We have band practice that Thursday, and true to her word, Catherin had called both Dwight and Pete, and they had agreed to join our band. Now our group consists of Catherin on guitar, me on fiddle, Cody on mandolin, Pete on banjo and Dobro, and Dwight on bass. In just a short time, we've become a bona fide band. Too bad we don't sound like one, though.

I soon discover that Catherin is always on the move. She has things for us to do every evening—places to go and songs to practice. It's too much for me. I'm the kind of person who needs time alone to unwind and restore my energy, more so than most people. By the following Sunday I'm exhausted. After a late breakfast I lie down on the couch to read the Sunday paper, content to relax and maybe take a snooze later on. But Catherin will have none of that.

"Let's go, Bry!" she says, pulling my arm. "You agreed to go hiking today. Remember?"

"A nap is more what I had in mind," I say, further settling into the couch. "Can't we just stay home and rest? Besides, I'm not finished reading the paper."

"You can read that darn paper later," says Catherin. "Let's go while it's cool. Come on. Don't waste time!"

I finally give in to her wishes, and we wind up at the same trailhead in the Superstitions where I had been only a week before with Dr. Thomason. Back then, I dared not think of Catherin as more than a wishful fantasy. Now here she is, no fantasy but a very pleasant and surprising reality.

A warm breeze greets us as we climb out of the car. Yet Catherin wraps a plaid scarf around her head and ties it in a knot. I wonder how it could possibly be cold enough for a scarf. This is Phoenix, after all, January or not.

"I don't want to get sunburned," she says, seeing my puzzled look.

"The scarf makes you look like an old lady," I say laughing, and then realizing my inexcusable blunder. "But I like you just the way you are," I add in haste.

There aren't any thunderheads in witness to tell me what a fool I am. It doesn't matter, because Catherin seems undisturbed by my remark.

Earlier we had filled a desert-camouflaged hip pack of Catherin's with water bottles, a block of cheese, a pocket knife, and a couple of apples. I strap the pack around my waist and we start up the trail. As before, lizards poise stealthily in the warming sun. I wonder if *they* have noticed the quick change in my life.

The day grows warmer as we hike the steep trail. I get thirsty and stop to retrieve a water bottle from the pack. Catherin uses this as an opportunity to catch her breath, and stops too. I notice her water bottle is the kind used in cycling.

"Do you ride a bike?" I ask.

"Well, I used to," she answers, still breathing hard. "My mountain bike was stolen out of the garage a few months ago."

I think back to the time she rode up to the ramada in Squaw Peak Park on a white mountain bike. That must have been the one stolen.

"That's too bad," I say.

"I once belonged to an outdoor club, and one time we took a field trip to California and rode our bikes through the hills of San Diego."

"That must have been quite a challenge."

"I was in much better shape than I am now."

Her shape looks fine to me.

"Years ago I lived a few miles west of Squaw Peak Park," I say, "and used to ride my bike along the canal to the park. Sometimes I would lock my bike to a post, climb to the top, and then ride home. It was quite a workout."

"I know that park well," says Catherin. "I lived for a while just northwest of Squaw Peak, in Sunnyslope."

So we *had* been crossing paths, only to miss each other until now.

We round a switchback and reach the top of the hill. Catherin stops to rest on a small boulder along the trail, and I plop down beside her. Below is the valley of the square bluff. Weaver's Needle beckons further south.

"I was just out here a week ago with a friend," I tell Catherin, as I remove my shoes to relieve tired feet. "We were going to hike all the way to Weaver's Needle, but we got lazy."

"I don't need to go any further," says Catherin. "I'm perfectly content right here."

We sit in silence, facing the southwest. A ridge of saguaros is framed in the mid-afternoon sun, each backlit cactus assigned its own halo. The wind dies down and the day grows quiet. In the silence, I feel a sense of timelessness wash over me. I blink my eyes, triggering my recursive memory game. As the sun burns down upon us, that moment is burned into my memories.

Later, restlessness overcomes me and I put on my shoes and pull Catherin to her feet. We pick our way back down the trail, discussing our personal histories. I ask Catherin about her childhood.

"I grew up in Pennsylvania," she says.

"Ah, yes, you'uns guys and all! So you lived in Pittsburgh?"

"Some of the time. We lived on a farm for a while, just outside the city. I had a horse I used to ride everywhere." Catherin stops to show me a scar on her leg where the horse once kicked her.

We come to a scenic overlook and survey the cactus-strewn desert.

"I sure miss the green fields of our farm," says Catherin.

"I've never been to Pennsylvania," I say. "So I have no concept of how green it might be. But you know, the Arizona desert is greener than most people give it credit. In western Nebraska, where I'm from, it's often brown much of the year. Arizona can actually look greener, especially in the winter."

"So you grew up in Nebraska?" asks Catherin.

"Yes, and for a few years in Kansas."

"How many are in your family?"

"There's eight of us, plus our mother." I rattle off the names in my family. "My parents divorced when I was three, so our mother raised all of us by herself."

"Impressive," says Catherin. "I can't imagine how much work that was. There's only four in my family."

Catherin names the rest of her family: Older sister Annette, mother Geraldine, and father Herbert.

"They sure have funny names, don't they?"

She smiles at her own remark, but that is quickly replaced by a frown, and she's a bit moody the rest of the way back.

As we're storing hiking gear in the trunk of her car, I notice a business folder with a shopping center logo on the front. It's from where she works.

"How did you end up a leasing agent?" I ask Catherin.

"It was a roundabout way," she replies. "I worked as a massage therapist at a natural health clinic. Vincent, my current boss, had a psychology practice next door. He eventually became a real estate developer and persuaded me to get my real estate license, and I became the leasing agent for his shopping center."

"So you were once a massage therapist, eh?" I lean over and rub my sore thighs and calves. "I'm betting I'll need some of your expertise later on."

Catherin laughs and says, "Only if you promise to write me that astrology program."

"Deal!" I reply. "Because I've already started."

Chapter 5.
The Magic Farm

The weeks pass and we settle into a routine, practicing on Sundays and Thursdays. After work, I spend most of the time at Catherin's, going back to my apartment periodically for a fresh set of clothes. Sometimes I stay home, though, for it's the only place I can truly rest.

In the early evenings before supper, we go for walks through Catherin's neighborhood. One evening Catherin announces she has a special place to show me, and guides me to a nearby irrigation canal. Strung along the dry, unused canal are high-voltage power lines that feed the ever-growing valley cities. As we stroll eastward along the graveled banks, each step seems to take us back in time. Surrounding both sides of the canal are a series of green pastures. Horses swish their tails, cows munch on closely grazed greenery, and goats mill about. The more curious ones come over to greet us, looking for handouts. I can almost imagine myself back in rural Nebraska. The nostalgic setting is jarred, however, by graders and bulldozers lurking nearby.

As we approach the east end of the canal, a small farmstead comes into view: an old farmhouse with cracked adobe and tattered roof, a dilapidated barn, water tower, outhouse, and rusting farm machinery lined up in a row under a grove of cottonwood trees.

"This is my secret place," says Catherin, as we saunter past the old farmhouse. "I call it the Magic Farm."

On the sagging front porch, an old man watches from a rocking chair as we cross over a small bridge covering a gate that controls water in an adjoining north-south canal. We proceed south alongside this canal. A wall of trees and underbrush partially obstruct the view of the farm now on our right. It's a noisy wall—a cacophony of calls from unseen birds. A flock of prancing peacocks stand guard while chickens sniff and peck in the farmyard dirt.

Indeed, this is a magical place. The old farmstead tells stories of hot and dusty Arizona summers, and a more peaceful, relaxed existence. The farm is an oasis in the midst of the suburban blight spreading across the valley. It's quite a contrast to the air-conditioned cars whizzing by on a nearby road.

Visiting the Magic Farm becomes an evening ritual. It's a way for us to unwind. During these walks we often discuss metaphysics, new-age spirituality, and astrology. Catherin knows far more about these subjects than I do. Though skeptical, I listen attentively, willing to ponder anything new.

On one such walk, Catherin explains my astrological chart as we stroll east along the canal, underneath the buzzing power lines. I'm struck by the trichotomy of our spiritual, new-age discussions, the close proximity of the high-voltage power lines of technology, and the rural, yesteryear setting of the Magic Farm.

"I think I've got your chart figured out," says Catherin.

I stop to scratch the small of my back, which has been itching lately. "So what did you find?" I ask.

"Well, you already know that your sun sign—your birth sign as some call it—is in Leo. So that means you have lion-like traits."

"Such as?"

"Such as being warm and sunny, for one. That's why I was first attracted to you, by the way." She reaches over to kiss me, and then adds, with a note of conspiracy in her voice, "That and the fact our charts are very compatible."

"I see. What exactly do you mean, very compatible?"

"The astrological configurations in a chart signify a person's traits and where their energy lies. Our traits and energies happen to mesh well—balancing each other, if you will."

"Oh? And when did you first determine this?"

"Not long after asking for your birth time and place over the phone," she says, wrapping her arms around me. "You know, our first full night together?"

She kisses me again in case I had forgotten that night, and then says, "My rough calculations told me everything I needed to know." She laughs, flashing her shining brown eyes, and then whispers, "That night confirmed it, too, by the way."

"Well then," I say, "I guess you won't need me to write you that astrology program—not when rough calculations will do."

We start walking again and I ask, "So tell me, what are other Leo traits?"

"Let's see," says Catherin. "Leo's are courageous, natural born leaders, and have a tendency to growl."

"Tendency to growl? That doesn't sound like me. And I don't see myself as leader of anything, nor do I feel particularly courageous. I'm quiet and shy, in case you haven't noticed."

Catherin ignores these comments and continues her explanation: "Leo's like to be the center of attention, and they can be overbearing and autocratic."

The thought that these traits might describe me stings a little. I don't like criticism, no matter how slight.

"I certainly don't like being in the limelight," I say. "As far as being overbearing and autocratic, I guess I've never been in a position to put that to the test. I've always tried to stay in the background."

"Are you sure about that?" Catherin asks.

We reach the end of the canal and turn south along the Magic Farm. There is no cacophony of sound in the trees this time, as the birds have settled down for the night. The small water tower that sits on the property is adorned with perching peacocks, silhouetting the twilight sky. We stop along the fence bordering the farm, and I mull over Catherin's question.

"Come to think of it," I say, "I've had people tell me—when I've asked for their honest opinion—that I come across as obstinate, aloof, and self-centered. When I first heard that opinion voiced, it really surprised me. I've always thought of myself as friendly, and ready to help—if someone asks. I've certainly never felt better than anyone else. I think my shyness causes the misconception. I tend not to say much when I first meet people, which gets misinterpreted. But I'll admit I can be stubborn, especially when I know I'm right."

"And one thing's for sure about Leos," Catherin says. "They never like to be wrong."

"Oh, I don't mind being wrong," I say with a smile, "as long as I'm the one who discovers it first!"

Catherin shakes her head in amusement, and then continues. "There's a reason you don't exhibit some of the Leo traits. It's because you were born near a cusp."

"Now *that* sounds scary."

Catherin chuckles. "Cusps are the locations on a chart where two zodiac signs meet. You were born towards the latter part of August, near the start of Virgo. Because of this, you have Virgo tendencies too."

"So what are Virgos like?" I ask.

"Well, Virgos tend to be analytical and detail oriented. They can also be picky."

"So having skills in engineering and computer programming confirms the analytical and detail oriented part?"

"Exactly," she replies. "There are other things in your chart that make these traits even more pronounced. For example, your rising sign."

"What's that?"

"The sign of the zodiac that was on the horizon when you were born, as opposed to the sign where the sun was positioned. Your rising sign happens to be Virgo, which adds to the influence of Virgo already in your chart. You are as much a Virgo as you are a Leo, maybe even more so."

"So what's *your* sign?" I ask.

"I'm a Virgo too," she says. "In fact, I'm what's known as a triple Virgo, because my sun and moon are in Virgo, and so is my rising sign. It's one of the reasons we're so compatible."

"How does the rising sign differ from the sun sign?"

"The sun sign influences your inner personality, potential, and ego, the rising sign your outer personality—how you appear to others. It's important to know that the rising sign can mask certain sun sign traits."

"So that explains why I don't come across as a leader, or want to be in the limelight?"

"Perhaps," Catherin replies. "Or perhaps those traits have yet to be expressed in your life. Remember, your sun sign represents your potential. Those traits may be latent in you, and it's entirely possible they will never surface."

It's getting dark and chilly, so we turn around and head home. Fortunately, the moon is high in the sky, mixing with the lingering twilight to light our path down the canal.

I contemplate Catherin's explanations, and then say, "Perhaps I do like being in the limelight. After all, what do musicians strive for, but to be playing on stage, at the center of attention."

"See? This does work!" she says. "There's one other thing about your chart that strikes me. Mercury was rising when you were born. In fact, it was right on the horizon."

"Geez, was everything on the horizon when I was born?"

Catherin laughs. "Actually, you do have a lot of planets on the east side of your chart. As far as Mercury is concerned, it's all about communication, information, intellect, logic, and reasoning."

"Sounds like computer programming to me."

"Exactly. And another thing, Virgo is ruled by Mercury, meaning that Mercury has a strong influence when it's positioned in Virgo. The traits of Virgo and Mercury are quite prominent in your chart. Other things to consider are the exact angles between the planets, and also between the planets and signs. But I haven't worked all that out yet."

"Sounds complicated."

"There's more to astrology than the horoscope in the paper," Catherin says. "Certainly more than your sun sign."

"Perhaps all that complexity was put in there to hide the fact that it doesn't really work."

Catherin seems unfazed by this remark. "That's possible. But so far, it has worked for me. People misunderstand what astrology is about. It's not about forecasting the future, and your destiny isn't cast in stone—or cast in the charts, I should say. Astrology is about understanding your own tendencies, and how you respond to the world and interact with other people. From there, you can take corrective action for the traits you don't like."

"So, it's a form of self-help psychology?"

"Some astrologers, the good ones I believe, treat it that way. You can use it as a way to work through problems in life. At the very least, it makes you ask questions about yourself. I study astrology because I'm trying to figure things out—why my life is the way it is, and what I'm supposed to be doing."

A hint of sadness and angst suddenly washes over Catherin. There were certainly struggles going on inside her.

"Astrology was just one of the avenues I tried exploring," Catherin continues, "and I've found that it works for me."

"I guess that's all that counts," I say, scratching the small of my back again.

~ ~ ~

A few days later we once again make a journey to the Magic Farm. Just as we reach the canal and turn eastward, Catherin pulls us to a stop. We are standing right under the massive high-voltage power lines, which are buzzing quite loudly.

"I can feel the vibrations of your spirit," Catherin says solemnly, touching my forehead lightly with her hand.

I laugh and point upwards. "It's no doubt just the 60 Hertz electrical vibrations from the power lines overhead."

"Perhaps."

We come to a culvert along the dry canal.

"I want to go through this culvert," says Catherin.

"Why?"

"Going through a tunnel is symbolic of reliving your birth experience," she says. "I must have had a bad one, for I'm afraid of tunnels. I've been thinking lately that I need to work through that fear."

She hunkers down and enters the culvert. I follow close behind. Crawling on our hands and knees, we make it out the other end without anything perceptible happening.

The sun sets as we reach the farmhouse and turn south along the eastern fence. Peacocks have taken up their posts atop the small water tower. We watch, spellbound. Later, the peacocks move to an old cottonwood tree, as huge in expanse as the Arizona sky used to be. We follow their lead and sit nearby, watching the evening grow darker. The view of the sky is quite rare for a metropolitan area. Few lights blot out the stars. Against these stars, the peacocks have become dark, mysterious shapes.

Cars whiz by on a nearby road, periodically interrupting our quiet solitude. It's like the traffic belongs to a different reality. And this reminds me of something.

"Did you ever read *The Mists of Avalon?*" I ask Catherin.

"Mists of Avalon?"

"A novel that came out a few years ago, set in King Arthur's time."

"I'm not familiar with it," says Catherin. "What's it about?"

"In the story, Avalon is a legendary island near the English coast, said to exist before the spread of Christianity. As more people convert to Christianity, the old ways, rooted in the cycles of the earth, sun, and moon, are forgotten and dismissed as works of the devil. Avalon, which resides partially in other planes of existence, becomes invisible, disappearing into the mists of other dimensions. It's still there; it's just that people lose the ability to see it."

More cars roar down the street nearby.

"Hear those people speeding by?" I continue. "In their busy, modern lives, they don't have time for this old place. It's a relic of the past, and they've lost the ability to notice or care. Places like the Magic Farm are vanishing right under their noses, disappearing into the mists of time."

"Disappearing into the mists," muses Catherin. "I like that."

"Or disappearing into the dusts," I say on second thought. "This is Arizona after all."

~ ~ ~

Late January in Phoenix often means warm and sunny days. The last weekend finds us with a free Saturday afternoon—a rarity in Catherin's whirlwind lifestyle. Late in the day, we take advantage of the nice weather and make another trip to the Magic Farm. This time, we head straight for the large cottonwood tree and prop our backs against its trunk, facing west. From there we can watch the golden, late afternoon sunlight rake across the green fields.

It's too early for the peacocks to find their evening perches, but we do hear doves cooing in the trees. They are mourning doves. Their coos are similar to Catherin's turtle doves, but slower, more subdued—more mournful. The slow, mournful coos and lack of traffic on the nearby road makes for an especially peaceful setting.

I blink my eyes, playing that private game of induced, recursive memories, which brings to mind a childhood memory of a particular afternoon on the farm in Kansas: I'm nestled in a rocking chair, alone in the living room, looking out a window that faces the south. The front door is open to the warm summer afternoon, and a wind chime tinkles gently in the breeze. For a moment, time stops, and an incredible feeling of peace and contentment wash over me. I want to hold on to that moment forever. But later, even if I duplicate the setting, I'm not able to get the magical feeling to come back.

As I sit underneath the cottonwood tree remembering this, I finally succeed in my quest, after all these years. There *is* a place where I can achieve that state of mind—the Magic Farm, with Catherin. Back in Kansas, it was the chimes on the porch blowing in the wind that did the trick. Now, it's the coos of mourning doves in an old cottonwood tree.

After the sun goes down, we begin our journey home along the canal, with only the lights of nearby suburbia to guide us. I stop frequently to scratch my back.

"What's going on with your back?" Catherin asks.

"It's been itching a lot lately. I can't seem to get it to go away."

"That and your fidgeting."

"You've noticed."

"Kind of hard not to."

I laugh. "The itching only happens around you, by the way."

"That's interesting."

We continue our journey down the canal. Catherin seems lost in thought. Eventually she speaks. "Maybe you are itching because you don't really like me, and your body is manifesting the real truth."

I laugh again, but the look on Catherin's face makes me wonder if she's serious. I gently pull her to a stop.

"You don't really think that do you?" I ask, searching her eyes. "Catherin, you are without a doubt the first woman I've ever felt totally comfortable with. I don't have any idea why I'm itching so much, but in no way is it because I don't want to be with you."

"I hope that's the case," she says. "But you have to admit, it would explain things." She raises her eyebrows and tilts her head in a conspiratorial fashion.

"I assure you that can't possibly be the problem," I say.

Catherin shrugs and we continue along, walking hand in hand in near silence, the only sound being our crunching footsteps.

"It's just that sometimes, you seem too good to be true," Catherin says, further down the canal.

"Well, that's how I feel about you, too," I reply.

~ ~ ~

That night, my back itches like crazy as we try to sleep. My feet are wiggling back and forth a mile a minute as well. Catherin sighs. "Turn over, and I'll give you a back rub."

I happily oblige, and soon find expert hands kneading and caressing my back and legs—the key word being *expert*. Catherin was once a massage therapist, after all.

"I don't know what I did to deserve you," I say, as she soothes my tense, itchy nerves, "but I sure am grateful."

"Perhaps *that's* why your back itches all the time. You just want an excuse to get a massage."

"Works for me," I reply. "Or maybe I'm itching to get on with our relationship."

"I like that better," she says.

The itching goes away the following week, just as mysteriously as it came. But my fidgeting continues. One day while sitting on the couch at her place, Catherin is knitting a sweater while I read a book. My feet are once again in motion.

Catherin looks up from her knitting and says, "What would happen if you stopped wiggling your foot?"

"I don't know," I say. "I think I would explode!"

Catherin chuckles. "Your chart points out that trait, you know. Astrologically speaking, it's your moon in Gemini."

"My moon in Gemini?"

"When you were born, the moon was in the sign of Gemini. Your moon sign indicates how you tend to handle your emotional self. Gemini is the constellation of twins, so it symbolizes indecisiveness—such as split careers, split feelings. It accounts for your fidgeting."

I stop wiggling my foot. "I'm not going to let some silly chart run my life."

"You know it doesn't work that way," Catherin replies. "Your astrological chart only points out tendencies and energies. It doesn't control who you are."

"I know. I was joking," I say, my foot soon wiggling again.

"That reminds me," Catherin says. "I've been studying a karmic astrology book. It also explains your fidgeting."

"Karmic astrology?"

"It's a system that helps analyze your life's direction. Two aspects come into play: your moon's north and south nodes."

"So what are these nodes?"

"The north node is the point where the moon crosses the ecliptic plane, ascending from southern to northern latitudes. The south node is on the opposite side. They form an axis pair—like a compass needle. The direction of this needle is determined by your time and place of birth, and points to your spiritual path. The other astrological positions flavor this path."

"Somebody sure has an imagination," I say.

"This system wasn't developed overnight," she replies. "It has taken centuries, over the course of many civilizations."

"So how does this compass needle work?"

"The south node represents where you are coming from—where your soul was in the previous life. The north node represents where your soul is supposed to head, in order to grow spiritually."

"I'd like to read this book you're talking about," I say. "But how does my fidgeting fit into all this?"

"Well, I looked up your north and south nodes in the book, and it mentions your nervousness in connection with your mission in life. You are constantly being reminded that you have a mission to fulfill, and your nervousness is your soul telling you to get moving."

Catherin chuckles, as do I. And I know exactly what I will do with such information.

One night as we are snuggling in bed, trying to drift off to sleep, my fidgeting becomes particularly intense. I wiggle my feet back and forth with rapid abandon. Catherin can take no more.

"Don't fidget!" she says, letting out an exasperated sigh.

"Why? Don't you know it's part of my mission?"

I say this with pretend innocence and we roll off and giggle to the floor, following that with a more passionate endeavor in bed.

~ ~ ~

One day I was reading Catherin's latest issue of *Sky and Telescope*, relaxing at a small table in her kitchen as she prepared supper on the stove. We had been going together for a month. I had been complaining how the driving back and forth between work, her house, and my apartment, was tiring me out.

As Catherin stirs sauce in a pot, she asks, "Why don't you move in with me? That would solve the problem."

"Move in with you?" I ask, looking up from the magazine.

"Yes, why not?"

"I don't know. Because I'm not ready?"

She stops stirring, spoon in hand. "Don't you like it here?"

"Oh, I like it just fine."

"Then what's the problem?"

I shrug, not having an answer at first. "It's just that I can only get truly rested back at my apartment. I need my own space to go back to."

Catherin continues stirring without comment and finishes preparing our meal. We move to the dining room table, eating in silence underneath the picture of a white dove flying through the clouds. I had grown so used to that picture that I scarcely noticed it anymore. Over in the aviary Mr. Bubba stirs, beginning his usual song and dance, bobbing up and down. Mrs. Bubba ignores him. She is sitting on her nest, keeping warm two eggs she laid a few days before.

After finishing our meal, Catherin looks up and says, "Not to put on any pressure, but it would be nice to have you here all the time."

I avoid a direct response by gathering up my dirty dishes to carry into the kitchen. Catherin follows with her own. Afterwards we sit down at the table to finish our drinks, and Catherin begins scrutinizing me, making me shift uncomfortably in my seat.

"It's not that I don't love you," I finally say. "And you do know that, don't you? But we've only known each other a few weeks. Surely it's too soon for the next step. Surely it would be logical to wait."

"Don't pay so much attention to what your mind is telling you," Catherin says. "You need to trust your heart."

She takes a sip of water and continues to watch me intently, as though trying to probe my inner thoughts. I feel weary from the scrutiny.

"I'll think about—"

"What did I just say?" Catherin shakes her head, chuckling in disbelief.

"I'll think—I think I need to go home and rest," I finally say. "Why don't you come and stay at my place tomorrow night? That way we can still be together, and maybe I'll recoup my energy."

"I understand. My Leo needs to spend time in his own den."

The next evening, Catherin comes over as planned and announces she has written a song about our relationship, showing me the lyrics and singing them on her guitar. I find one particular line amusing: *In ten or twenty years or so, we'll know if you should stay or go.*

Be Still My Love

Be still my love, and take your time
Let your heart decide, and not your mind
Cause it knows if you really care
If your home is here, or if it's there

　　You want to know your heart is pure
　　To give me love that will endure
　　But when your heart feels really safe
　　It just might be too late

Now take it easy, take it slow
In time my dear our love will grow
And if apart we start to drift
We'll take the best, and leave the rest

　　It's just a trial, it's just a start
　　Whoever said that hearts were smart
　　In ten or twenty years or so
　　We'll know if you should stay or go

I have a lot of love to share
I knew someday that you'd be there
I prayed to meet you in my songs
Been waiting for you much too long

　　Be still my love and take your time
　　Let your heart decide, and not your mind
　　Cause it knows if you really care
　　If your heart is here, or if it's there

— *Catherin Delaney, 1987*

Late that night, I wake and can't get back to sleep. A melody spins through my head. Words form, prompting me out of bed. I don my bathrobe and move to the living room to fetch Catherin's guitar, sitting on the couch and experimenting with words and chords, developing the melody further. I strum and sing softly, trying not to wake Catherin. She's soon beside me anyway with pen and notepad, jotting down phrases as they come to me by free association.

In my mind, I see the Magic Farm in the early morning, with the old man who lives there sitting on his front porch. I know the Magic Farm can't last, what with the massive housing developments springing up all around. I've seen the bulldozers parked nearby, threatening. It's just a matter of time before the farm disappears. I sing words to this effect.

Then I see a vision of the farm in a night setting. I see candles, and feel a sense of loss. The phrase *burning candles in the night* blurts out. I stop strumming as chills spread down my back.

"Ooh," says Catherin. "I like that last phrase."

"I do too," I say. "Though it's a bit spooky."

"Now that you mention it, it *is* a bit spooky. What made you think of candles?"

I shrug. "As a memorial, I guess. Lighting candles in memory of the farm ... of it disappearing."

"Into the dusts?"

"Something like that. Who needs green fields and goats and peacocks, when a more profitable housing development can be built?"

"Kind of sad," says Catherin."

"Yes, it is. But you know, the burning candles imagery seems more than that, somehow. I can't explain it."

"Maybe it's a premonition," Catherin says.

"Maybe so."

The lyrics Catherin records in her notepad find their way into her guitar case. When the time comes later for me to finish this song, I forget these recorded lyrics, and the burning candles. What I do write is the following:

The Magic Farm

There is a special Magic Farm
Just south of Guadalupe
It's there for all the world to see

> *But, it's not on their way*
> *It's not in their time, their day.*

We used to walk the Magic Farm
Just south of Guadalupe
Holding on to each other's arms

> *Along toward the end of day*
> *The Magic Farm was on our way.*

We'd sit amongst the grass and leaves
The birds were singing in the trees
The peacocks with their feathers bright

> *Silhouetting the dark of night*
> *They presented quite a sight.*

They'd like to buy the Magic Farm
And tear down all the trees and barns
To make their profits where they can

> *The old man sits on his front porch*
> *Between the golf and tennis courts.*

The days are numbered at the farm
Just south of Guadalupe
But it can come to no more harm

> *For it has moved on to our dreams*
> *Still, it is real, more than it seems.*

> — Bryan Flamig, 1987

Chapter 6.
Desert Skies

February 13-14, 1987

After placing the *Red Knuckles and the Trailblazers* album on the stereo, I collapse on the couch with a sigh. I'm sure glad it's Friday. Lately, I've been staying home more than usual, trying to restore my energy and sense of balance, for the Catherin whirlwind is leaving me frazzled. We tried alternating between her house and mine, basing our schedule on regular band practices, but that was only partially successful. I never felt fully rested unless I was home alone. When Catherin mentioned Cecilia was performing at a talent show and wanted her to come, I said it was a good excuse for a "girl's night out," and that I was content to stay home and do nothing.

The next thing I remember is waking up to the sound of the phone ringing, and the phonograph needle popping and clicking around the inner grooves of the record—the turntable not having shut off as it should. With a back stiff from lying on the couch all night, I shuffle across the room to answer the phone, and then move to turn off the stereo, dragging the phone cord behind me. Yawning into the phone, I say hello to Catherin on the other end.

"You sound sleepy," says Catherin.

"Your phone call woke me up," I say. "I fell asleep on the couch last night, and now I'm ready to go back to bed. So what's up?"

"You *do* remember we were going to Tucson this morning?"

Oops.

"I do now."

Earlier in the week Catherin had mentioned she needed to meet leasing customers in Tucson that Saturday, and we decided to go together and make a nice trip of it. But I had completely forgotten these plans.

"Bry! What am I to do with you?" asks Catherin. "We have to leave soon—my appointment is at ten."

The clock on the wall reads ten after seven. With the phone in one hand, I use the other to begin pulling off the rumpled clothes I had slept in.

"I'll be ready by the time you get here," I say. "Do you still want to go to the Desert Museum afterwards?"

"Yes, and Irene and Guthrie are coming as well."

I hang up the phone and take a quick shower. Catherin and company arrive at my apartment twenty minutes later, and soon we're on our way to Tucson. I sit up front with Catherin. Irene and Guthrie are in the back.

"I almost forgot to tell you," Catherin comments as she steers the car onto the freeway. "We have baby birds!"

"Baby birds? So the eggs hatched!"

"Both of them. Right on schedule. It's been two weeks."

"Your aviary is going to get crowded with all these babies. What are you going to do if Bubba and Mrs. Bubba keep having them?"

"These two are already spoken for. Pete said he'd like to have one, and Cecilia may take the other."

"Speaking of Cecilia, how was the talent show last night?"

"Her voice lessons are really helping. She says coming to our band practices has also motivated her."

"That and a certain bass player," I remark.

Since Cecilia lives just down the street, she frequents our band practices and has taken a liking to Dwight.

Irene speaks up from the back seat, "How's the band going, by the way? I'm sorry I haven't been around much to hear you play."

"That's a good thing," I say to Irene. "You haven't been subjected to our noise."

"Don't listen to him," says Catherin. "We're far from perfect, but I think we'll be ready for our debut at the coffeehouse next week. By the way, Bry, I lined up another performance for us, at a women's prison in Phoenix."

"A women's prison?" I ask.

"Minimum security. On Friday night in two weeks. It's part of their series of cultural programs."

"I don't know how you manage to find these things," I say, shaking my head, "and I'm glad you're doing the planning and not me, but that's going to be one strange night. I can see it now. We'll play badly, and they'll decide to lock us up for good."

"We'll do fine," says Catherin.

"If you say so, boss lady," I say, tongue-in-cheek.

We reach Tucson with just enough time for Catherin to make her appointment. The rest of us wander around the University of Arizona while Catherin attends to business. We rendezvous for lunch and head west out of town to the Desert Museum, over a small range of mountains. Thick stands of saguaros dot the hillsides, reminding me of that conversation with Dr. Thomason about lurking gargoyles. There were no gargoyles today. At least none I could perceive.

The Arizona-Sonora Desert Museum is actually a combination botanical garden and zoo. It's a great place to learn about the plants and animals of the desert. Along with an exotic collection of cactus and succulent plants, there are jaguars, coyotes, desert wolves, big horn sheep, tortoises, birds, butterflies, snakes—and river otters of all things.

As we stroll along the cactus-lined pathways of the museum, I search for and locate a white object that looks like a giant aerosol can, sticking up out the side of a mountain, some distance away to the south.

"Hey guys," I say to the others, "there's Kitt Peak Observatory. Can you see the telescope?"

All eyes strain in the direction I'm pointing.

"I can just barely pick it out," says Guthrie. "How did you know where to find it?"

"I've been out this way many times," I say. "That's the Mayall Telescope you are looking at."

"I've always wanted to go to Kitt Peak," says Catherin.

I make some mental calculations. "There's no reason we can't go today. We should have enough time to see it before they close, if we leave soon. Kitt Peak is about forty miles from here, if I remember correctly."

When we planned this trip to the Desert Museum—or should I say, when *Catherin* planned this trip—I don't know why it didn't dawn on me to mention Kitt Peak. On numerous occasions, I've visited both places on the same day.

"Can we stay and look through the telescopes in the evening?" asks Catherin.

"I believe they have a scope they use for public viewing—a sixteen-incher," I say. "But I'm pretty sure we would need reservations."

"That's too bad."

"It's still a great place to visit," I say. "There are soaring views from the top." I turn to Catherin's friends. "You guys up for it? It's only one of the finest sites for telescopes in the world."

"Then by all means, let's go," says Guthrie. Irene nods in agreement.

We leave the museum and take back roads down to the highway leading to Kitt Peak.

"We haven't gone to any star parties," I say to Catherin as we're driving along. "You still belong to the astronomy club, don't you?"

"Yes, but as you know there hasn't been time to attend any meetings."

"Maybe we should skip some of our visits to prison," I say.

Catherin rolls her eyes at me, chuckling.

We pass a sign that says we are entering the Tohono O'odham Reservation. Soon we're at the base of the mountain and begin the steep, twelve mile, three thousand foot climb to the top. The climate changes dramatically, from the lower Sonoran desert of saguaros and mesquite, to oaks and pines. The cool mountain air is refreshing, the 360-degree views, staggering. From on high the desert looks like a vast brown sea, with mountain ranges off in the distance reaching up like islands. It's partly the reason mountain tops like Kitt Peak are called 'sky islands.'

We park our car near the visitor's center and climb the pathway to the Mayall Telescope building. The chilly wind picks up to almost gale force intensity. I've encountered such winds before at this spot, almost every time I've come here. That's probably why the building housing the telescope was designed to withstand one hundred and twenty mile per hour winds, according to a sign I see.

We reach the door of the observatory, after struggling in the wind, and Catherin discovers we have to ride ten stories up an elevator to the telescope observation deck. I push the 'Up' button and the elevator door opens. I step inside.

Catherin hesitates, a worried look on her face.

I press the 'Hold' button. "What's wrong?" I ask.

"It's nothing," she says. "Okay, I'm a little afraid of elevators." Catherin apparently sees my look of puzzlement. "It's the same fear I have of tunnels."

"As in reliving your birth experience?"

"Yes, but don't worry. I'll manage."

She steps into the elevator and I let the doors close. Catherin remains silent for the short trip.

When the doors re-open we are presented with the sight of the huge Mayall Telescope. It's ninety-two feet long, and the surrounding dome weighs five hundred tons. The main mirror is four meters in diameter. The dome and telescope move together, separated from the building by huge rollers. It's all very impressive. I try to imagine what it would be like to be here late at night, with the dome open to the distant galaxies. My previous job was with a group that designed control software for instrument pointing platforms, to be mounted in the bay of the Space Shuttle. I would feel right at home controlling telescopes—and that had almost happened a few years before.

"I once interviewed for a job up here," I tell Catherin.

"Really?"

"They were looking for a 'mountain programmer'—someone to keep the computers running while astronomers collected images and data from the night sky."

"That sounds like a great job for you," Catherin says.

"Yes, but I didn't get it."

"So what happened?"

"I don't really know. I was certainly qualified. Ironically, after starting the job I currently have—which was my second choice—the recruiter from Kitt Peak called and said the person they hired hadn't worked out, and asked if I was still interested. I had only been at my new job a few weeks, and didn't think it was fair to leave them hanging. So I turned down the mountain programmer position."

"That's too bad," Catherin says.

"In retrospect I should have taken it. What a life that would have been: Living in the desert, working on a mountain top, being in the sunshine *and* the starlight, and not to mention working on computers as well."

"Maybe you should reapply."

"Maybe so."

We explore the rest of the observatory grounds. There are many optical and radio telescopes sprinkled about, each housed in its own building. Numerous star photographs line the walls inside some of these buildings. We make a game of picking out which stars we'd like to visit, and at one point we come to a large photograph of the Pleiades star cluster.

"That's the place to be," I say.

"I've always liked the Pleiades," says Catherin.

A plaque below the photograph informs us that the Pleiades—also known as the Seven Sisters—are located in the constellation of Taurus.

Catherin adds her own astrological knowledge. "The Pleiades turn up in the folklore of many cultures. In astrology the star cluster is often associated with sorrow and mourning."

Sorrow and mourning. Perhaps we best not go there after all.

The plaque divulges another interesting fact about the stars of the Pleiades cluster: "Look at this," I say, pointing to the plaque. "It says here that the group of stars making up the Pleiades are all moving at the same speed and direction. Unlike some star clusters that *look* like they belong together, the stars in Pleiades actually *do* belong together."

While gazing at the photograph I have an idea. "Perhaps this cluster is a group of souls that have evolved into stars, and are taking a stroll through the universe together."

"Like us," says Catherin, smiling and placing her hand in mine as we continue the stroll of our own—alas, only here on planet Earth—and eventually end up at the McMath-Pierce Solar Telescope.

This telescope, the largest instrument of its kind in the world, is used to study the surface of the sun. It's housed in an odd-shaped structure consisting of a vertical shaft and an angled shaft. As a unit these shafts look like the number seven laid on its side. The main imaging mirror rests at the bottom of the angled shaft, several hundred feet underground. Inside, at ground level, is a video screen where you can see the image of the sun—and any sunspots—as caught by the mirror.

Standing next to the Solar Telescope, I scan the view to the south, and point out landmarks to Catherin. Mexico lies a short thirty miles away. Before the mountains of Mexico, however, lies Baboqui-vari Peak, the center of the universe in the Tohono O'odham tribe's cosmology. Given the way the peak juts out from the surrounding mountains, it seems like a plausible center of the universe to me. It also resembles the dome of a telescope. That aspect of Baboquivari Peak has always intrigued me.

I turn my head to the southwest, where the afternoon sun fills the sky. A hundred miles in that direction lies the Gulf of California.

"Remember when we sat along the trail in the Superstitions on our first hike together?" I ask Catherin.

"I'll never forget it," she says. "It was a lovely, peaceful after-noon."

"What I remember most was a sense of timelessness," I say. "We were facing the southwest, just like now."

And just like in the Superstitions, I'm now having that same timeless feeling. During numerous visits to Kitt Peak, I've built up layers of memories—of standing at this very spot and looking off to the southwest. Each time, I'm spellbound, as though gazing into infinity. I always walk away re-energized.

"Did you ever read any of the Carlos Castenada novels?" I ask Catherin.

"I vaguely remember them," she says.

"In his books, he talks about 'power spots,' places where your spirit can draw energy. We must be on a power spot now."

"That figures," says Catherin after a short pause. "Since we're standing right next to the Solar Telescope, of course a Leo would find this to be a power spot!"

I smile at her keen observation. We stand hand in hand a while longer, soaking up the serenity and beauty of the desert vistas. Finally, Catherin mentions she wants to go to the gift shop at the visitor's center.

"I want to see if they have any souvenir patches," she says, look-ing at her watch. "We'd better hurry. The visitor center might be closing soon."

"Afterwards we'll have to see where Irene and Guthrie have wan-dered off," I say.

Catherin has no success finding a souvenir patch in the gift shop. For some reason, her wanting to collect patches touches something in my heart. Catherin could be pleased by such simple things, it seemed.

We eventually find the others and make it back to the car, soon beginning the steep descent down to the valley floor. We head east through the reservation. I'm driving, with Catherin by my side. Guthrie and Irene snooze in the back.

We are passing through a raw landscape of seemingly barren mountains and plains, but one that is actually filled with a surprising amount of vegetation: cholla cactus, prickly pear cactus, ocotillo cactus, Palo Verde trees, mesquite, sagebrush, and of course, the giant saguaro cactus unique to the Sonoran Desert.

"I've always liked this stretch of highway," I tell Catherin, as we skirt around a small range of mountains. "When I lived in Nebraska, I always pictured Arizona to be miles of sand dunes."

"It's nothing like that at all, is it?" she replies.

"My favorite song when I was in college back in Nebraska was *Desert Skies*, by the *Marshall Tucker Band*."

"I'm not familiar with it."

"The lyrics talk about a cowboy riding along a sandy trail on his horse, with the moon hiding in the desert skies."

At that description Catherin begins clucking on the roof of her mouth with her tongue, making the syncopated sound of horse hooves, clopping along.

"Are you making fun of me?" I ask.

"No, I actually like the imagery."

"I was always spellbound by that song, but it never occurred to me that I'd be living in the desert someday."

We continue northeast towards Tucson.

"I used to walk along a creek bed on the outskirts of Lincoln, with *Desert Skies* running through my head," I continue. "I never understood why that song captivated me then. The desert was a long ways away."

"Perhaps your spirit knew what it needed, and was just trying to tell you," she says.

When I was growing up, I always figured that someday I'd be living in the Rocky Mountains. During my teenage years I spent summers on a ranch in eastern Colorado, working for an old cowboy who hired me mainly to keep him company. Our work day, if you could call it that, often consisted of nothing more than saddling up the horses and riding all day to count cattle. The ranch was comprised of low, rolling, grassy sand hills that were too far from the Front Range for me to see the mountains, but that didn't stop me from riding to any high spot I could find to search the horizon. Like my recurring Kansas childhood dreams of sitting on a roof looking westward, I would try to wish those shimmering white peaks into existence.

During my life I've had the opportunity to spend time in the Rockies, and have learned I don't need to be *in* the mountains, I just need to see them. I don't care as much for the forested valleys, but I do love being high on the peaks. I'm used to the wide-open prairies and need to have a view. I'm even happier when there is 'broken sky' on the horizon.

When I came to the deserts of Arizona I realized what I had really been looking for. The desert mountains are perfect, for I can be in the heart of them without ever feeling claustrophobic. There are few trees to block the view.

That's certainly the case now as we drive east towards Tucson. We eventually reach the city and swap driving duties after stopping for gas. Catherin and I move to the back seat, and Irene and Guthrie sit up front. As we head northwest on the freeway back to Phoenix, it dawns on me what day it is.

Sheesh, it's Valentine's Day! I don't have anything for Catherin, not even a card!

Things like cards and gifts never seem to enter my mind, even in the most obvious situations. Actually, I *had* thought about them the day before, while I was at work. But that thought had gone in one neuron and out the other. Maybe I'm a self-centered Leo after all. Or maybe I'm just a space case. I prefer the latter explanation.

"I'm sorry I forgot to get you anything for Valentine's Day," I say to Catherin, giving up on finding a more inventive apology.

"It's no big deal," she says, staring out the window towards the rosy glow of sunset on the Santa Catalina Mountains northeast of Tucson. "And I think Valentine cards are silly."

But then, further down the road, Catherin reaches below the seat in front of her and pulls out a package.

"This is for you," she says.

A present? For me? After pretending she didn't care about Valentine's Day? Boy, did I feel like a schmuck.

Inside the package is a tape of many different versions of *Pachelbel's Canon*. I have a dreamy recording of this classical work that is played at a slow, relaxing tempo. It's a peaceful, yet haunting rendition, and to me it speaks perfectly of the joys and tragedies of being alive. I had played that version for Catherin a few weeks earlier, and she had really liked it. It had become 'our song.' Catherin thought I might enjoy these alternate versions as well.

"I have the album I bought for you back home," she says.

We listen to the taped copy on a cassette recorder Catherin also pulls from under the seat. I look out the car window to the east. An orangish, glowing orb is rising over the desert mountains, soon to be swallowed by silvery, fluffy clouds.

"Well, I'll be damned, the full moon is rising!" I tell Catherin, pointing out the window. "It's really huge tonight."

"How beautiful!" she says, gazing out the window with me. "On Valentine's Day no less."

Then I have an idea.

"It's my gift to you," I say, whispering in her ear, hoping she will pretend I planned all this.

Catherin gives me a kiss confirming my hope, and as the scenery drifts by, we settle into each other's arms, gazing at the rising moon now partially hidden in the desert sky.

I blink my eyes, wanting this moment to last forever.

~ ~ ~

At band practice the following day, Catherin hands out a sheet of lyrics.

"I've got a song I wrote a few years ago," she tells us. "I'd like to sing it and see what you'uns guys think."

The lyrics are more country than bluegrass, but that fits Catherin's voice better anyway. She has a deeper, folksier kind of voice than is usual for bluegrass singers.

She sings the song for us and teaches us the chords. It's clear to me that Catherin has talent as a songwriter. Her song, titled *Treat Yourself to Me*, seems appropriate for the Valentine's Day weekend:

Treat Yourself to Me

Treat yourself to me babe
I'm sure you will agree
It's good to take some time out for yourself

Let me hold you in my arms
And thrill you with my charms
Please dream of me and think of no one else

> *But remember babe, I'll spoil you beyond compare*
> *With our secret selves, and our souls to share*
> *Remember babe, my passion it runs deep*
> *I want a lasting love, one that's mine to keep*

Don't deny yourself to me
Let your feelings all run free
And take your heart down from the shelf

Let me hold you in my arms
And thrill you with my charms
Please dream of me and think of no one else.

> *But remember babe, I need love in the morning too*
> *When the moonlight fades, and the world's in view*
> *Remember babe, I'm looking for happiness*
> *My one and only love, to give me sweet caress*

Treat yourself to me babe
I'm sure you will agree
It's good to take some time out for yourself

Let me hold you in my arms
And thrill you with my charms
Please dream of me and think of no one else

— Catherin Delaney, 1985

~ ~ ~

One evening after work, I don running clothes and jog down the canal to the Magic Farm. A storm is brewing in the desert sky, and by the time I reach the farm it grows dark and windy. I begin thinking I should head back before the weather gets worse.

Thunderstorms in Arizona don't always involve much in the way of rain. Dust from the advancing storm kicks up and is blown onto your car, and then the storm sprinkles on just enough rain to coat said car with a thin layer of mud. You can almost hear the thunderclouds laughing and mocking you as they go by.

But they aren't laughing today. The peacocks begin their evening calls—sharp cries which can be quite eerie, especially with the backdrop of an approaching storm. All of this conjures up the tornado scene from *The Wizard of Oz*. As a child growing up in tornado-prone western Kansas, that movie was mighty scary, causing numerous nightmares. We didn't have a storm cellar underneath our house for nothing.

Usually the Magic Farm was a peaceful, inviting place, but those distant fears from childhood, the increasing winds, and the eerie cries of peacocks had me turning around and running as fast as I could back to Catherin's place, dodging dust and raindrops along the way.

Chapter 7.

Lessons to be Learned

C atherin straps the guitar over her shoulder and steps on stage. She projects poise, confidence, and exuberance. The rest of us are lined up in various states of the opposite. Dwight tentatively tests the strings of his bass, I nervously pluck the strings of my fiddle, and Pete tunes and re-tunes his banjo, never quite getting it right. Cody is his usual laid back self, having performed many times in various bands.

I look out into the audience and marvel at the recent turn of events. It's the third Friday of February, and we're at the *Desert Sky Coffeehouse*, ready for our first performance. Just a few short weeks ago on the night of New Year's, Catherin and I were out there, in the audience, not quite a band yet—and not quite an item.

"Good evening folks," Catherin announces, in that professional sounding radio-voice of hers. "I'd like to introduce our band, *Dusty River*." She laughs and turns to Pete. "It's Pete's fault we have that name."

She continues, "Along with Pete, we have Dwight on bass, Cody on mandolin, Bryan on fiddle, and I'm Catherin."

We begin our first number, *Fox on the Run*, a standard bluegrass tune. We all sing a bit of harmony on the chorus, but other than that, I only have to worry about a short fiddle break. While we're playing, Cody begins to balance on one leg like a flamingo, the other leg folded across. I mimic his behavior, which brings laughter from the audience.

After we finish the song, Catherin turns away from the mike and whispers, "I know we planned on doing *Billy in the Low Ground* here, but do you want to try *Blackberry Blossom* instead?"

"*Blackberry Blossom?* … I-don't-think-so," I reply softly, shaking my head. "Let's stick with *Billy*."

I still don't have *Blackberry Blossom* up to snuff, though I've worked on it diligently.

Catherin turns back to the mike. "It's time for a fiddle tune," she announces to the crowd. "Bryan's going to kick it off." Catherin chuckles. "Byron!—we call him Byron sometimes, after a famous fiddler by the name of Byron Berline."

As soon as I play the 'four potatoes'—a four beat shuffle used to set the tempo and start the tune—Cody assumes his one-legged flamingo pose. I try to do the same, but there is no way to hold balance *and* concentrate on playing. I stumble, bringing more laughs from the audience. *Oh well*, I say to myself. *If you can't wow them with your fiddle prowess …*

~ ~ ~

The next day I go over to Larry and Amy's for a small party. Cecilia has come from across the street. Catherin isn't there yet; she had planned on stopping by later. As we're having drinks in the kitchen—me with my usual club soda—Cecilia hands me photos she had taken over the holidays. I sit down at the table and thumb through the collection. In the stack of photos is one of Catherin, sitting on the couch in her living room, a sad and lonely look on her face.

"When was this photo taken?" I ask.

Cecilia puts down her drink and studies the picture. "That was on Christmas day. I remember Catherin being very depressed."

"Do you know why?"

"No, not really. It may have something to do with her parents. I know she hasn't spoken to them in over a year."

It tugs at my heart to see Catherin looking so forlorn. It put her suggestion of practicing on Christmas day in a whole new light. This sadness was in stark contrast to the enthusiastic, self-confident stage presence conveyed the night before at the *Desert Sky Coffeehouse*. I could only hope that the coffeehouse version of Catherin was the true one.

~ ~ ~

The following Friday we play at the women's prison. Never having been anywhere near a prison, the complex looks ominous to me. We are greeted by a guard and escorted through the entrance. As the prison gates close behind us, I repeat my joke about us being "locked up for good" if we don't play well. Everybody resolves to play their best. The guard leads us down a few hallways, and we discover that our so-called stage is the hard-tiled floor of the fluorescent-lit, bare-walled cafeteria. We proceed to set up sound equipment and tune our instruments.

"This is going to be an acoustic nightmare," says Cody, eyeing the walls and floor.

"That's for sure," I reply. "The bad notes are going to bounce off those walls and come right back at us. It's like instant karma."

Catherin chuckles at my comment and shakes her head. She plugs in a tape recorder to record those bad notes for posterity.

Tattooed inmates file into the room and park themselves at the cafeteria tables. They don't seem to be likely bluegrass fans—their jaded, scowling looks provide little hope of that. Most of them leave within minutes of hearing our first song.

"So much for our captive audience," jokes Cody, after we finish the first tune.

"Captive audience?" I remark. "More like captive band!"

We don't play too badly that night, at least, that's what I think until the next practice, when Catherin plays back the recording of our performance. The rest of the band sounds fine—Pete did a good job on the banjo, Cody's always good on the mandolin, Dwight's bass was for the most part steady, and Catherin's singing was smooth and clear; but I cringe every time I hear myself on tape.

"Listen to that sour fiddle!" I growl, placing my hands over my ears. My lips stick out in a pout.

Upon seeing my pouting, Catherin immediately quips, "Birdsgonnabuildanestonyourlips!"

She talks so fast that the words run together, and I don't catch what she is saying. I give her a puzzled look. She turns off the tape recorder so I can hear what she's saying.

"Bird's-gonna-build-a-nest-on-your-lips," she then says, slowly drawing out the words.

I quickly move my lips back to normal, trying to keep a straight face, pretending not to have ever pouted. I don't want any birds on my lips, not even Catherin's turtle doves.

"You sure are a picky sort," says a laughing Catherin. "That's the Virgo in you. And that sulking face—that's pure Leo."

Catherin's birds-building-a-nest quip soon became an inside joke for us, and she would say this any time I would sulk. She thought it funny that I denied ever being a grouchy, growling lion.

~ ~ ~

The next evening I take Catherin to her first contra dance, held in an auditorium at a school near downtown. The band is still setting up when we arrive, while the caller teaches a beginner's lesson.

The standard contra dance formation consists of pairs of long opposing lines. The caller guides the dancers through a series of moves where you dance with your partner and your neighbors. The moves are drawn from a repertoire similar to that of square dancing: allemandes, promenades, balance and swings, dos-à-dos, and courtesy turns, among others. These moves are choreographed into sixteen-beat cycles. During each cycle the couples *progress*, or move up or down the hall one or more positions, and dance with another set of neighbors. That way, you end up dancing with everybody.

It's the progressions that make a contra dance pure poetry in motion—if the dancers know what they're doing. When things are clicking, it's like weaving a fabric of humanity. But if someone makes a mistake and temporarily rips this fabric, it's not a problem. For the most part, contra dancers are forgiving. They'll laugh *with* you (and usually not *at* you) and someone will help get you back into position. It's not about style and grace, but about having fun.

It's an open band, so Catherin and I scramble for seats on stage. The more experienced musicians are given the exalted chairs with microphones. Everyone else gathers around as best they can. Cody is there, as well as his friends Tom and Lisa.

Soon it's time for the first dance to begin. Tom, the band leader, pounds out the 'four potatoes' to start the proceedings. He plays hammered dulcimer, a trapezoid-shaped wooden instrument strung with rows of strings. It's played using wooden sticks with felt tips. The hammered dulcimer is found in many cultures, and is in fact the forerunner to the piano. Lisa plays the modern version of the piano—an electric keyboard. The rest of the band consists of a few fiddlers, including myself, an assortment of guitar players, including Catherin, and a few banjo and mandolin players, including Cody.

It's crowded on stage, but we don't all play on every tune, and no one knows all the tunes anyway. I myself only know a few. There is some overlap to those played in the bluegrass circles. The tunes gravitate to the lowest common denominator—the classic ones that probably every fiddler learns as a beginner: *Soldier's Joy, Saint Anne's Reel,* and *Cold Frosty Morning,* among others. Some people play by ear while others read sheet music. We play many tunes out of the *Tucson Book*—a collection of tunes compiled by our Tucson counterparts.

Halfway through the evening there is an intermission—a time when a waltz is traditionally played. I ask Catherin if she wants to dance. We step off stage and onto the dance floor with numerous other couples. The music begins and I try to move my feet in the standard box step pattern, only to step on Catherin's toes. She's not bothered by this but simply laughs. I eventually get the hang of it. With tentative leading skills I whirl her around the dance floor, trying my best not to guide her into the other couples.

As we circle the hall, Catherin comments, "I really like the tune the band is playing. Do you know what it's called?"

"I believe it's *Midnight on the Water,*" I say, raising her arm for a twirl. "I've never played it, but I recognize the melody."

Somehow, we manage to complete the twirl without tying ourselves into knots.

The waltz ends and Catherin says, "That's such a pretty tune. I want to learn it."

"I'll try to remember to find the music for it," I reply.

~ ~ ~

February progresses into March, and our band plays at a park in central Phoenix on a chilly and windy day. The overcast skies make for a dreary outing. It's the band's first outdoor performance. The park system is promoting a series of cultural events in the city parks, and like the women's prison gig, Catherin somehow makes connections and signs us up to play.

There have been changes to our group. Cody didn't have the time to practice twice a week after all, and had decided to leave the band. He still played with us occasionally. Catherin recruited another mandolin player, Darrell. He's a fine player, and a fine singer—the best singer of us all. That makes him a great addition. At the park we have a guest vocalist. Cecilia had been practicing some of our songs in conjunction with her voice lessons, so Catherin invited her to sing with us.

Along with chilly gusts of wind, sour notes drift my way from Pete's corner of the stage. He's trying to tune his Dobro, and whenever he plays his 'D' string, it sounds nothing like the 'D' string on my fiddle. They clash badly. After listening to this for a minute or two, I can take no more.

"Hey, Pete," I say, turning towards him. "Tune it or die!"

At first I scowl at him, but then break into a laugh. The "tune it or die" phrase was a popular joke in the bluegrass circles. I had been waiting for an opportune time to use it. Pete chuckles at my comment, and then proceeds to retune his 'D' string again, but unfortunately, it still isn't the same 'D' that I have. Oh well.

I should have listened to my own advice. During the warm-up I come to the conclusion that my fiddle is as off-key as Pete's Dobro. Unlike our first rehearsal at Catherin's house, Bubba and Mrs. Bubba aren't there to laugh with their repetitive coos at our sorry attempts at music.

The sound system isn't helping matters. It's a cheap setup, but the occasion doesn't warrant anything better. I glance out onto the park grounds and survey our audience.

"Look at this record turnout," I remark to Catherin. "I count all of three people."

Catherin laughs and shrugs. "I guess we have to pay our dues somewhere."

As usual, Catherin is vibrant on stage, adding a cheerful presence to an otherwise dreary day. I don't share her enthusiasm. My fingers are stiff with cold and I'm not feeling confident about our performance. Catherin had been prompting me to sing harmonies with her on one traditional song, Columbus Stockade Blues, which I hadn't spent much time practicing. I give it my best shot and hope it's not too disastrous. One stanza makes me think of the women's prison:

Last night as I lay sleeping
I dreamed that you were in my arms
When I awoke, I was mistaken
I was peeping through the bars

I'm supposed to play a short fiddle break, but lack of practice means I have to improvise. Amazingly enough, my solo isn't half bad. It has a gypsy feel that seems to work, and we subsequently incorporate the short interlude into our rendition of the song, giving our band its second unique feature—the first being Cody's one-legged flamingo stance.

~ ~ ~

Beautiful sunny and 70 weather prompts me on a hike with Catherin to the summit of Squaw Peak the following weekend, up the steep and well-worn trail—a popular hiking mecca in the center of the city. We join hundreds of hikers picking their way up and down the mountain. The moving throng stretches out in a long line, like ants on a giant anthill.

After a half hour of heavy breathing we reach the summit and plop down on a small outcropping of sharply cut boulders—a tilted chunk of Precambrian schist, one and a half billion years old. I note this fact to Catherin and add, "It's geologically the same layer of rock that's at the bottom of the Grand Canyon."

"That's amazing," says Catherin, her breath finally slowing. She rubs her hand on the rock's surface, perhaps trying to reconnect with the ages.

"The Canyon is one of my favorite places," I say. "I like sitting on the rim and gazing at the multi-colored layers and formations. Just think how many millions of years those layers have witnessed. It's like each layer has its own set of frozen memories."

Catherin likes my depiction of layers of frozen memories.

The sharp contours of the Precambrian schist beneath my seat become uncomfortable, so I stand up and stretch my stiffening legs. Catherin follows my cue and stands up to stretch too.

"I've always been intrigued by the layers of memories that are built up each time I visit a place," I say, bending over to work out kinks in my legs. "I like to probe into these layers, and recall what I was doing, how I was feeling, and who I was with."

"And what will you remember about this particular time on Squaw Peak?" asks Catherin.

"I'm sure it will become one of my favorites," I say, wrapping my arms around her and giving her a kiss. "After all, it's our first time here together."

"Hopefully, there will be other times too," she says.

Arm in arm, we survey the sweeping views. Mountains surround us on all sides in the distance.

"I know these mountains by heart," I say to Catherin, pointing out the landmarks in a clockwise direction and rattling off names: The Sierra Estrellas, White Tanks, Bradshaws, Mazatzals, McDowells, Four Peaks, Superstitions, San Tans, Camelback Mountain, and finally South Mountain.

After my sweep of the valley I glance down to the picnic ramadas below us, which sparks a memory of the first time I had spoken to Catherin.

"Do you remember our conversation down there last fall, when you had asked about my favorite bands and artists?"

"No, I don't," says Catherin, looking downwards. "I didn't realize we had met before the Christmas party."

"I told you I didn't pay much attention to the names of bands or artists. To be honest I don't pay much attention to the names of people in general. But if you ask me the name of a mountain, pretty much anywhere in the Southwest, I can probably tell you."

"You certainly aren't very people-oriented," says Catherin. "But you should work on that. Your purpose in this life is to learn how to interact with others."

"Oh? How do you know that?"

"I see it in your chart. Remember that book on karma and astrology I told you about? It's described in there."

We move to a different side of the summit where smoother boulders provide more comfortable seats. Catherin takes two apples out of her waist pack and hands me one.

I continue our conversation. "It's funny. I've been shy and afraid of people ever since I can remember—for no apparent reason."

"Perhaps you had a bad experience in a past life," says Catherin. "Perhaps you didn't treat people very well, so early in this life you tried to make up for it by being nice. Maybe your fear of harming others has led you to overcompensate by avoiding people altogether."

"That's very perceptive," I reply. "What you are saying rings true."

"I've been told I would be good at helping others through their psychological problems."

I take a bite of my apple and think of the photo taken at Christmas time of a sad and lonely Catherin. "What about your own problems?" I ask.

"That's another matter," she says, diverting her eyes and focusing solely on her own apple, munching away.

I want to know more about that photo, but it doesn't occur to me to directly ask Catherin about it. This particular manifestation of absent-mindedness is a curious trait of mine: I might think of something internally; but that never gets translated into action—not out of laziness, but because the thought to take action simply doesn't appear. This trait seems related somehow to the way it never occurs to me to remember the names of artists and bands, or authors and characters in a book—even ones I like.

We finish our apples, half listening to the conversations of other hikers around us. Catherin then has an observation to share.

"You should take your affinity for the mountains and try to channel that somehow—to help you learn how to get along with others."

"If learning to get along with others is my purpose in life, what's yours?" I ask.

"I'm here to be of service."

"Hence the massage therapy?"

"Yes, that's part of it."

"But why the real estate?"

"I'm tired of not making enough money," she says. "I'm tired of putting so much energy into helping others and not getting anything in return."

We sit quietly for a moment, gazing westward at the harsh desert landscape being swallowed up by urban sprawl.

"I'm tired of the desert too," Catherin continues. "I need to be around water."

"What about down there?" I ask, pointing to numerous pockets of water down on the valley floor—swimming pools sparkling like so many turquoise jewels.

Catherin laughs. "I was thinking more like a lake, or the ocean. I've been told that water is supposed to restore my energy—help renew my spirit."

"Like mountains for me?" I ask.

"Yes, something like that."

It's getting late in the day, so we start back down the steep, rocky trail, dodging a seemingly endless supply of hikers coming the other way. Some of the female hikers we encounter are quite attractive, sporting halter tops and well-toned legs. I catch myself staring as they pass by. Then I feel embarrassed and hope Catherin doesn't notice.

We round a bend and climb onto an outcropping, turning to face the southwest. This reminds me of the time on Kitt Peak where I had envisioned the far-off ocean. An idea pops into my head.

"If you're needing a water fix, maybe we should make a trip to San Diego."

"San Diego is a great place," Catherin says. "I used to live there."

"I didn't know that."

"My friend Michelle lives there now."

I look at her, questioning.

"You wouldn't know her," says Catherin. "She moved there last fall, before I met you."

Catherin tells me briefly about Michelle, and then says, "I've only known her a short while, but we seemed to hit it off. I miss her. She has a new boyfriend she'd like me to meet."

"Why don't we go and see her?" I ask. "In fact, why not next weekend?"

"That could work," says Catherin, after some thought. "Our next performance isn't till the second week of April."

"I bet we could get cheap airline tickets. I've gone to San Diego for as little as thirty-nine bucks round trip."

"You really want to go?" asks Catherin.

I shrug. "Why not? I'm always up for travel, especially on the spur of the moment. I got that from my grandfather, my mom always says."

"I'll call Michelle and see if she'll be around next weekend," says Catherin.

Off to the southwest and across the valley lie the Sierra Estrellas—Spanish for "Star Range." The name reminds me there are mountains near San Diego, one in particular.

"We could even see telescopes," I say.

"Telescopes?"

"On Mt. Palomar, northeast of San Diego. I went there once with my brother. On the road to the top were roadside stands selling the best strawberries I've ever tasted. Maybe we could go there Saturday, and then the beach on Sunday. We'd get to see mountains *and* ocean."

"Sounds like a plan," says Catherin.

"Plan?" I remark with a chuckle. "Oh, don't call it that. Plan is a four letter word, don't you know?"

"I see."

"Seriously though, having a set schedule tends to make me claustrophobic. I'd rather take things as they come."

"We'll still need to plan *some* things," says Catherin with an amused voice. "We need to make airline reservations. Suppose you can handle that?"

She chuckles, and then rambles on about how this will help me work on my "flaws."

~ ~ ~

Catherin makes the call to San Diego that evening, and Michelle says she would love for us to visit, so I book the tickets. We leave for San Diego early the next Saturday.

As we land at the airport, Catherin begins fretting.

"I haven't known Michelle all that long," she explains. "Maybe we won't have that much to talk about."

"You picked a fine time to think of that," I say, shaking my head as we sashay down the narrow aisle of the plane, bags in tow.

Catherin's worries are all for naught, for as soon as Michelle and her friend Tony meet us at the gate, the tensions ease immediately. They make a friendly and attractive couple. She is healthy and wholesome looking, with light brown hair and a winning smile. He's of Polynesian descent.

As we head for Tony's car in the airport parking lot, Michelle asks, "What do you guys want to do while you're here? Tony and I are free today, but only in the afternoon tomorrow."

"We thought about going to Mt. Palomar," I reply. "Do you guys want to do that? And then tomorrow morning Catherin and I can go to the beach by ourselves."

"You understand," says Catherin to the others. "This isn't a plan in Bryan's way of thinking. He claims he's not into planning things."

"You can call it a tentative schedule of events," I say.

They laugh and agree to my 'schedule of events,' and we leave the airport, heading northeast for Mt. Palomar. The city of San Diego will have to wait. Alas, so will the tasting of strawberries, as it apparently isn't the right season. We find no open roadside stands on the way.

After reaching the top, we pair into couples to explore the grounds separately. I'm not as energized on Mt. Palomar as I was on Kitt Peak. To be sure, the main telescope on the site—the five-meter Hale Telescope—is larger and older than the four-meter Mayall Telescope of Kitt Peak, and that's impressive in its own right. But the top of Mt. Palomar is a different world than Kitt Peak. Mt. Palomar is forested, and there are few views of the surrounding landscape from the observatory grounds. No Baboquivari Peak, no center of the universe, no solar telescopes. It's not a power spot to me.

We finish touring the Hale Telescope, and then wander through the information center, finding a bench where we can sit and gaze at star photographs, much like we did at Kitt Peak. Catherin seems lost in her thoughts, and more subdued than usual.

"Anything the matter?" I ask.

"It's nothing," Catherin says with a quickly fading smile.

Later we enter the gift shop and Catherin hunts for a souvenir patch. But having found one, she puts it back on the rack, saying she's not going to buy it after all.

"I don't understand," I say. "Here you find a patch and you don't want it?"

"I shouldn't waste the money."

I look at her, even more puzzled.

"I'm having trouble leasing space at the shopping center," she explains. "I've haven't had much in the way of commissions come in. Plus, I don't know if I told you, but Irene is moving out at the end of the month."

"Irene is moving out? What's the problem?"

"There's no problem," says Catherin. "She's decided to move back to Minnesota."

"I'm sorry to hear that. I've always liked her."

"I don't know how I'll handle the mortgage," says Catherin. "I'll probably have to find another housemate."

Catherin continues to look wistfully at the patch.

"If you want that patch, I could buy it for you," I say.

"No. I don't want any gifts."

"Not even from me?"

"My finances are my problem, and I should handle them."

As she says this, a fair amount of concern colors her face.

Catherin turns to leave the shop. "I'm ready to head back to San Diego. Let's go see where Michelle and Tony went."

I linger a moment to reflect on Catherin's revelations. If I move in with her I can help with the house payments, and her problems will be solved. But I don't feel ready for that type of commitment, and it doesn't sound like Catherin would let me help directly with her finances, either. She won't even let me buy her a souvenir patch.

I find Catherin outside with Michelle and Tony. They had noticed a sign for a trailhead, and wonder if I'm up for a hike. There is still plenty of time left in the day, so why not? We locate the trail and soon enter a damp coastal forest of oaks and pines. As usual, Catherin and I discuss metaphysics and other related subjects. Michelle and Tony stroll behind us, involved in a private conversation of their own.

"I've been reading your book on karmic astrology," I say at one point. "It's an interesting read, although your description of my life's purpose seems to be from the wrong section. Did you calculate the position of my moon's nodes properly?"

"The calculations are correct as far as I can tell," she says. "But you're right; the results for you don't seem to match up. I'm still trying to figure that out."

"Before reading that book, my understanding of karma was very simplistic, I now realize. I've always thought of karma as a law of cause and effect, of reward and punishment—a 'reap what you sow' rule. You know: good karma, bad karma. I see there is more to it than that."

"Here's how I understand it," says Catherin. "Karma is the result of your actions, and is imprinted on your soul. It comes in different flavors—depending on your actions—which either help in future endeavors, or are obstacles to overcome. It's not that useful to think in terms of good karma, bad karma. No matter the flavor, karma is there to help you learn the lessons of life. If you don't learn a lesson when it's presented, the applicable karma stays imprinted, and you are presented with that lesson again and again."

"What happens when you *do* learn the lesson?" I ask.

"Then the karma dissipates. It's no longer needed."

"I've heard karma described like a bank balance," I say, "with a list of credits and debits—good deeds and bad deeds. But given what you are saying it's not so much about balancing out the good and the bad, but growing spiritually—learning lessons."

"That's a better way to think of it."

I tell Catherin that from what I've seen, many Christians dismiss the whole concept of karma. Or if they do acknowledge it, their view is that the 'grace of God' negates karma, so why worry about it? I've always sensed an agenda behind this viewpoint. Since karma is emphasized more in the Eastern religions, and since grace—a concept given emphasis in Christianity—can overcome karma, the inference is that Christianity is superior.

"I find that attitude off-putting," I say to Catherin.

Catherin says nothing about this. I wonder if I've offended any Christian sensibilities she might have. Actually, I know nothing of her religious background. And true to my absent-minded nature, it never occurs for me to ask, even in such an obvious situation.

We walk along the trail as the intermittent sunshine slowly transforms into cloudy, misty weather. I'm still thinking about karma and grace and then have an idea.

"Perhaps grace and karma are of the same nature," I say. "Isn't grace a form of forgiveness? I know in the view of Christianity, grace is thought of as primarily coming from God, but really, can't we all be graceful to others? Whether it's from us or from God, it's still forgiveness. And I'm thinking it's karma as well. Because if I forgive someone, the karma of forgiveness may eventually come back to me—as forgiveness."

"As you forgive others, so will you be forgiven?" asks Catherin rhetorically.

"Yes, exactly."

I help Catherin over a log blocking the trail and she falls into my arms. After a moment or two, she says, with a soft, playful, suggestive voice, "And as you love others, so will you be loved back."

She reaches up to kiss me. We soak up the silence in each other's arms, under the cool pines of the damp forest.

"All this talk about love and spiritual growth reminds me of something," I say as we step further down the trail. "I once read a book that talks about these things from the viewpoint of a psychologist who uses case studies as examples. The book was given to me by Catholic roommates I once had. It's called *The Road Less Traveled*. I should go back and re-read it."

"I would like to read it too," says Catherin. "I'm always looking for new views to consider."

I tell her I admire her inquisitive nature, and that I will try to find my copy of the book and loan it to her.

By this time we are deep in the forest. The tall pines and black oak trees are closing in, the fog lurking not far away. We stop to admire a tree with red bark that when peeled away yields a greenish, silvery wood. It's a Pacific Madrone—a beautiful tree that isn't found in our Arizona climate. The fog drifting up the slopes isn't common for us either. We continue along the trail in silence, the day turning noticeably colder. At one point, Catherin speaks up.

"You know Vincent … my boss?" she asks.

"Yes?" I say, absent-mindedly. I was thinking about the fog and how it reminded me of the *Mists of Avalon* book that I had mentioned to Catherin a few weeks before.

"He met his girlfriend Arielle at a supermarket," Catherin continues. "Arielle is a psychic, and claims she knew she would meet Vincent there. She claims they both dreamed about each other beforehand."

I'm not sure how I feel about claims of psychic abilities, but I can't dismiss them out of hand. Indeed, I probably had some ability of my own. In my childhood I had a recurring dream where, using my tongue, I would push on my teeth, causing them to come out as a unit—at least that was the sensation. I never understood that dream until years later. I had to wear braces in college, and after that, retainers. The feeling of popping off the retainers with my tongue was exactly the same feeling I had in that dream. Was it a premonition? Seems plausible.

We round a bend and the fog completely covers the trail in front of us.

"We must be entering the mists of Avalon," I say. "You know, the story about medieval England, just before Christianity took over? Perhaps we can be transported straight into the dusts of the Magic Farm."

Catherin chuckles at this notion, and hooks her arm through mine as I escort her into the mist.

Alas, nothing magical happens. The canal, water tower, and peacocks of the Magic Farm never appear. Nor does any Arizona warmth. Just more fog, cold and damp.

"I vote for turning around," says Catherin, beginning to shiver.

"Can't argue with that," I say.

We reverse course and head back towards the observatory. Michelle and Tony are still down the trail, coming the other way, and when we reach them they turn around with us. The sun breaks through by the time we make it back to the parking lot, and the afternoon turns pleasant.

Catherin had brought her camera, and she takes pictures of me and of Michelle and Tony. Then I take one of Catherin and Michelle. They are both smiling cheerfully—two attractive girls out enjoying the day. But later I take a picture of Catherin by herself as she poses on a boulder, and underlying her smile is the mysterious darkness that seems to follow her around.

We drive down the mountain and back to San Diego, eventually ending up at the house where Michelle lives. As we are climbing out of the car, Tony mentions going back to his apartment. Michelle and Tony stay behind to talk while Catherin and I lug our bags up the steps to the house.

"I just assumed Michelle and Tony lived together," I say to Catherin.

She shakes her head no. "Michelle rents a room from the owner of this house."

Michelle soon catches up and introduces us to the owner after we go inside. Sporting long, straggly hair and military camouflage, Vic holds a glass of whiskey as he greets us. We drop our bags and enter the living room to sit and talk with Vic while 1960s rock music blares from his vintage stereo. Scattered throughout the living room are pictures and mementos of his service in Vietnam. He's divorced, he says, with two daughters. After finishing his drink, Vic grabs his car keys and says he's going out to meet friends.

Michelle gives us a quick tour of the house and shows us her bedroom. "You can sleep here tonight," she says. "I'll be staying with Tony."

We move our bags to the bedroom. As we pass through the hallway Michelle points out numerous pictures of Vic's young daughters plastered along the wall.

"That's a lot of photos," I say to her.

"Yes, he really seems to love his daughters," says Michelle. "They spend a lot of time here."

"Where do they sleep?" asks Catherin. "I saw only two bedrooms, yours and Vic's."

"Oh, they sleep with him," says Michelle.

"His daughters sleep with him?" asks Catherin.

"How old *are* they?" I interject.

"They're ten and twelve," Michelle says. "I must admit he does fawn over them a bit."

Catherin and I look at each other with raised eyebrows.

"That doesn't sound so good," says Catherin.

Michelle looks at her, a bit surprised, and then says, "Nothing is going on there. Vic's a nice guy."

"Are you sure about that?" asks Catherin.

A frown forms on Michelle's face. "Now that you mention it, I want to show you something." She goes back to her bedroom and returns with an anonymous letter. "I found this the other day, addressed to me."

Catherin and I look at the letter. Whoever wrote the letter says that he is "devoted" to Michelle, and that he considers Michelle his "princess."

Michelle continues, "Another thing that's odd is that I've had several letters sent to me that I never received. I know this because the senders—who were boyfriends at the time—asked me about them later."

"You think Vic is hiding the letters?" asks Catherin.

Michelle shrugs. "I wouldn't have thought so, but now I'd have to say yes. It's starting to make me uncomfortable."

No shit, I say to myself.

Michelle is quite attractive and it's not hard to imagine that a guy living in the same house would fall for her.

"Don't you think you should find another place to stay?" asks Catherin. "I'd say the sooner the better."

"Oh, I don't know," Michelle replies. "I've been looking a little, but nothing's come up."

"Why not move in with Tony?" Catherin asks.

"Well, I like Tony a lot, and we get along great, but I'm not ready to move in with him."

So Michelle is not ready to move in with her boyfriend. Now that sounds familiar …

~ ~ ~

The next morning Michelle lets us borrow her car and Catherin and I drive to Old Town—a historic district north of downtown San Diego—and we have breakfast at a Mexican cafe. Afterwards Catherin says she has something to show me nearby and suggests we go for a walk. She leads me to an area called Heritage Park, filled with historic Victorian houses.

"It's around here somewhere," Catherin says, looking up and down the street.

"What's around here?"

"A house I want you to see."

After a few more blocks Catherin stops in front of a yellow Victorian-styled house that has been converted into a bed and breakfast.

"I first discovered this place a few years ago," she says. "I was riding my bike through this area and saw this house, and for some reason I was compelled to stop and go inside. The house seemed familiar to me, like I had memories of how its interior looked—how the rooms were arranged. These details were confirmed when I saw the interior."

"So that means what, exactly?"

"Well, I don't see how I could have known what it looked like inside. As far as I know, I had never been here before, at least in this life."

"So you think you were here in a previous life?"

"That's what I'm thinking."

"Maybe you saw pictures of this house in a brochure or something."

"Maybe, but that doesn't explain why I was drawn here."

Before meeting Catherin, I had never given the idea of previous lives much thought. I had been thinking more about it lately, after perusing books Catherin loaned me on the subject. I didn't have a clear opinion on what I believed, but it was fascinating all the same.

Catherin wants a picture of herself by the house, so I take one of her sitting on a bench near the front sidewalk. Then I say, "If you want to see the ocean, we better get going."

"Okay Bry, you be the boss. You do the planning."

We find our way back to Michelle's car and drive to a series of cliffs near the Point Loma peninsula on the south side of San Diego. After parking the car at the top of these cliffs, we scramble down a short, steep trail to a small beach, and stroll barefoot along the shore, eventually resting on a boulder near the water and gazing hypnotically at the rolling, shimmering waves of the Pacific Ocean. I rub my bare feet back and forth in the soothing sand. That makes me think of a story to tell Catherin:

"When I was in graduate school at Arizona State, I was lonely, even with all those tens of thousands of students. I was feeling isolated, with few friends and absolutely no female companionship. I started to lose touch with the physical world, and felt as though I was just an intellectual head and mouth, with no body attached. Being in engineering and computer science didn't help matters. At one point, I was hiking by myself along a trail in South Mountain Park, and I swear it was as if my body disappeared, and all that was left was my head. It's not that my arms, legs, and chest were invisible, but they felt like they weren't there. It was a strange experience."

"It sounds strange," Catherin says. "What do you suppose it means?"

"I think it was a manifestation of my general disconnectedness. I discovered quite by accident on a subsequent outing by a lake that if I took off my shoes and rubbed my feet in the sand, I would begin to feel whole again. It was as though I needed to be reconnected with the Earth, and rubbing my bare feet did the trick."

A stiff wind blows in from the ocean, carrying shore birds along effortlessly. They scan the surf for a meal of exposed clams and crabs.

Catherin then tells me a story: "When I worked at the massage clinic, I used to dream of the ocean. It was so dark and stuffy in the room where I worked that I would get depressed, so I imagined myself on a sunny beach. That made me feel better."

Our conversation tapers off as we are cast under the spell of waves crashing along the shore. The wind has calmed into a pleasant breeze, ruffling our hair—and tasting of salt.

After a while, Catherin breaks the ocean's spell. "There's something I've been meaning to say."

"Okay."

"Your chart indicates you may have a tendency to be secretive. Did I ever mention this to you?"

"I don't remember, but I can certainly see that about myself. Why do you bring this up?"

"I have those same tendencies. It's hard for me to confide in people, especially those close to me. But I want you to know, I feel you're the first person I'll be able to completely open up to."

Catherin proceeds to tell me more about her life. She had lived in various places in the northeast, and also in San Diego, and was married once. But when I ask her a few probing questions, she hesitates. "I'm not ready to tell you everything."

Catherin's revelations make me acutely aware that she had way more experience than me, even discounting my sheltered Nebraska upbringing. She must have seen the wheels turning in my head.

"I've got a confession to make," she says. "Remember when I told you was thirty? Well, please don't be mad, but I'm really thirty-five."

"I had a hunch you were older than you said."

"How does that make you feel?"

"What else have you lied about, I wonder?"

"Just that … I promise. I'm really sorry. I was afraid of losing you if you knew my real age."

"It doesn't matter," I say, shaking my head in dismissal. "Don't worry about it."

Was it a problem? I honestly didn't know. The issue wasn't so much the difference in our physical ages, but our emotional ones. I not only looked younger, I felt and acted younger too. Being shy and alone during a big part of my life, I lacked the experience most people would have, given my age, especially when it came to relationships. It left me feeling inadequate.

The boulder we're sitting on grows uncomfortable—perhaps my feeling of inadequacy has something to do with this. So I help Catherin up and we venture further down the shore, where a more inviting park bench presents itself. It's inland, away from the chilly surf. We sit down and wiggle our bare feet in the warm sand. The waves of the Pacific Ocean roll in, like they have since time immemorial, bringing with them that sense of timelessness.

Are our souls timeless? How long will we be together? Had we known each other in previous lives? And what lessons are we supposed to learn in this one?

Chapter 8.
"Ain't no moon in my Gemini"

April, 1987

W e hear fluttering from across the room, then two dull thuds and the sound of flapping wings.

"Look, Bryan!" says Catherin. She untangles from my embrace and rises off the pillows we are lying on. She hurries over to the aviary. "The babies have flown the nest!"

Bubba and Mrs. Bubba begin heh-heh-heh-ing and cooing to announce this happy occasion.

I push up from the living room floor and follow Catherin. The two fledglings scuffle on the ground and stare intently at the nest above, as though willing themselves upwards. When one gathers up enough strength and willpower, it flaps its wings and attempts a launch. At first, this only amounts to a series of short hops, but eventually, both reach the nest, even if this does entail a prodigious amount of flapping and fluttering.

"I guess they are almost ready for new homes," says Catherin.

"Didn't Pete say he wanted one of these birds?" I ask.

"Yes, and Cecilia too. I'll have to let them know they need to start looking for bird cages."

The adventures of the young birds are entertaining, but we eventually return to our pillows. It had been a cozy, amorous evening up to this point, and I'm sure we both want that to continue. Supposedly, we were going to watch a few videos, but somehow, that hasn't happened. A fire crackles in the fireplace as we snuggle close by. The warmth of the fire feels good on my back.

So do the caresses from the woman lying next to me.

"I'm glad you suggested getting wood for the fireplace," I say. "Though I have to admit, fireplaces seem out of place in Phoenix."

"But it is romantic, isn't it?" says Catherin. She kisses me and runs her fingers through my hair—or at least what's left of it. The day before she had given me a haircut, and sorry to say, it was a botched job. My hair was too short now. The cowlick I prominently sported as a kid had made its reappearance. Catherin lazily plays with that cowlick now; seemingly amused by the way it bounces up after she brushes it down with her fingers.

"It sure is nice to have the house to ourselves," she says, further twirling my cowlick.

I close my eyes momentarily and indulge in Catherin's caresses. "It's hard to believe Irene moved out just a few days ago," I say.

"Yes, it does seem longer than that."

"Irene's a nice person, but I have to admit, it felt awkward having her around."

"Having her here did have its benefits, though," Catherin says. She stops her caresses. "I wish I could close a few leases at the shopping center."

Catherin watches me carefully. Is she thinking what I'm thinking? Her financial difficulties would be solved if I moved in, and this did seem like the perfect time to make such a move. While part of me likes this idea, the rest of me is unsure and afraid. I remain silent in confusion. Catherin looks away, but not before I see a hint of disappointment on her face.

"I suppose we should actually watch the videos we rented," she says, leaving my embrace and going over to the entertainment center. "Which one do you want to see first?"

"It doesn't matter," I say. "You picked them out."

"Actually, they were recommended by a friend. I don't know anything about them."

Catherin chooses one of the tapes, pops it into the VCR, and turns on the TV. I barely remembered she had a TV. It was a rare occasion for it to be on in her house, as we were usually too busy practicing or performing with the band somewhere, or out hiking the local trails.

Unfortunately, her friend's recommendations prove unworthy. The movies are so bad that we fast-forward through most of the two tapes, hoping to find scenes where surely, the script writing and character portrayal get better. That never happens.

Halfway through the second tape, the absurdity of the situation strikes me.

"Well, this sure is romantic," I say, as the scenes flicker by in full fast-forward mode.

"I'm sorry these movies are so bad," Catherin says. She gets up to turn off the TV and VCR. "Would you like me to read you some poems instead?"

"That sounds like an excellent idea."

Catherin leaves the room and returns a few moments later with several poetry books. "Which of these do you want me to read from?" she asks.

I choose a book of poems by Emily Dickinson and rest my head on Catherin's lap while she reads out loud at random. At one point, she flips to a poem I recognize from high school English class. Catherin recites the first few lines:

> I heard a Fly buzz -- when I died
> The Stillness in the Room

A chill spreads down my shoulders, leaving goose bumps in its wake. Dying embers in the fireplace crackle and pop as Catherin's pure, clear voice lulls me to sleep.

~ ~ ~

One evening after band practice we relax on the couch in the living room. Catherin had been her usual enthusiastic self during practice, but now looks worried and a little down, twiddling her thumbs like knitting needles. I think I know what she is thinking.

"I'd be more than happy to move in," I say to her. "If you want me to. That way, I can help with the house payment."

"No!" Catherin says, shaking her head.

My normally wiggly feet stop moving. "No? Why not?"

"I don't want you to move in because of that. I don't want your help."

"I don't understand."

"I want you to move in because you want to *be* with me."

"I *do* want to be with you. Surely you know that."

"You could have moved in before this. Something's holding you back."

"Your financial situation serves as an opportunity to get over that."

"To get over what? What are you afraid of?"

"I just need more time to—"

Catherin interrupts with a sigh. "Seems like we've been through this before."

A stern look comes over her. "I can't wait any longer. I've already put an ad in the paper for a housemate. In the meantime, you need to sort through your feelings. You need to decide what you are going to do. Are you with me, or not?"

"I'm sorry I'm having so much trouble figuring that out."

Catherin's sternness softens into a look of understanding. "I know it's hard for you to make a commitment. It's the same reason you're always fidgeting. It's your moon in Gemini."

"I remember you saying something about the Gemini Twins sign symbolizing split careers—"

"And split emotions. You want to be here, yet you don't. You say you love me, but I saw the way you stared at those women on the trail a while back."

"What are you talking about?"

"Coming down the Squaw Peak trail."

"You noticed that? It was nothing—just an old habit."

Well, that wasn't entirely true. Although I loved Catherin very much, sometimes I had contradictory feelings that she wasn't the one for me. So my eye would wander. This confused and embarrassed me. Surely I was above that. Surely I did love her.

"The Virgo in you doesn't help matters," says Catherin.

"How so?"

"It's your analytical, critical, picky nature," she says. "Virgos tend to over-analyze things. I ought to know, since I'm a Virgo too. Your moon in Gemini just exacerbates things. I suspect you easily see both sides to a situation, and can see them quite well—so well you have trouble committing to a particular side."

"That sounds just like me," I say. "I'm always afraid I've missed something—that more facts might come in. I don't like being wrong."

"Not wanting to be wrong—that's the Leo in you," says Catherin.

"I can see how that *also* exacerbates things," I say.

I place her hands into mine. "I really do love you Catherin. I promise I'll try to be more decisive."

"Well, I love you too," says Catherin, allowing me to kiss her, and then removing her hands and getting off the couch to go into the kitchen for a drink. "But don't say you want to move in with me until you are truly ready."

~ ~ ~

Two weeks fly by and we are again in the living room for band practice. "I've got an announcement to make," says Catherin to the band. "You know how we're supposed to play at the Phoenix Folk Festival on Saturday? I didn't realize it when we lined up the event, but we're scheduled to play at the coffeehouse that evening as well. Is that okay with everybody?"

"How did you manage to book both the same day?" I ask. "Did our boss lady mess up?"

"Well, Cody actually booked us for the folk festival," says Catherin, "even though he's not in our band anymore."

"So Cody's becoming a planner and organizer too?"

Catherin smiles at this remark. "He's leading some of the festival workshops, so he had the connections."

After band practice finishes and the others leave, we sit in the living room. Catherin works on her knitting, and I study a computer printout from work.

"I'm having trouble finding someone to rent a room," says Catherin at one point. "I haven't received any response from the ad I put in the paper. Have you decided what you want to do?"

"About what?" I look up from the printout, my mind still absorbed in the details of the code I was working on.

"About moving in with me."

Catherin sighs, and her knitting needles work their way through the yarn a little more forcefully.

"Who's that sweater for anyway?" I ask.

"I'm knitting it for Arielle." Catherin stops for a second and looks at me. "You haven't answered my question."

"I guess I haven't come to any decision."

Actually, I had forgotten about it, in my typical absent-minded style. I wait for the onslaught. Were the thunderclouds ready to admonish me? I was ready for them. I'd even take a whack from the cosmic two-by-four. Either would be better than what I imagined was coming next.

Catherin throws her knitting down beside her. "What am I to do with you?" She rises off the couch and goes over to stand by the window in the sitting room. The turtle doves, who had been making their usual noise, suddenly grow quiet.

I follow Catherin and sit down to watch apologetically from a chair nearby. She stares out the window with the same sad and lonely look I had seen in that photo taken at Christmas time. But this time, disappointment also colors her face. And I think I see tears. My heart sinks.

I rise from the chair to go and comfort her.

"I know I promised to make a decision," I say, softly touching her arm and then moving my hand down to hold hers. "And I know I haven't given this the attention it deserves. It's not much of an excuse, but I've been so involved with work. And you should know, programming makes me more of a space case than I usually am."

Catherin continues to stare out the window.

"I'm sorry," I say. "I don't mean to hurt you. I want us to be together, but it feels too soon for me. I need a place to go back to. I need my time alone."

Catherin's demeanor turns into one of determination. She pulls away from me and says, "Well, you're going to get what you ask for. I think we should spend some time apart, perhaps several weeks, starting … right now."

"But—"

"I want you to leave."

I sheepishly gather up my printouts and fiddle. Catherin stops me by the door.

"Remember, we're playing the two gigs on Saturday," she says with an even tone, without hint of emotion. "I suppose I can come pick you up, since your apartment is on the way." She then hands me a tape. "Here is a song I've been working on. It would be nice if you learned the harmony part."

When I leave, she surprisingly gives me a kiss, but only on the cheek. I have a tearful drive home.

The next evening, I don't have anything else to do, so I listen to the tape Catherin had given me. She had recorded an old western song by the *Riders of the Purple Sage* called *No One to Cry To*, and this was followed by a recording of Catherin playing and singing the song in a key more suited to her.

I have always liked the old western songs. I didn't know Catherin liked them too. I figure out the chords and sing along with the tape, trying out any harmonious notes I can conjure up, wondering if my relationship with Catherin will ever be harmonious again.

The next morning, Catherin comes by to pick me up. I open the door and find Catherin standing there wearing a cowboy hat and western style clothes, looking more attractive than ever. She seems friendly enough—*friendly* being the operative word, for I receive no kiss and no hug. I feel my heart breaking. I don't want to be just friends with her—not at all.

Catherin drives as we head down the freeway on our way to the folk festival in downtown Phoenix. Normally, she didn't wear a lot of makeup—at least since I had known her, but today she's wearing more than usual. She fusses with her appearance in the rearview mirror while steering between lanes. I'm surprised by her carelessness.

Riding in a car with someone I'm not supposed to see for 'two weeks' is tense and awkward. I can only imagine what it's going to be like on stage. When we reach the festival grounds and park, I turn to Catherin, and she looks over to me. I can see a mixture of sadness, hope, and love in those shining brown eyes.

I laugh tentatively. "Aren't we something? You know I love you, and I'm pretty sure you love me."

Catherin responds with a tentative smile and a small laugh of her own. But her smile quickly vanishes, replaced with a determined look. "You're still not to see me for two weeks," she says.

The festival is held at *Heritage Square*, a city block filled with old historic houses, including the Victorian-style *Rosson House*. Next to the house is a pavilion where the stage has been set up for the performances.

It's a warm, beautiful, sunny day—just the opposite of our first outdoor performance in March. That day had been chilly and dreary, with Catherin supplying the warmth. Now any chill in the air comes from her. Although she's exuberant on stage, I can tell she's not herself. I don't think anyone else notices.

If vocals can make or break a band's success, our band is on its way, as Darrell and Catherin both put in a good performance. The rest of us are improving too. My chops are better, my backup shuffles tighter, and my solos more nuanced. I still can't play *Blackberry Blossom* worth a darn, though.

My friend Alden had come to watch our band play and brought his girlfriend Kimberly. I see them sitting on the grass in the front row of the audience, and after our performance I climb off stage to greet them.

"What did you guys think?" I ask.

"You were great!" says Alden, with Kimberly nodding in agreement.

"I know we weren't *really* … but thanks for saying so."

Catherin soon joins us. The performance must have energized her, for she seems more cheerful than before, and seems to be warming up to me again.

"Have you met Catherin?" I ask the two of them. I then make introductions.

Alden says to Catherin, "So you are the mystery woman that Bryan always talks about."

"What has he been saying about me?" she asks.

"That you're a complete mystery to me, of course," I interject.

Catherin chuckles and smiles a genuine smile—the first I've seen today.

"Do you want to hang out for a while with Alden and Kimberly?" I ask Catherin. I have no expectation she'll say yes. But she surprises me by doing just that. I realize later that she probably agreed so that no one else would know we were having problems.

We watch a few other bands play, and then wander around the festival grounds, eventually ending up at the *Rosson House*.

"This reminds me of our visit to *Heritage Park* in San Diego," I say to Catherin. "We're once again at an old Victorian house. Have you been here before too?"

Catherin smiles. "Well, yes, but only in this lifetime."

Arts and craft exhibits are set up both inside and outside the house. Catherin and Kimberly spend time browsing through racks of knittings and weavings as Alden and I wander off by ourselves.

"How's Wacky the Robot doing these days?" I ask Alden.

"Well, right now he's a plant stand in my apartment," he says.

"A plant stand? You're not experimenting with him anymore?"

"Not at the moment. I need a faster computer. Plus, you never did help me figure out how to get Wacky to recognize empty space."

"Ah, yes, the old figure-ground problem. Sorry about that. I've been, um, rather occupied."

"Apparently," Alden says, eyebrows rising.

"Wacky the Robot, turned into a plant stand," I muse. "Maybe you should call him Marvin, after the depressed robot in *Hitchhiker's Guide to the Galaxy*."

Alden laughs. "At least Marvin got to open elevator doors. Wacky just gets to sit there and hold up plants."

Poor Wacky, under-utilizing his brain cells. Seems a lot of humans do that too, and certain humans under-utilize their hearts as well. I think of the lyrics to one of Catherin's songs:

> *Be still my love and take your time*
> *Let your heart decide, and not your mind*

We rejoin Catherin and Kimberly, and since it is now early afternoon, we eat lunch on the festival grounds. Afterwards I ask Catherin, "What are we going to do the rest of the day? We don't have to play at the coffeehouse until this evening."

"Do you guys want to see a movie?" Alden interjects.

"A movie? You know what, Catherin and I have never been to a movie together."

"Do you know what's playing?" Catherin asks.

Kimberly replies, "There's a new comedy that was filmed locally. I think it's called *Raising Arizona*. Maybe there's a theatre nearby that's showing it."

We head for the movie theatres at Chris-Town Mall, and sure enough, *Raising Arizona* is playing. We find the movie extremely funny and it seems to relieve the tension between Catherin and me. At one point I sneak my hand into hers and she doesn't push it away. Instead she gives me an encouraging and sympathetic squeeze. If this is how we are going to spend our time 'not seeing each other,' well, it's not so bad.

After the movie, Alden and Kimberly leave to go home. Catherin and I are left in the middle of Phoenix with another two hours of 'not seeing each other.' Catherin remembers there's a metaphysical bookstore nearby, but locating the store and browsing through its shelves doesn't use up much time.

We eventually wind up sitting in Catherin's car in the parking lot outside the coffeehouse, waiting for the evening performances to begin. I drum my fingers on the side of the car, firing in a rapid, syncopated motion—probably driving Catherin nuts, I finally realize. I stop my drumming and wait in silence. I'm not sure how to act and I'm not sure Catherin does either.

Our performance goes well. We were already warmed up from the Phoenix Folk Festival earlier in the day, and for the first time, I feel good about our playing. We're no *Hot Rize* and I'm no *Byron Berline*, but I'm pleased with our progress.

When the coffeehouse closes, I accompany Catherin out to the parking lot, knowing that after she drives me home, it will be time for us to part. I walk with her slowly, wishing to delay this parting. I need to convince her there is no need for us to *be* apart, broken promises or not. She needs to know there are no doubts about my love for her. As we reach the car, I happen to see the silvery moon shining through the trees. A thought immediately comes to mind.

"There ain't no moon in *my* Gemini!" I say in jest, turning my head and raising a hand to block the sight of the moon. I look back towards Catherin.

Her eyes flash with amusement, if only too briefly.

Chapter 9.
Here We Go Again

I climb the steps to Pete's place and knock, but it's Dwight who opens the door. I glance in, only to be greeted by the sight of Catherin giving Pete a massage on the floor of the living room, the two of them deep into some kind of discussion. My long-time insecurities reassert themselves.

Pete was saying to Catherin, "... there's the coin toss method and then the traditional method involving a set of fifty yarrow stalks." He looks up and sees me at the door.

"Hey, Bryan, come on in."

Catherin says nothing, acknowledging me only with a distant smile. She and Pete then continue their discussion—something about current and future hexagrams, interpretations, and meaningful coincidences.

I step into the doorway and ask Dwight, "What are they talking about?"

"Something called the *I-Ching*."

"*I-Ching?*"

Dwight shrugs, "Some kind of Chinese system of fortune telling, I guess."

I stand uncomfortably in the entryway, still holding my fiddle, not sure how to join the discussion. Not sure I want to.

The band had agreed to start rotating practices between each of the band member's houses. Tonight was Pete's turn. It had been five seemingly long days since I had seen or spoken to Catherin—the last time being the previous Saturday at the folk festival and coffeehouse, when I had made the jest, "There ain't no moon in my Gemini."

I hear the fluttering of wings coming from the kitchen, followed by feeble, high-pitched coos. I put my fiddle down and go to investigate, finding a young turtle dove pacing back and forth on its perch in a small cage.

Returning to the living room I ask Pete, "You've got one of the baby doves?"

Catherin answers instead of Pete, "I brought it over tonight. Cecilia is picking hers up tomorrow. Darrell should be here shortly, by the way."

Well, at least Catherin is still talking to me, I say to myself. I look for further signs of encouraging behavior from her and finding none, I go back to the kitchen and take the young dove out of his cage, stroking his feathers, thinking: *This poor bird looks as lonely as I feel.*

I place the bird back in his cage and wait in the living room for practice to start, finding a chair in the corner. Catherin seems content to confine her discussion about *I-Ching* with Pete, and I notice she has cut her hair into a shorter, more fashionable style. Has she done this to symbolically distance herself from me? Not only should it be me down on the floor getting the massage, I should be the one involved in any metaphysical discussions. Despair settles in. I languish in the corner chair and revert to my old wall-flower mode— pretending not to pay attention, but doing just the opposite.

Dwight spends time tuning his bass. There's a knock at the door and he puts down his instrument to answer.

"Sorry I'm late," says Darrell after the door opens. He's sporting his usual crew cut and thick, square-rimmed glasses. In his hands are a mandolin and a bag of fast food. "I was hungry so I stopped for something to eat."

"Hey, that reminds me," says Pete to the group. "There's a new Ethiopian restaurant that's opened in Tempe. We should go there before practice some time."

This is followed by someone telling an Ethiopian joke—something to do with the size of portions on the menu. More Ethiopian jokes ensue. It's all in bad taste, but that doesn't stop the laughter from the other band members. "No joke is too low," someone remarks. I'm still in full wall-flower mode, and don't participate.

We spend most of practice going over gospel tunes that Darrell suggests we learn. Darrell does a fine job singing, and Catherin picks right up on the melodies and harmonies. As usual, she tape-records the session so we can work on the songs later. All through the evening Catherin treats me as just one of the boys.

After practice, I catch up to her in the parking lot, before she reaches her car.

"How are you?" I ask.

Catherin ignores me at first. She steps past and stores her guitar, notepad, and practice tapes in the trunk of her car. As she skirts around to the driver's side, she says, "I'm okay." She hesitates for a moment with her hand on the door handle and seems in conflict, as though she isn't sure whether to continue getting in the car or not.

"Would you like to stop by my apartment for a while?" I ask.

Catherin looks at me with disbelief. "Bryan, why are you asking this? I thought it was understood you were to spend some time by yourself—to sort out your feelings. Two weeks, remember?"

"I already know my feelings," I say. "And I'm pretty sure you do as well."

Catherin opens the door, tosses in her purse, and climbs inside. She stops short of closing the car door, though, and asks, "What do you want from me?"

"Just for you to stop by, so we can talk. Please?"

After much persuasion, (actually, more like me standing there without any clue what to say), Catherin finally says, "We *do* need to practice harmonies on the gospel tunes we learned tonight. I guess we could do that over at your place."

It sounds like a convenient excuse, but that is fine with me. Catherin follows in her car back to my apartment, and after unlocking the front door and entering the living room, I'm not sure what to do next. Catherin solves that problem by going over to the entertainment center, saying, "Let's practice those harmonies now."

She inserts one of the practice tapes into the cassette player and sits on the floor, humming along to the gospel songs and periodically rewinding the tape to revisit certain phrases. Eyes closed, I sit next to her and listen, my back propped against the entertainment center. Such a fine voice she has, with just the right timbre.

One of the selections on the tape is titled *Where the Soul Never Dies*, a traditional song that begins with the following lyrics:

To Canaan's land I'm on my way
Where the soul of man never dies
My darkest night will turn to day
Where the soul of man never dies

Catherin hums a few more verses and then stops to ask, "Don't you want to practice with me?"

"I'm sorry, but I'm not really in the mood," I say, opening my eyes, and shifting to lie down on the floor. "Besides, I'd rather listen a while and get more familiar with the songs before I try singing with you."

After a few minutes of humming by herself and winding the tape back and forth, Catherin sighs and removes the tape from the player. I look up. She looks dejected, eyes moist.

"I don't like this any more than you do," she says. "But you were the one that said you needed time alone. I was just giving you that time."

I sit up and scoot closer, tentatively placing her hands in mine— only to be surprised to find her reaction warm and friendly. I must have misinterpreted her cool and distant demeanor earlier in the evening. She's not really mad. She's hurting, like me.

"I don't like being alone the way I used to," I say, "back before we met. Now I feel lost when you're not around. But I need my own space, too. It's very confusing."

"I have a hard time understanding why you want to be by yourself so much," Catherin says. "I hate being alone. I get crazy and depressed—and really spacey."

That reminds me of a certain photo. This time, I bring it up.

"Cecilia showed me a picture of you at Christmas time, taken in your living room. You looked desolate. Is that what was going on then? You were depressed from being alone?"

"Partly," she says.

"And the other part?"

"Just my own self-destructive shit."

"Such as?"

Catherin turns away and grabs one of the practice tapes, flipping it over in her hands absent-mindedly.

"Could you get me some water?" she asks.

I get up and go into the kitchen to fill a glass with water. On the way back, I notice a record album propped against a chair next to the entertainment center. It's that haunting version of *Pachelbel's Canon*. An idea forms. I hand Catherin her glass and pull out the record and place it on the turntable. Soon, the sweet strains of violins fill the air with the signature progression of notes that make up the famous canon, each note sustained several seconds for maximum emotional effect. I lower next to Catherin and take her into my arms, running my fingers through her dark hair, giving her a hesitant kiss.

"I don't want us to be apart anymore," I say.

She responds with a more passionate kiss of her own.

"Nor do I."

That was the end of our so-called breakup, which lasted all of seven days, and on one of those days we had spent the whole day together, supposedly 'not seeing each other.' It was a long seven days, though, for both of us.

Later that evening, Catherin plays me a song on her guitar that she had written during that time, titled *Bryan and Catherin*. I'm not particularly thrilled with the line about me waiting to grow up:

Bryan and Catherin

Maybe you're not the one for me now
Maybe I made a mistake somehow
Maybe it wasn't love that I felt
But your smile could always make my heart melt

Maybe it's true love to set you free
Like the old cowboys on the lone prairie
Maybe you're not for me anyhow
But your warm embrace could always make me smile

> *You know I'm waiting to be perfect*
> *And you are waiting to grow up*
> *But one good thing that I can say*
> *We always talked but not quite soon enough*

Maybe we ignored the signs that we gave
That told us that we'd go away
But we were so taken and fantasy bound
To think a true love we'd finally found

Chorus

We always dreamed of our true lover
One who'd make our lives over
And take away that lonely ache
We never dreamed that we would feel our hearts break

Chorus

— *Catherin Delaney, 1987*

~ ~ ~

April is in full swing, with dry, sunny, warm days—and temperatures in the 80s. The weather is as good as it gets in Phoenix. I'm out in Catherin's garage, preparing to install new speakers in her car, drilling screw holes into the interior door panels. The garage door is open to a soothing breeze that wafts in, along with music coming from an album playing on the stereo in the living room. Catherin is inside, doing housework. Whoever is playing on the record holds me spellbound, and the music merges with the warm breeze to produce a magical state of peace and contentment.

The album is a mixture of folk, bluegrass, and country, and as a new track begins, I hear the sweet and mournful strains of a pedal steel guitar. I have always loved the sound of the pedal steel; in fact, it's what originally drew me to country music as a kid. Ironically, back then I figured I would be playing pedal steel someday, not fiddle. I never paid much attention to the fiddle before taking lessons at the *Phoenix School of Country Music.*

The exquisite interplay of pedal steel and fiddle is too much. I put down the drill and go into the house.

"What album is that playing?" I ask Catherin, after finding her in the living room washing windows. More riffs from the pedal steel fill the room, followed by lively harmony fiddle.

"It's something Pete loaned me," Catherin says. "It's called *Restless Rambling Heart*, by someone named Laurie Lewis."

Catherin drops her wash cloth and retrieves the album for me. We sit on the couch and scrutinize the back cover.

"I've never heard of this artist," I say, scanning the credits, noticing that the album was mastered in Phoenix, and also noticing that my favorite bluegrass star, Tim O'Brien, of *Hot Rize* fame, was co-producer. I had once told Catherin I didn't pay attention to the names of artists or bands, but I guess that was no longer always true.

We continue listening to the album, which is filled with sweet harmonies and rich and powerful fiddling. The tasty licks of a pedal steel are just icing on the cake.

"This is an excellent album," I say to Catherin.

"That's why Pete brought it over," she says. "He thought we'd like it."

"He was right about that."

Since everything was back to normal between us, I had privately forgiven both Catherin and Pete for any jealousy they caused me to have that night over at Pete's place. It wasn't their fault of course. It was just my own insecurity.

A song begins called *Here We Go Again*, a slow, country ballad with beautiful harmonies:

Here We Go Again

Here we go again
I love you so again
Once more it starts to end
The moment it begins

I thought I'd never see
Your love come back to me
But there you stand in front of me
And here we go again

> *It took a long time*
> *For me to learn to live without you*
> *When you were gone*
> *I thought I'd laid it all to rest*

> *But darling, I remember everything about you*
> *And the only thing I'm learning*
> *Is you are still the best*

Here we go again
I love you so again
Once more it starts to end
The moment it begins

I thought I'd never see
Your love come back to me
But there you stand in front of me
And here we go again

— *Judy Sanders, 1980*

I ask Catherin to dance and we circle across the living room to the enchanting elixir of steel guitar, fiddles, and harmony vocals. I might be a bit clumsy in the dance department, but the music is magnificent. So is the woman in my arms. That now-familiar sense of timelessness washes over me. We circle the floor, spinning around like miniature dancers on top of a music box, dancing our way through life together.

~ ~ ~

One day I ask Catherin about her and Pete's discussion of the *I-Ching*. She explains that the *I-Ching* is also called the *Book of Changes* and is an ancient Chinese system of divination. She loans me a book on the subject.

The basic idea with *I-Ching* divination is to pose a question, and then toss coins (or more traditionally, select different length yarrow sticks) and construct hexagrams from the results. Each hexagram is made up of six lines, and each line is one of two types: a solid line called a *yang* line, and a broken line called a *yin* line. Two hexagrams are formed, the first representing the current situation, and the second, the future trend. Each hexagram has a symbolic meaning, listed in the *Book of Changes*. From this symbolism, you can determine a proper course of action for the question posed. Of course, the trick is in interpreting the symbolism.

"So let me get this straight," I say after having skimmed through the book. "You toss some coins and from them you are supposed to know the future?"

"It's not about fortune telling," Catherin replies, "and it's not about predicting specific events. It's about helping to determine what the situation is and what to do about it."

"A form of self-help, then. Like the way you treat astrology?"

"Yes, exactly."

"But the random coin tosses, surely that can't mean anything. It reminds me of those silly Magic 8-balls, where you ask a yes/no question, shake the ball, and an answer appears in the window from a plastic die floating in the liquid. If I recall correctly, the die has something like twenty faces, so there are twenty possible answers that appear at random."

"Well, for one thing," Catherin says, "in the *I-Ching* system you don't ask yes or no questions. Instead you ask questions about how things will affect you, or how you should react to a given situation. Secondly, there are many possible combinations of answers. More than twenty."

Using my computer programming experience, I recognize that each hexagram forms a six digit binary number, with zero representing *yin* and one representing *yang*. There are 64 possible hexagrams (two to the sixth power) and 4,096 (64x64) possible combinations of two hexagrams.

"Yes, there are 4,096 combinations to be exact," I say to Catherin. "But one could look at that skeptically and say that by having that many combinations, it's obscuring the fact that it's all based on chance, and the more combinations, the more likely something in the results will make sense to you, especially if the situations are described in vague, generalized terms."

"It's not really based on chance," Catherin replies, "at least not in the way you are thinking. The theory is, if you ask the questions with respect and sincerity, and have your mind in the proper receptive state, the coin tosses will land according to the situation you find yourself in and the needs of your soul."

"Sounds pretty hokey to me."

"Have you heard of Carl Jung?"

"The famous psychologist? Something about archetypes and collective unconsciousness ... that's all I remember from college."

"He studied the *I-Ching* for many years. He developed a theory for how the *I-Ching* works. It's called the Principle of Synchronicity."

"Synchronicity?"

"A coincidence that has meaning. The idea is that everything is interconnected, even if we can't see that. When a coincidence occurs that has special meaning to you, something that makes you sit up and take notice, then you are seeing a portion of that interconnectedness. When you ask the *I-Ching* oracle a question in the proper receptive state, and do the coin tosses, you are tapping into this interconnectedness. The results of the coin tosses aren't just random events, but meaningful coincidences. They come out the way they are supposed to, in order to help guide you through the problem posed."

It still sounded suspect to me, but I had to concede it wasn't impossible. After all, it was I who had suggested to Dr. Thomason on our hike in the Superstitions that our view of the world is affected by the rules of perception we use, and that there is a mysterious portion of the world we can't ordinarily see. Perhaps these meaningful coincidences are just the consequence of tapping into a different type of perception and are in fact glimpses of that other world.

From studying artificial intelligence in college, I was familiar with the concept of self-awareness—really just a name for self-reflection. Perhaps the world is like a mirror that reflects our own selves back to us. When we perceive the world, are we just perceiving ourselves? If so, then any synchronicities we experience could be patterns of our own consciousness.

I couldn't recall ever experiencing a synchronicity—a coincidence with meaning. So far, this was just intellectual pondering.

Chapter 10.
Life's Railway to Heaven

Mid to late April, 1987

A car door slams. I put down my sandwich and peer out the kitchen window. There's a man, late 40s or 50s, wearing jeans, long sleeve shirt, and cowboy hat. He skirts around the driver's side of an old beat-up Cadillac, and I hear the clomping of cowboy boots as he comes up the sidewalk.

Catherin answers the door. The man is there to see about the room for rent, and she invites him in, showing him the living room, kitchen, and guest bedrooms. I follow behind, feeling awkward and uncomfortable, my hackles raised. With shifty eyes the man looks at Catherin more than he looks at the house, and I don't like the way he keeps staring at her figure.

Catherin had been trying to find another female housemate, someone like Irene, but to no avail. She wanted a single, non-smoking, working woman, preferably in her 30s or 40s, with no children. That's what the ad in the paper said. Those were tough requirements. Not many single women wanted to commute the long distance to the working centers of the valley. There weren't many single women childless at that age, either. After no response from the first ad, Catherin relaxed the requirements, advertising for male *or* female.

Numerous men responded to the ad, a few coming over to see the place. I tried to be there for the meetings. I wasn't keen on the idea of having another man in the house—particularly this latest prospect.

After the cowboy drives away, Catherin turns to me and says, "Well, he seemed like a nice enough guy."

My jaw drops open.

"We need to talk," I say.

I motion her to sit with me at the dining room table. "Under no circumstances are you to allow that man to move in. Do you understand? Didn't you see the look in his eyes?"

Catherin gives me a puzzled look. "No, not really."

"I'm telling you, that guy is nothing but trouble. Promise me you won't let him move in."

"Okay," she says, shrugging her shoulders. "I still need to find a renter. I don't think I can be picky."

"But you don't want to be foolish either."

I see the frustration in her eyes. What is she to do? The house payment needs to be covered, which I offered to help with, but she doesn't want me to move in just for that reason. There has to be a way out of this impasse.

"I know we've been over this before," I say. "I'm sorry I'm not ready to move in with you, but why don't you at least let me help you make the house payment until you find a renter. That way you can take your time and make a good choice."

Resentment flashes in Catherin's face momentarily, but she regains her composure. "I appreciate your wanting to help," she says. "Really, I do. But don't you understand how you not wanting to move in makes me feel? It makes me feel like you don't really want me—like you can't make a commitment. It seems you are just talk."

I bristle at these words. "We've only been together four months," I say. "Surely, wanting to get to know you a little longer isn't too much to ask, is it? It's not that I don't want you. And if you don't know that, well, I don't know what to say."

We both stew in frustrated silence.

"I'm just trying to be practical," I eventually say. "Doesn't it make sense for me to help you out until the time comes when I feel ready to move in? And isn't that what you said you wanted—for me to move in only when I feel ready?"

"That's what I said, sure."

"You're always saying to listen to my heart, not my head. But I think in this case, it should be the other way around."

"I just want you here," Catherin says, with tears in her eyes.

I reach across the table to hold her hands, and say, "We'll be together—I know we will. Just give it time. But meanwhile, promise me you'll let me screen any prospects."

"Okay."

"Promise?"

"I promise."

~ ~ ~

Our band is slowly improving. We incorporate multi-part harmonies and practice the new set of gospel tunes suggested by Darrell. Catherin seems to enjoy the gospel music, which I find ironic, coming from this supposedly New Age woman. I like the tunes too. There's something about them that appeals. They remind me of my days as a child, going to church every Sunday—even though I had since given up on organized religion for the most part and rarely attended church now.

We have another performance at the coffeehouse the next weekend. Catherin is on form: confident, jubilant, and very entertaining. On one of the gospel numbers, *Life's Railway to Heaven*, Catherin's voice keeps cracking, and at one point, she almost loses her voice altogether. But she recovers gracefully, laughing at herself and keeping the audience amused.

Life's Railway to Heaven

Life is like a mountain railway
With an engineer so brave
You must make this run successful
From the cradle to the grave

Heed the curves, the hills, the tunnels
Never falter, never fail
Keep your hand up on the throttle
And your eye upon the rail

> *Oh blessed savior, thou will guide us*
> *Till we reach that blissful shore*
> *Where the angels wait to join us*
> *In God's grace, forever more*

As you roll across the trestle
Spanning Jordan, spanning time
There you'll see the union depot
Into which the train will glide

You will meet the superintendent
God the father, God the Son
There you'll have a joyous union
Weary pilgrim, welcome home

Oh blessed savior, thou will guide us
Till we reach that blissful shore
Where the angels wait to join us
In God's grace, forever more

— Traditional

In late April our band plays at a bluegrass festival put on as a charity benefit. It's a day of firsts. All the more established local bluegrass bands are there, and this is the first time we are heard by our peers. We play our best set, and for the first time, I feel we aren't the worst band to play. I even sing harmonies with Catherin on *Columbus Stockade Blues* without completely embarrassing myself.

That evening we play another charity gig at a benefit for Guatemalan refugees. Catherin had double booked us again, just as she had done the day of the Phoenix Folk Festival. We play after a set by Walt Richardson, a local reggae musician. Bluegrass is a long ways from his style of music. It's also a long way from Guatemala. How Catherin found this gig, I'll never know. It was a typical Catherin move. She could charge in and do things without worrying whether they made any sense. Nevertheless, the audience seems to enjoy our show.

~ ~ ~

The weeks of April come to a close. I arrive at Catherin's one day after work, and find her clearing out one of the guest bedrooms, having already organized things into boxes.

"I've found a renter," she says, after seeing my puzzled look.

"What?"

"He moves in tomorrow—would you help me carry these boxes out to the garage?"

Before I have a chance to register her words, she picks up a box and heads out of the room. I'm momentarily frozen in place with shock, trying to gather my thoughts. I'm still standing there when she returns.

"Aren't you going to help?" she asks.

"Sure, but not before you tell me what's going on. Who is this guy?"

"Oh, an ASU student." She says this casually.

"I thought you promised I could screen any prospects, especially guys."

"I'm sorry, but he came by on short notice."

I help with the rest of the boxes as I try to absorb this unsettling news. We go to relax in the living room afterwards, and I plunk down on the couch beside Catherin, still in a state of shock.

"You promised," I say after a few moments.

"He'll be fine."

"So what do you know about him?"

"Well, he's a political refugee from Ethiopia. Seems like an interesting guy."

Something about Ethiopia rings a bell.

"Wasn't somebody telling tasteless Ethiopian jokes at band practice a while back?"

"You're right," says Catherin, first pausing and then lightly chuckling. "I guess he's my karma."

~ ~ ~

I meet the Ethiopian the next day. Though he speaks little English, he seems okay on the surface, and I resign myself to his presence in Catherin's house. She goes out of her way to help him. As he didn't have any bedroom furniture, Catherin arranges to borrow some from her boss and we spend a morning moving in a bed and dresser. Catherin also successfully refers the Ethiopian to a job prospect she finds in the paper.

A few days later, Catherin rents the other guest bedroom to another guy. Again, I have no warning. Being overwhelmed by all the rapid changes, I let the matter drop. Besides, the new guy seems like a nice person, even to skeptical me.

I spend little time at Catherin's the next few weeks, apart from band practice. I'm focused at work, developing software that is a streamlined, mini-version of the company's main product. I'm the sole programmer. The project is due in a few weeks, and I work a lot of late nights both at the office and at home. For better or worse, I don't have much interaction with Catherin's new renters.

Chapter 11.
The Promise of Summer

Early May, 1987

Jagged peaks loom off to our right, four in number. "Did you know there's an old amethyst mine at the base of Four Peaks?" I ask Catherin, pointing out the window as we zoom up Beeline Highway, northeast of Phoenix.

"That's interesting," she says, not looking up, absorbed in knitting that sweater for Arielle.

"There's nice hiking up there," I say. "A trail skirts around the base of those peaks, and near the old mine, you can still find chunks of purple amethyst lying about. We should go there sometime."

"Uh-huh," says Catherin. She works her knitting needles with abandon, using energetic twists and turns that seem more forceful than necessary.

"Are you okay?" I ask.

"Just 'pied."

"'Pied?'"

"Preoccupied," she explains.

"About what?"

"Nothing."

A frown forms on her face. She doesn't look at me, but stays intent on her knitting.

"How are the new renters working out?" I ask.

"Fine," she says, pausing and finally looking up. "Well, I admit the Ethiopian is a bit strange, but it's probably a language barrier. His poor English makes him hard to figure out."

Something in her voice doesn't sound right, but she offers no further details, and I don't press for any. I don't want to spoil our nice Saturday outing by worrying about things. Catherin resumes her knitting.

Wiping a trace of sweat from my brow, I crank up the car's air conditioner. It's the first weekend of May, and the oppressive heat of summer has settled into the lower deserts of Phoenix, prompting us to head north to cooler climes. Highway 87, otherwise known as Beeline Highway, is our escape route. Our destination? Tentatively, the Mogollon Rim, a set of escarpments and bluffs that run diagonally through the heart of Arizona, marking the southern boundary of the Colorado Plateau. There are several small villages along the Rim, including the town of Payson. Might be a good place for lunch, I'm thinking.

As we climb to higher elevations, the saguaros and chollas of the Sonoran desert give way to short-grass and prickly pear cactus, which cover the rocky slopes. We reach the summit of Sunflower Pass, and descend down its northern slopes. Soon we come to a junction, where another highway heads east down a broad, desert valley to the northern reaches of Roosevelt Lake. If you know where to look you can see the shoreline off in the distance. This brings back memories of a hot summer weekend I once spent on that lake, sailing on an eighteen-foot Hobie Cat with friends and sleeping under the stars.

One of the best kept secrets of Arizona are the summer nights. Although they can be oppressively hot, with temperatures past a hundred even after midnight, more often than not it's a pleasant, dry, eighty-five degrees—at least if you get out of the concrete-laden metropolitan areas and into the surrounding desert. The summer nights are perfect for camping by the shores of a lake. You don't need a sleeping bag, and you can lie on a folding chair with no blankets and never get cold. There are few flying insects to distract you, though scorpions and tarantulas on the ground are a bit of a problem, I admit.

I remember lying on a flimsy aluminum lounge chair beside Roosevelt Lake that long ago summer evening, staring up at the stars, which were quickly being blotted out by an approaching storm. An angry thundercloud threatened off to the southeast, lit up by lightning deep within its turbulent bowels. I gazed into the dark sky for a long time, listening to the intricate guitar work of jazz artist Pat Metheny on the headphones of my portable cassette player.

When the cassette finished, I removed the headphones and stared at the flashes of heat lightning spreading through the clouds, now overhead. I could hear occasional distant rumbles of thunder, far enough away that I wasn't too concerned for my safety. For a moment I had a sensation of projecting upwards and floating amongst the clouds, speaking to them in the language of thunder. I drifted off to sleep, and the thunder continued to roll well into the night, telling ancient stories in my dreams. It never did rain, which is not unusual for an Arizona storm. By early morning, the thunderclouds had finished their conversation with me, and a quiet and peaceful dawn awakened.

I realize now, five years later, that the thunderclouds had spoken to me recently, calling me a "fool" for not being able to strike up a meaningful conversation with the dark-haired, white mountain bike woman, upon our first meeting at Squaw Peak. No matter, for she is here beside me, and we've been together long enough that we no longer feel the need to have any conversation at all. We can be together in silence like we are now, Catherin knitting her sweaters, and me watching the scenery and day-dreaming of trips from long ago.

Gray peaks of another range of mountains loom off to our left, sending a small thrill through me, triggering further wanderlust. These desert mountains don't have the grandeur of the Colorado Rockies, but for me, having grown up in the flatlands, any sort of hill, cliff, bluff, or mountain is a welcome sight.

"That's the Mazatzals," I say to Catherin, pointing to my left. "They always remind me of the Rockies. Every time I see them I want to drop everything and head to Colorado."

Catherin suddenly stops knitting. "I almost forgot to tell you," she says excitedly.

"Tell me what?"

"I've got a surprise. I ordered tickets to the *Telluride Bluegrass Festival* a while back, and they came in the mail yesterday."

"You bought tickets to Telluride? That's awesome!"

Telluride is a small skiing town in southwestern Colorado, surrounded by some of the most spectacular scenery anywhere, supposedly. I had never been there. I knew of the bluegrass festival held every year in late June, and figured someday I would go, if for no other reason than it involved being in the mountains.

"I thought you'd like going," Catherin continues. "That's why I went ahead and ordered the tickets."

"You're the best girlfriend ever," I say, reaching over and patting her leg affectionately. "And such a planner!"

Catherin smiles, and goes back to her knitting.

A sign appears along the highway, announcing a trailhead on the left.

"There's a nice trail up those mountains that leads to a waterfall," I say to Catherin, motioning towards the west. "This is a good time of year to hike up there. The water may still be running. Most of the year it isn't."

Catherin looks to see where I'm pointing: a dusty trail meandering off into parched, scrubby brush. The prospects of running water seem slim in that direction.

"We can go hiking there someday, if you want," says Catherin. "But not today. I'm too tired."

"I know what you mean. With the band and all, it seems we've had little time to rest. Plus, that project at work is really making me spacey."

"And goodness knows we don't need you to be any more spacey than you already are," Catherin says with a small laugh. "I'm surprised you remembered to pick me up this morning."

"I would never miss an excuse to ramble about the countryside," I say. "I'm sorry I forgot to call last night. I was on computer time, which is always warped. That new computer I have at home is pretty fast, by the way. But how about you? I never asked how your day went yesterday."

"I spent most of the time at the office. Cecilia came over in the evening and we practiced harmonies."

"You sure have our schedule filled up. At least it seems that way to me."

Catherin nods her head. "We do have a lot of gigs planned. I think next weekend is the only one we have free for a while."

We continue up the Beeline in silence, now just a few miles out of Payson. Catherin resumes knitting, and I daydream about trips to exotic mountainous locales. My thoughts drift to past encounters with thunderclouds.

Catherin then says something, but it's as unintelligible as those conversations with the clouds.

"I'm sorry," I say to her. "I missed what you said."

"'Pied?" she repeats.

"Yes, I'm 'pied."

I tell Catherin about my experience with the thunderclouds at Roosevelt Lake.

"You sure have interesting fantasies," Catherin says, after I finish my story. "Right now, I like the thought of clouds and rain … a lake … water!" She lets out a deep sigh.

"Is another trip to San Diego warranted?" I ask. "I know, we could turn around and head for Roosevelt Lake. It's not far."

"Sounds hot," she says. "Let's keep heading towards the cool pines."

The traffic picks up as we reach Payson, and the town seems busier than usual, with cars and people milling about. I guess the ideal weather of the pine country has attracted more than just the two of us.

"Do you want to stop here in Payson?" I ask. "We could get something to eat."

"I'd rather we keep driving, away from all these people," Catherin replies. "Besides, we've got plenty of snacks with us."

I think of other possible destinations, and finally pick the closest one. "Let's head further north to Strawberry."

Strawberry is a quaint but growing little town—well, more like a wide spot in the road—northwest of Payson, higher up on the Mogollon Rim. The town is rapidly becoming a favorite summer retreat for the heat-weary residents of the Phoenix area. A hodgepodge collection of cabins, mobile homes, and yuppie mansions are popping up everywhere.

Driving the narrow, curvy roads to Strawberry further triggers the wanderlust lurking in me. Cruising along a scenic highway always does that. It's funny, I'm always reluctant to make the effort to get away, but once I do, I wonder why I don't do it all the time. I guess like most people I'm too complacent, not willing to take action to change things, even if I'm not particularly satisfied with the way they are. That reminds me of my current job. Although I'm busy enough, the work isn't satisfying. Perhaps I *should* re-apply for the job at Kitt Peak. And speaking of observatories, I remember there's one in Flagstaff.

"Maybe Strawberry isn't far enough," I say. "We could drive all the way to Flagstaff. There's an observatory there, did you know? It's where Pluto was discovered."

"Driving to Flagstaff is stretching it a little, don't you think? We were going for a short ride, remember?"

"Yeah, I know."

"But whatever you want to do is fine," says Catherin.

Once I'm on the road and the wanderlust takes hold, I've been known to drive five hundred miles on what starts out as a mere Sunday morning drive. But that's by myself, with no other commitments, and no companions with other interests. Now I settle for pretending we are driving all the way to Flagstaff, or even further north to the Grand Canyon, and beyond. In reality, I will turn around whenever Catherin wants. But of course, she'll have to ask …

We come to a curve in the road with a red bluff situated on the left, and the East Verde River gurgling below, wooing us to its banks. We are easily persuaded. We park the car and stroll hand in hand along the banks of the river, soaking up the beautiful scenery and cool breezes. Catherin spots an inviting patch of grass near the riverbank, and we stretch out lazily alongside the river.

"I sure miss seeing green," Catherin remarks, running her hands through the damp blades of grass. She sits up to take off her shoes and rub her feet in the grass. I follow suit, my feet reconnecting with the Earth. There's a boulder nearby with room enough for us both, and soon we dangle toes in the water from atop the boulder.

"I'm really getting tired of the city," Catherin continues, sloshing her feet in the water. "I keep thinking it's time for something else. My astrologer says major changes are in store for me this summer."

"You have an astrologer?"

"Didn't I tell you about him? His name is Michael. I've taken classes from him and he interprets my chart from time to time."

"What major changes does he see?"

"He says something significant."

"Such as?"

"It's hard to be specific," Catherin says. "You should know that."

"So what would you do if you could make any changes you wanted?" I ask this as we put our socks and shoes back on.

"I don't know." Catherin sighs. "It would be nice to have a place in the country, with horses and green pastures, like I had back in Pennsylvania. And it would be nice to have a small circle of friends nearby—no more being surrounded by millions of strangers."

Her wishes bring to mind a song from the bluegrass album we had discovered the month before:

Green Fields

We used to live just on the outskirts of town
When I was a little girl
The bright skies, the dark forests
And the green fields were my world

Then we moved away into the city
And left the fields of home behind
And now when solitude's so hard to find
My memories take me back in time

> Where are my green fields now?
> No, nowhere around
> So I'll steal away, with my memories
> And in green fields, I'll lay me down

Now I've got concrete for my front yard
And it's the same way out in back
But still it fills my heart with happiness
To see green grass push through the cracks

> Where are my green fields now?
> No, nowhere around
> So I'll steal away, with my memories
> And in green fields, I'll lay me down

I guess I share the same time-worn dream
With folks in cities everywhere
To find a little place on God's green earth
And live in peace and quiet there

> Where are my green fields now?
> No, nowhere around
> So I'll steal away, with my memories
> And in green fields, I'll lay me down

— Laurie Lewis, 1980

I help Catherin to her feet and we continue our stroll down the banks of the East Verde, eventually finding another patch of grass beneath huge cottonwood trees. Catherin is wearing her favorite blue T-shirt, and she looks youthful and girlish. Being outdoors seems to do her wonders. It's clear we need to spend more time out-side—perhaps a camping trip is in order. But where, and when? We *could* camp during our trip to Telluride. But no, it needs to be sooner than that, and right now it's too early in the season for the moun-tains. We need something scenic, at a lower elevation. And I know just the place.

"We have next weekend free, right?" I ask Catherin.

"It's the only time we have until Telluride."

"Then how about going to Zion?"

"Zion?"

"You know, the national park in southern Utah?"

"I don't know if I've ever been there," Catherin says.

"You'd remember. It's an amazing place, filled with majestic pink and white sandstone cliffs, and a beautiful canyon floor."

"Sounds wonderful."

"We'll go next weekend, then. I'll bring my tent and we can go hiking. There are plenty of places to explore in the canyon."

Catherin laughs a big hearty laugh.

"What are you laughing at?"

Catherin tries to imitate my deeper voice. "I don't like plans! They're a four letter word!" She laughs again, and then switches back to her own voice. "That's what you told me."

~ ~ ~

The following week is hectic as I try to finish the programming project that's coming due. Catherin's week is busy too, with the pos-sibility of her closing a few deals at the shopping center. We plan on leaving for Zion at noon the following Friday, and when the day comes, we're both psyched and ready to go.

I'm also psyched about the upcoming trip to the *Telluride Blue-grass Festival:* mountains, bluegrass, and being with the woman of my dreams—a woman who would love the music as much as I would. How could it get any better? Summer promised to be such a wonderful time.

Catherin calls me at work mid-morning and says we can't leave at noon as planned. Important things have come up at the leasing center. They are getting ready to move their office to a new location, and she needs to handle the details. I still have plenty to do anyway, so I plunge back into programming. At two o'clock Catherin calls again and says we'll have to postpone the trip. Now I'm bummed.

I finish what I can on my project and drive home. I resign myself to the trip being postponed, and look forward to relaxing and getting much needed rest. Stumbling into the bedroom, I shed my work clothes and conk out as soon as my head hits the pillow.

At seven-thirty, a phone call wakes me up.

"Let's go," I hear from the other end. "Are you ready?"

"Ready?" I ask, still a bit groggy. "Ready for what?"

It takes a while to figure out who is calling and for what reason. "You mean leave for Zion tonight? Are you crazy?"

"Don't you want to go?" asks Catherin.

"We should have left earlier," I say. "Seems too late now."

"Come on, Bry, don't be a deadpan! I thought you said you were always ready to travel at a moment's notice. Why not now?"

I have no desire to get out of bed, let alone drive all the way to Utah in the middle of the night. But no doubt about it, she has me. I quickly estimate our driving time to Zion.

"You do realize we'd be getting there very early in the morning," I say. "Around four by my calculations."

"That's better than not getting there at all," she says. "I'll be at your place shortly, so be prepared."

Catherin comes right over. She brings along a bag of cassette tapes, most of them audio books, including *Hitchhiker's Guide to the Galaxy*. But Catherin's car doesn't have a tape player. Even though I had successfully installed speakers for her, she had yet to purchase an in-dash audio system. So I find my portable stereo cassette player and try one of the tapes to make sure the machine works. It doesn't.

"I guess the batteries are dead," I say. "We'll have to stop at the store and get new ones."

"Okay," Catherin says. "We can also pick up snacks for the trip."

I need to get cash too, and believe there is an automatic teller machine near the supermarket. To save time, Catherin shops for groceries while I search for the teller machine. Unfortunately, I discover my bank card has expired. I return to the supermarket and find Catherin waiting at the checkout line.

"My card's out of date," I tell her. "I can't get any cash."

"No problem," she replies. "I've got plenty."

We finish checking out, ready to be on our way, except I won't let us go.

"I must have received a new bank card in the mail," I say. "I want to go back to my place and find it."

"What for?" she asks. "We don't need any more money. Let's go! Don't waste time!"

"Not until I find my card first."

Back at my apartment I search a good fifteen minutes without success. That shouldn't have been surprising. My filing system consists of throwing mail on the table, and when that gets full, stuffing it all in a box. Catherin watches me sort through piles of letters.

"Forget about that silly bank card," she says, following me around. "We can do without it."

By this time, I'm in a grouchy mood. I don't feel like traveling in the middle of the night, and not being able to get money of my own makes it even worse. I always feel the need to have extra cash, to be prepared for anything.

"We're not leaving till I find that card!" I growl. My lips stick out in a pout while I continue my search.

When Catherin sees my pouting lips, she seizes the opportunity. "Birdsgonnabuildanestonyourlips!"

That stops my grouchiness in its tracks.

"See?" she says. "You *are* a growling Leo after all."

I shake my head with a smile. She has me, again.

"I'll be fine by the time we get to Zion," I say. "It *is* one of my favorite places, after all."

"I sure hope so!" Catherin says, first trying to act concerned, and then proceeding to laugh.

But that doesn't stop me from looking for the card. I finally find it, and we drive back to the automated teller to get the cash I so adamantly have to have. By nine-thirty, we're on our way. We head north on Interstate 17, bound for Flagstaff and the Utah canyons beyond.

Chapter 12.
Endless Starry Nights

City lights recede in the distance as we cruise up the freeway, Catherin at the wheel. The plan is for me to take over during the wee hours of the morning, so I should be resting. But the further north we go, away from the busy, congested city, the more alert I become. It's the charge of adrenalin that comes from traveling the desert at night, after the day's oppressive heat subsides and there's relief from the sun's dazzling glare.

We listen to *Hitchhiker's Guide to the Galaxy* on the tape player, laughing and thoroughly enjoying the radio play, especially the character of Marvin, the Depressed Robot. In *our* corner of the galaxy, the waxing moon, high in the sky, adds ethereal light to dark canyons lurking on both sides of the road.

By the time we reach the Sedona area, I have completely transformed from the grouchy old lion who can't find his bank card, to a content but alert and curious creature, watchful of the moonlit bluffs and outcroppings off in the distance. The next thing I know, we have climbed into cool pine country, a very different world from the lower deserts. We stop at a gas station on the northern outskirts of Flagstaff and I take over the driving duties, steering us northward past the western edge of the Painted Desert, and then along a major fault line known as the Echo Cliffs, thirty miles south of Page.

The taped radio play finishes and I say to Catherin, "Marvin, the Depressed Robot, reminds me of Wacky."

"Wacky?"

"I guess I've never mentioned him. Wacky is a robot my friend Alden is programming to navigate down hallways, all on its own. A big puzzle is whether to have Wacky recognize objects, or just the opposite, to recognize empty space, like the floor. Alden hasn't worked on this for a while. Poor Wacky is now just a plant stand."

Catherin is amused by my description of Wacky, the Plant Stand. I explain my thoughts on the figure-ground illusion, and how we might see other things if we change our rules of perception, and that perhaps synchronicity plays into this theory—that meaningful coincidences occur because we become receptive to them.

"That reminds me of the *I-Ching*," Catherin says, as she rummages through the bag of tapes she brought along. "Before you do the coin toss, you have to prepare your mind to be receptive to the outcome. That's when the synchronicity occurs."

"The question is," I ask, "are you merely becoming receptive, or are you actually affecting the outcome?" I raise and lower my eyebrows several times, whistling the *Twilight Zone* theme music.

Catherin laughs and says with a low voice, "Only the shadow knows." She then presents a tape of plays from *The Shadow*—an old radio series—which she had literally pulled out of the bag. "Do you want to listen to this?"

I see the tape and say, "I'd rather have silence for a—"

I do a double-take. Catherin's joke dawns on me.

"Very funny," I say. "I see you've cleverly constructed a coincidence using that tape. I'm not sure it's a synchronicity, though."

"Why not?" she replies, with mock offense. "That tape appeared at just the right time, didn't it? I was just being receptive."

"*And* you were affecting the outcome," I point out, laughing.

Our banter dies down as we reach a junction, and we begin heading up a long grade, climbing the Echo Cliffs and topping out on a plateau, eventually reaching the city of Page near the southern shores of Lake Powell. I steer the car across the bridge at Glen Canyon Dam. Below, the impressive Colorado River plunges south on its way to the Grand Canyon. We pass the Utah state line and head west through very scenic Colorado Plateau country—at least I *remember* it being scenic from previous trips. In the late night hour the landscape is rather dark, the moon having traversed into the western sky, partially hidden behind scattered clouds.

Very few cars pass. The road is straight and monotonous.

"What music did you bring along?" I ask Catherin, stifling a yawn.

She is lightly dozing, but opens her eyes as soon as I speak.

"Well, I brought a tape of Laurie Lewis," she says, reaching for the cassette bag.

"You mean the one Pete loaned you? That's a great album—and great planning on your part for bringing a copy."

Catherin smiles at my planning remark and digs through the bag. After finding the right tape, she plugs it into the player. The songs of Laurie Lewis fill the air, and I get that familiar sense of timelessness that seems to arise whenever something special is about to happen. The moon reveals itself from behind the clouds as a silvery-golden orb in the west, and the twinkling stars in the Utah sky are nothing short of spectacular. I feel myself drifting into a magical realm.

At one point we stop alongside the road and climb out the car to gaze at the moon and stars. We are in the middle of nowhere, just the two of us and the starry Utah sky. We lean against the hood as the sounds of fiddles, guitars, and sweet harmonies drift out the open car doors, merging with the winds of the Colorado Plateau.

On the tape is a song about a maple tree whose wood is turned into a stringed instrument. Featured in the song is a *hardingfele*—a special kind of Norwegian fiddle having additional sympathetic strings that resonate when the main strings are played, giving the instrument a haunting, almost unearthly sound. The song's lyrics speak of endless starry nights, perfectly matching the occasion:

The Maple's Lament

When I was alive the birds would nest upon my boughs
And all through long winter nights the storms would 'round me howl
And when the day would come, I'd raise my branches to the sun
I was the child of earth and sky, and all the world was one

But now that I am dead the birds no longer sing in me
And I feel no more the wind and rain as when I was a tree
But bound so tight in wire strings, I have no room to grow
And I am but the slave who sings, when master draws the bow

But sometimes from my memory I can sing the birds in flight
And I can sing of sweet dark earth and endless starry nights
But oh, my favorite song of all, I truly do believe
Is the song the sunlight sang for me while dancing on my leaves

— Laurie Lewis, 1985

Listening to these lyrics sends a tingling down my neck, spreading to my arms and back.

"That song gives me goose bumps," I say to Catherin, rubbing my arms.

"I know," she says. "It does me too."

As the song finishes we climb back in the car, and I shut off the tape player so the spell won't be broken. The strains of the harding-fele reverberate in my head as I navigate down the road and contemplate the fate of the poor maple tree, which is no longer able to experience the joys of life. This thought sends shivers down my spine a second time. I glance over to Catherin, and notice goose bumps have reappeared on her arm as well.

I blink my eyes, adding this moment to my list of unforgettable memories.

After twenty miles, the drone of car tires makes me drowsy again. I turn the tape player back on. Soon I hear a familiar song— one we had danced to in Catherin's living room a few weeks before:

> *Here we go again*
> *I love you so again*
> *Once more it starts to end*
> *The moment it begins*

I'm captivated by the harmony fiddles and poignant sighs of the pedal steel. Goose bumps reappear once more.

"What great music," I say to Catherin. "I wish my fiddling sounded like that."

"That is a wonderful song," says Catherin. "Maybe we should add it to our band's repertoire."

"Except it's more country than bluegrass."

"So?"

I shrug. "Good point."

The song ends, only to be followed by another superb selection, which also has a familiar refrain:

> *Where are my green fields now?*
> *No, nowhere around*
> *So I'll steal away with my memories*
> *And in green fields I'll lay me down*

The lyrics remind me of Catherin's stories about riding her horse through the green fields of Pennsylvania, how she has to eventually give that up for the city, and how she misses those green fields, wanting nothing more than to live in peace and harmony. I think of the Magic Farm, whose own green fields are threatened by lurking bulldozers and graders.

I should pay more attention to lyrics, I realize. Too many times I just sing along to my favorite songs, without really understanding their intended meaning.

The last song on the tape is *Haven of Mercy*, a gospel-like tune about the loss of a loved one. The first two stanzas send more shivers down my spine:

> At the end of just another day
> That's when I miss her most
> When her memories gather 'round me
> Like an old familiar ghost
>
> Then high above this rocky coast
> There's a place that I can go
> To heal the wounds of a heartbreak
> And soothe a lovesick soul

The song fades as we reach Kanab, Utah. We slow down at a junction in the road, and in silence, turn to head north and west for the mystical canyons of Zion.

Chapter 13.
Feelings of Restlessness

The moon hovers low in the western sky. Intermittent clouds diminish any light offered by the golden orb, rendering the landscape beyond our headlights a black void. It's just as well. I know from previous trips along this lonely highway that we are passing through a country of unsightly, scrabbly hills composed of clumpy gray soil. There is no indication of what lies twenty miles up the road: some of the most beautiful scenery in the West, the towering cliffs and buttes of Zion National Park.

Dazed by the hypnotic effects of whirring tires, I try unsuccessfully to shake off the wee morning hour, using repeated eye-blinks that have nothing to do with my induced recursive-memories game. It's time for more music. As the moon disappears beneath a ragged horizon off in the west, the setting reminds me of songs from my favorite western band, *Riders in the Sky*. I momentarily reach for the bag of cassettes, thinking it would be nice to play a tape of their music. Yes, it would be nice, had I planned ahead and brought tapes of my own. Realizing I had not, I abandon my search and resort to humming and then softly singing songs I know from the *Riders in the Sky* albums.

Catherin nuzzles against my shoulder, bringing a particular song to mind: *Blue Bonnet Lady*, a *Riders in the Sky* original that talks of a lonely gal needing a shoulder to lean upon. Catherin shifts her head a little closer on my shoulder, eyes closed. I sing the melody to her, wondering how she would look wearing a blue bonnet from the old days. I'll bet she would look mighty fine. Mighty fine.

The monotonous drone of the roadway is interrupted momentarily as the road surface changes and we enter and exit a short tunnel. This startles Catherin awake and has her sitting up. A few curves later we enter a second tunnel, much longer than the first. The tunnel is lit only by our headlights.

I notice Catherin twiddling her thumbs as though using knitting needles. She looks a little worried.

"How long *is* this tunnel?" she asks.

"A mile or so."

Catherin continues her thumb-twiddling.

"I forgot you aren't entirely comfortable with tunnels," I say.

"I'll be okay."

"If it's any consolation, there are five or six windows along the way, off to our right."

An arched window soon appears that I point out to Catherin. She leans over to peer out as the window goes by, only to have nothing revealed but a black abyss. It's as dark out there as it is in the tunnel.

"You'd never know it, but we're actually skirting the side of a sheer canyon wall," I say.

I can tell from Catherin's furrowed brow that this was not the best thing for me to say.

"In the daytime the views from those windows are really quite impressive," I say. "Even though there's not much time to look."

More windows into the abyss pass by and then the tunnel exit comes into view.

"I'd like to say there's light at the end of this tunnel," I say, "but at four in the morning ..."

Catherin laughs softly at my joke. Worried look notwithstanding, she seems more at ease than in previous encounters with enclosed spaces. I remember our time at Kitt Peak, when she was nervous about going up the elevator to see the Mayall Telescope.

We emerge into pre-dawn darkness, the stars beginning to fade. Had it been later in the morning we would have been presented with the awesome sight of a massive layer of white sandstone that caps the western wall of the canyon. Most of the bluffs and escarpments of Zion are made of a mixture of red and white Navajo Sandstone, and there are several volcanic plugs sticking up, most prominently a formation called Watchman's Tower that stands as sentinel near the park's campground, our destination.

We descend a series of switchbacks to the canyon floor, and are soon rolling quietly into the campground. During the busy season, an empty campsite would be nearly impossible to find, but the summer crowds are still weeks away. As such, an available site readily presents itself.

Seeing as how it's four-thirty in the morning, we have no desire to pitch a tent in the dark and don't want to disturb neighboring campers by hammering stakes, so we roll out a ground cloth, plop down sleeping bags, and go to sleep immediately.

A few hours later I open my eyes and stretch. I sit up to the glorious sight of the sun rising behind Watchman's Tower. Though backlit, the front of the tower is glowing from rosy light bouncing off dazzling sandstone opposite the canyon. Admiring this display of reflected light brings reflections of a different nature—memories of other times I have camped in this canyon. The first time was during spring break five years earlier, when I had pitched a lonely tent, just me and an old guitar, not far from where we are now.

Catherin stirs beside me, a pleasant reminder that those lonely days are thankfully over. I lie back down and turn over to watch Catherin as she sleeps. The sun clears the eastern cliffs and the slanting morning light catches fine wrinkles on her face—wrinkles that foretell the end of her youth. How will I react as we get older? Will her fading beauty upset me? Will we still be together?

I rub my eyes. Except for a few aches and pains due to sleeping on the hard ground, I feel surprisingly refreshed. Catherin wakes a short time later and doesn't seem tired either. This should not have been the case, for we had slept only a few hours—and this after seven hours of night driving. We have a quick breakfast of orange juice and rolls, and then set up the tent so no one else will claim the campsite after we leave for the day's adventures.

As I hammer in the last tent peg, Catherin puts away our breakfast and then throws sleeping bags into the tent.

"Okay, Bry, what's your plan now?"

Spying the inviting sleeping bags, I plunge into the tent and motion with raised eyebrows for Catherin to follow. She does, giggling.

~ ~ ~

"We can't spend all day in here," Catherin says afterwards. "Seriously, what do you want to do the *rest* of the day?"

I briefly describe the lay of the land. Zion National Park covers several hundred square miles, much of it remote. It's the inner canyon—through which the Virgin River runs—that most people associate with the park. The campgrounds are situated on the banks of the river towards the south end of the canyon, but most of the attractions are on the north end. About halfway along are a series of waterfalls known as Emerald Pools, and north of that is a trail winding up an imposing bluff known as Angel's Landing, which has the quintessential view of the park. Further north, at the end of the road, are the Narrows, where the canyon closes in on both sides to the width of the river. It's a popular hiking and wading destination.

"We should definitely hike up Angel's Landing," I say to Catherin as we clamber out of the tent. "That's my favorite place in the park."

Though we are shaded from the sun by cottonwood trees, tendrils of heat are already spreading through the canyon. I know what it's like to be hiking up the trail to Angel's Landing in the heat. I had made that mistake once, and had no intention of making it again.

"The trail is steep up to Angel's Landing," I continue. "It's best if we avoid the heat of the day as much as possible. We should pack a quick lunch and start hiking soon. We can explore Emerald Pools afterwards, and maybe go to the Narrows tomorrow."

Catherin nods her head with each suggestion, looking as though she's suppressing a laugh. When I finish, she remarks, "You can sure plan things when you want to."

"Well, then, let me rephrase that," I say, laughing. I adopt an exaggerated and fake western Nebraska cowboy dialect: "Maybe we can mosey on up the trail and maybe by accident climb to the top of one of them there bluffs where angels supposedly land, and then I s'pose we could ramble around a bit and if we're lucky maybe stumble across some waterfalls by sheer coincidence. And I hear't rumors of a narrah canyon where a man cain't barely but see the sky and where lots of water critters on two legs can be found millin' about. Maybe we'll just happen to discover that canyon tomorrah."

Catherin chuckles at my antics and packs a lunch while I fill water bottles and finish tidying up the area. It's a short drive to the Angel's Landing trailhead. With our daypacks securely attached, we proceed to cross a footbridge over the Virgin River, which is swollen with snow melt from mountains far to the north. At the end of the bridge is a junction: one path goes to Angel's Landing, the other to

Emerald Pools. I point out the latter, and say that's where we can head later, if we feel up to it.

The trail is easy at first, but grows more difficult as we climb a series of long, moderately steep switchbacks. The view becomes more impressive with every step, with the highway and river receding in the distance. After a mile or so we come to another bridge, where the trail turns north and levels off into an area called Refrigerator Canyon—a narrow chasm filled with junipers and occasional pine tree. We hike gratefully in the coolness of the shaded canyon, alongside a small burbling stream, our footsteps echoing across the narrow and otherwise peaceful canyon walls.

We round a bend. Suddenly the trail pitches steeply and wildly upwards, making us pause.

"I forgot about this," I say, pointing upwards to a seemingly endless series of short switchbacks. "These switchbacks are known as Walter's Wiggles."

"We're not going up there, are we?" asks Catherin. "And who's Walter?"

"I believe Walter was one of the early park superintendents that helped in the construction of these trails."

Catherin laughs. "I wonder if Walter fidgeted as much as you do. Maybe we should rename these Bryan's Wiggles."

"Well, then, I should be able to power us easily to the top." I take Catherin's hand and help her up the first of the wiggles, before climbing on ahead of her.

The steep switchbacks of the Wiggles look formidable, but they really aren't. It's not long before I reach the top and step onto an aptly named saddle known as Scout's Lookout. Catherin has fallen behind, and lets out a big sigh when she catches up. That sigh quickly changes to a gasp when she realizes what's in front of us.

The saddle gives way to a sheer drop down to the canyon floor. It's a thousand feet, maybe more. Catherin immediately finds a place to sit—and not very close to the edge, I notice.

"I'm glad we're at the top," she says. "I'm not moving another inch."

"Oh, we're not there yet," I say, turning my gaze southwards and motioning with a nod. "That's the top, over there."

The trail follows a steep, narrow ridge that goes right up the side of a bluff—the actual site of Angel's Landing—with nothing to block a fall on either side. It looks like an impossible climb, like something out of a nightmare.

Catherin follows my gaze. "No way!" she says. "We can't possibly be going up there."

"It's not as bad as it looks," I say. "Besides, there are cables and rails to hang on to the whole way."

Catherin looks at me with disbelief. "Oh, *that's* reassuring!"

She unpacks our lunch, and we take in the sights while we eat. A couple of hikers pass by and head towards Angels Landing, looking nonchalant about the whole affair. We watch them climb the ridge, using the cables and rails that snake all the way to the top.

"I remember the first time I came here," I say, finishing a sandwich. "I was just like you, thinking there was no way I could climb to the top. But then I saw others do it—ordinary people, like you and me, with no special gear. I figured if they could do it, I could do it."

We pack up the leftovers and start up the trail, soon encountering boulders where the first cables appear.

"Just hang on to the cables if you need to," I tell Catherin. "It's not that bad. Trust me."

"Right," says Catherin, the doubt apparent in her voice.

After climbing the first boulders, I pause and turn to her. "I have to admit, I did get apprehensive the first time I hiked this ridge, about halfway up. But I persevered. Subsequent climbs were no big deal. They seemed easy. I'm sure it'll be the same for you."

"Well, I'm not so sure," says Catherin.

"It's what I've observed over the years," I say, shrugging. "You think something isn't doable until you see others do it, or you try it yourself. Then you are surprised it's not so hard after all."

But little do I know that Catherin is afraid of heights. We come to a spot where the trail narrows to a path six feet wide, with nothing but an eight-hundred foot fall on one side that seems to draw you towards the edge. Scanning further up the trail, I can see that both sides of the trail are exposed. Catherin sees this too and looks appalled.

"You go on, Bry," she says, stopping. "I'm going to stay right here."

Catherin searches for and then backs down to a wider spot in the trail. She nervously huddles against the wall as far away from the edge as possible, as though wishing she could glue herself to the boulder she now uses as a backrest.

"You sure you don't want to come?" I ask.

Catherin acts as if I'm asking her to jump off a cliff. I have to admit, it might seem like that.

I've always wanted someone to share my love of the outdoors, and of this special place called Zion National Park. I particularly wanted to share the top of Angel's Landing with Catherin. But nothing I say will move her. I finally give up and scramble towards the summit by myself. Partway up I turn around, and hanging on to one of the cables, I yell back to Catherin. "See, it's not so bad."

She stares back, not budging a muscle, a "he's crazy" look clearly visible on her face.

On top are spectacular views of the sandstone bluffs of the canyon, with the Virgin River snaking through the valley a staggering distance below. Winding alongside the river is the road to the Narrows, now filled with what appear to be tiny moving cars and buses, dramatically providing a sense of scale.

Despite the inspirational view, I don't spend much time on top. I'm restless—and lonely.

While definitely afraid of heights, Catherin seems more worried that I will stop liking her because she wouldn't go to the top. I find this out after making my way back down. She clearly looks distressed.

"Are you okay?" I ask.

"I'm alright."

Catherin is silent for a moment and then says, "I feel bad I didn't go with you." She bites her lip and looks down and then sideways up at me. "You still want me?"

I think she is joking—till I see tears.

"It doesn't matter that you couldn't make it," I say, giving her a consoling hug. "Really, I love you, and nothing will change that." I stroke the beautiful hair of this puzzling, dark-haired, white mountain bike woman.

Her tears flow.

"Why are you crying so?" I ask.

"Just because."

I hold and soothe her a while longer and then say, "We should get going. I suspect it's going to get hot soon."

We work our way to the canyon bottom in silence. After reaching the trail along the Virgin River, we turn up the fork that will take us to Emerald Pools. These pools are actually a series of waterfalls situated along the western side of the canyon. According to a sign posted along the trail, it's one and a half miles to the waterfalls. I'm thinking we'll have no trouble with that.

Ha! The hike up Angel's Landing has left us sore and tired—as we quickly realize when our feet sink into the deep sand that makes up this unexpectedly steep trail. The morning coolness has been chased away by the dazzling sun—though clouds are beginning to form, and along with them comes a touch of humidity. Soon we are soaked in sweat.

We reach the first set of waterfalls, and I mistakenly believe the others are just a little further, so I have us press on without stopping. As it turns out, the trail goes for another half a mile, and is quite steep in spots. The shifting, slippery sand robs our strength.

"He-ee-ere we go again," I sing as we round another sandy switchback, referencing the song on the Laurie Lewis tape. To Catherin's amusement, I sing the refrain, "He-ee-ere we go again," every time the trail turns uphill.

We finally make it to the upper pools and sit along on the bank to rest and enjoy the view. A large group of hikers had been trailing us, and they are now milling about. A particularly attractive gal walks by in shorts and a revealing halter top. My head swivels. My eyes follow.

"Whoa!"

The exclamation slips from my lips before I realize what I'm doing. I look sheepishly over to Catherin. Is that hurt in those eyes? And to think I would behave this way, after the episode on Angel's Landing. I'm not yet used to the fact I already have someone of my own, and that she is right here beside me. *I'm sorry*, I want to tell her. But I don't say it out loud. I rub her thigh tentatively, apologetically, and then find a hand of hers to slip into mine. I hold her hand for a while, feeling ashamed.

That dang moon in Gemini. I'll blame it on that.

~ ~ ~

On our hike back to the canyon floor, we hear a series of loud claps off in the distance. Catherin winces at the sound and quickly moves a hand to her chest.

"Were those gunshots?" she asks, as we stop momentarily.

"I don't know," I say. "I wouldn't have thought guns were allowed in the park."

Catherin seems visibly shaken, and remains that way until we reach the trailhead and cross the bridge over the Virgin River. Near the river bank we spot a large patch of grass and head that way. With a sigh, Catherin lowers down, tucking her knees into her chest, wrapping her arms around. She is wearing her favorite blue T-shirt and her favorite plain silver bracelet.

Though I'd been carrying Catherin's camera in my pack, I hadn't snapped more than a few photos. But the composition in front of me grabs my attention. I pull out the camera and lift it to my eye. Through the viewfinder I see Catherin smiling, restrained though that is. She turns her head to follow as I maneuver around, searching for the most photogenic angle. In her eyes, I see love. Inexplicably, though, I also see sadness and … longing? Yes, a longing that seems to transcend time—for what was, for what will never be. At least, that's the feeling I get. Strange.

I angle the camera down, cropping out everything but Catherin and the green grass surrounding her. And what of that expanse of grass? It seems like a refuge for her, a place of solace.

When I snap the shutter, this now familiar refrain from the Laurie Lewis tape comes to mind:

Where are my green fields now?
No, nowhere around
So I'll steal away with my memories,
And in green fields I'll lay me down

~~~

It starts to rain just as we make it back to camp, and we escape into the tent. The fact that we had driven all night and only had a few hours sleep finally catches up with us. Dead tired, we collapse on top of our sleeping bags. The afternoon storm is perfect timing—it cools the air and quickly lulls us to sleep.

I wake up hot and thirsty. Though the rain has stopped, a few drops still splash down from the trees above. The sun is bearing down on the tent, which now acts like a greenhouse. I open the front, and unzip the no-see-um netting on the back, to let in more of the breeze. I have a splitting headache—probably from being out in the sun and heat too long. I never do seem to drink enough water when hiking.

I find a water bottle and take a long drink, and then settle back down next to Catherin. She is slowly waking up, her mouth in a yawn, her eyes fluttering.

"Bryan and Catherin," I say, almost as much to myself as to her. "I think our names sound good together."

"B and C," she replies absent-mindedly, staring off into space.

I roll over and prop my chin on an elbow, gazing into her shining brown eyes. That seems to dissipate my headache. *B and C*, I say in my thoughts. *Yes, we are good together.*

"Hey, let's start a word game," I say to her. "Let's see if we can think of all the word pairs that begin with B and C."

Catherin is silent for a moment, and then says, "Okay, how about Bill Cosby?"

"That's good!"

I try to think of another pair, but my mind grows fuzzy.

"Boulder, Colorado," I finally say.

"Cuddly Bear," she answers, almost immediately. She snuggles close.

"Sorry," I say. "It has to start with a 'B' first."

She pulls away. "A little chauvinistic, don't you think?"

"I guess you have a point."

Catherin snuggles close again; apparently satisfied she has gotten her way.

The weather grows cloudy again and a light rain starts, cooling off what's left of the afternoon heat. We fall back asleep in each other's arms, waking once again as evening approaches and the skies clear for good.

I start a small campfire and Catherin fixes supper. While the food is cooking, Catherin pulls out her guitar and starts singing *Here*

We Go Again. I join in with whatever harmonies I can conjure up, trying to remember the actual harmonies on the recording.

"Hey, we don't sound half bad on that song," I say, as Catherin stops to tend to the camping stove.

"Well, I *would* like us to sing more together," she says. "Just the two of us."

A certain tone in her voice is understood immediately. It was true; I hadn't worked much on the harmonies Catherin had planned for us. I wasn't too keen on singing in public, so I hadn't been trying all that hard.

Heaven forbid my harmonies improve enough that Catherin is inclined to use them, you see.

Catherin places her guitar back in its case on the picnic table bench. I have nothing better to do while supper finishes cooking, so I grab the guitar and strum absent-mindedly, day-dreaming about what it would be like to have our own little band, just the two of us, like she is suggesting. Thinking back to the harmonies she wants us to work on, I remember the other 'Riders' band, the *Riders of the Purple Sage*, and their song *No One to Cry To*. Yes, we *could* do old western songs like that, with me playing the fiddle, and Catherin playing guitar and singing lead. And wasn't I telling her earlier that just because something seems difficult, doesn't mean it is. Singing harmonies in public shouldn't be *that* hard. Perhaps Catherin can help pull me further out of my reserved shell. She's the perfect person for that—the perfect companion.

"Bueno Companions," I say, turning to Catherin.

Catherin glances up from the table where she is dishing out our meal, a questioning look on her face.

"B and C," I explain.

Catherin rolls her eyes after she gets the joke. She pauses for a second, and then says, "Well, if you don't put that guitar down, you'll be having Cold Beans for supper."

~ ~ ~

We go for a walk in the cool, pleasant evening. The stars are not yet washed out by the glow of the moon lurking behind the eastern cliffs. At the end of the campground we find a dirt road that leads to another camping area, still closed for the season. With no one to disturb us, we step carefully into an eerie silence and darkness that brings us closer to those eastern cliffs.

Two deer jump across the trail in front of us. They stop. We stop. They look at us, and we look at them. Somehow, I know this encounter is special.

"Those are our spirit deer," I whisper to Catherin. "See them? That's you and me, going through life together."

The deer trot off into the darkness. As they do, the masked glow of the hidden moon, the twinkling stars above, and the silence of the night all contribute to a mystical feeling that descends on us.

As we reach the end of the deserted campground, a meadow stretches out towards the cliffs, bathed in the faint glow of star light. The meadow seems to beckon us, and we oblige. Unfortunately, our way is composed mostly of itchy cheat grass, which is sticking to our socks, causing much aggravation.

"I remember the first time I encountered cheat grass when I was a kid," I tell Catherin, as I stop to pick at my socks. "I hated it then and I hate it now."

We walk further into the meadow, and notice a boulder out in the middle that looks like a good place to sit. Indeed, surrounded by cheat grass, it looks like an oasis. We swish through the itchy grass towards the boulder.

"This stuff sure is irritating," I say, stopping again to pick at my socks. Catherin looks on with indifference. The sticky tufts don't seem to bother her.

The boulder is fairly flat on top, and makes an excellent place to sit. We gaze at the stars, which are shining brilliantly. The sky is as clear as I've ever seen it. It's brighter off to the east, as the moon is about to clear the cliffs, and later it gives the canyon a soft glow that—combined with star light—holds us spellbound.

"I think we just found another power spot," I say to Catherin, as we pick the last remnants of cheat grass from our socks. "You know, like in the Castaneda books?"

Catherin murmurs a response.

We lie down on the boulder and Catherin rests her head in my lap, settling in. I stare at the stars in a hypnotic gaze. I suspect Catherin is doing the same.

Whenever I am out in nature, I always feel a long yearning, a yearning to stop and rest, to soak up the serenity, to think about who we humans are, and what we are doing here on this Earth. The stars seem to bring about this effect more strongly than anything else. The peacefulness they project is enough to make me pause and sit still. Yet I always get a secondary, contradictory feeling of restlessness, as though I'm not to linger.

I guess that's the way life and death are. Death is the ultimate peace, the final rest. It seems we go through life searching for this peace, never understanding that taken to its limit, this peacefulness we so desire is nothing more than our own death. We must sense this, though, because we never stop for long, lest death overtake us. We have to be in motion, using the energy given to us for our journey through this world. The restlessness is just life calling us back.

The stars try their best to hold me in their trance, but they don't succeed. Soon my feet are wiggling, bringing a familiar sigh and chuckle from Catherin.

I stop wiggling and say, "I'm ready to head back."

"Can't we stay a little longer?" asks Catherin. "I'm happy right where I am."

"You should be," I say, trying to nudge her up. I'm lying un-cushioned on the hard rock surface. Catherin on the other hand, looks as comfortable as can be with her head in my lap.

She reluctantly sits up, and I jump off the rock to help her down. While doing this, another clump of cheat grass burrows into my socks. And to think we have an entire meadow of this itchy stuff to wade through on the way back.

"This grass is really annoying," I say, stopping to pull out more of the tenacious tufts as we hike along.

"I know, I know, that's the umpteenth time you've said that," says Catherin in a mockingly irritated voice, as she picks out tufts of her own.

When we reach the end of the meadow, I have finally had enough. The itchiness is driving me crazy. I pull off my shoes and socks and step barefoot down the sandy path. Instantly, the feeling of sand beneath my feet reconnects me with the Earth, and a wave of contentment sweeps over me. Perhaps the cheat grass had been trying its best to remind me I needed the reconnection.

We journey back through the dark, closed campground. The spirit deer are nowhere to be found. No matter. I somehow know they are close by, if only in spirit.

So far, this has been a wonderful vacation, with the perfect companion. Too bad it's already half over. Ah well, there will be plenty of time for other vacations, won't there?

Chapter 14.
Out of Nowhere

The next morning finds us up bright and early at the campsite, with Watchman's Tower bathed in the early glow just like the day before. Catherin fixes breakfast while I roll up the sleeping bags and take down the tent. As breakfast cooks, I hear Catherin humming and then singing an old cowboy song—something about bacon frying in the early morn, and drinking coffee from a can.

What a rare find, this Catherin. I've always had a hankering for these old western tunes, but never thought I'd find anyone to share this affinity, let alone someone of the female persuasion. It hadn't dawned on me until yesterday that Catherin was that someone.

There's no bacon or coffee on our breakfast menu, just oatmeal and juice, which we eat and drink at a leisurely pace. It's as though we're both trying to stretch out the short time we have left of the weekend.

"When do you want to leave for home?" asks Catherin, as she pulls two apples out of a bag and hands me one.

"Never," I say.

"You and me both. But I've got appointments early tomorrow morning."

We munch on our apples while thinking things through.

"We'll have to leave by mid-afternoon," I say between bites. "But we still have time to see the Narrows this morning. It's too bad we can't stay another day. Bryce Canyon isn't far from here."

"Bryce Canyon?"

"Another great national park," I say. "It's not really a canyon. It's basically a giant escarpment—cliffs of pink sandstone sprinkled with hoodoos and other weird formations. Some people like Bryce better than Zion, but I don't. I find Zion a more spiritual place."

Catherin is putting things away when she suddenly laughs.

"What's so funny?" I ask.

"Bryce Canyon," repeats Catherin. "As in B and C?"

I almost cough up my last bite of apple.

"Very clever!" I say, laughing. "You win the prize for today."

"Oh? What's the prize?"

"You get to choose what tapes we listen to on the way home."

"Is that all?"

I think for a moment.

"Well, the tent is already down, so certain prizes aren't available—at least not until we get back."

Catherin says she'll be sure to claim one of the temporarily unavailable prizes when the time comes. She's still chuckling about this later, after we pack the last of our gear and leave for the Narrows.

In the car, I punch the start button on the cassette player, and the tape of Laurie Lewis picks up where it left off. Strains of fiddle and pedal steel guitar follow us up the road and swirl in my head the rest of the morning. The tape has become this trip's de facto theme music.

The Narrows are at the north end of the inner canyon, past Angel's Landing and around a bend. This area is called the Narrows because the further up river you go, the narrower the canyon. Eventually, there is no trail at all alongside the river. The river *is* the trail. The canyon eventually narrows to twenty or thirty feet in width, with walls high enough that just a sliver of sky can be seen.

We reach the parking lot for the Narrows, and begin hiking the trail. A short distance later we find a spot where the river is easily accessible. With walls so close together, the Narrows area is not the place to be during a flash flood. It *is* a great place to get your feet wet. Well, in theory anyway. We take our shoes off and plunge eagerly into the river, not realizing the water has yet to lose its memory of the high country snowmelts to the north.

Catherin yelps in surprise. "This water is cold!" she says, high-tailing it back to shore. I'm right behind her, and almost tumble into the freezing water.

"And slippery too!" I add.

The uneven river bottom makes for tricky wading, filled with painfully sharp yet ironically slippery rocks.

We recover from the initial shock of cold, and plunge in again, for the canyon walls looming overhead are beckoning us up river. We just have to see what's around the bend. We don't get far. Our journey lasts all of a few yards, due to all the slipping and sliding.

"Boy are we pathetic," I say, as we wade back to shore a second time.

We resort to sitting on a boulder along the bank, letting our dangling, bare legs dry in the breeze, taking in the sight of rippling water below and flying ravens above, the latter which are soaring between the canyon walls. Though the sound of rushing water is hypnotic, my feet eventually begin their customary wiggling.

"I wish we could stay here all day," I say. "But we should probably get going."

I begin putting on socks and shoes. Catherin does the same. Not ready to say goodbye to the river, we linger a while longer.

"We could slowly make our way out the canyon," I say, tying my last shoe string, "and stop at some of the scenic turnouts."

"Giving the canyon a long farewell?"

"Exactly what I had in mind."

Her mutual thoughts make me smile. "I just want you to know how happy I am here with you," I say, taking her hands into mine. "It's great being with someone where you can completely be yourself. We don't have to fight over what we're going to do, or how we're going to do it."

"I know," she says. "I was just thinking the same thing."

"Of course you were."

We hike back to the car and drive south until we come to a scenic turnout at the northern base of Angel's Landing. Catherin says she wants to get out and explore.

A historical marker points towards the Great White Throne—a massive hunk of granite off to the south that looks like a tower or temple. The marker indicates how the first Europeans to see the tower were struck with awe, having what could only be described as a religious experience. The formation is sacred to the Native Americans of the area, as most such places are throughout the southwest.

There's a reason for all this reverence and awe, as we soon find out. We sit on a concrete sidewalk with our backs propped against the marker, gazing at the Great White Throne. Although it's only early afternoon, the sun is ready to sink behind the western cliffs. It's warm, but not so much as to be unpleasant. And even though the concrete is undoubtedly hard, neither of us seems to notice. That sense of timelessness washes over me.

I shift my gaze to the heights of Angel's Landing, noticing rock climbers dangling from ropes as they carefully pick their way across the sheer eastern face. I point them out to Catherin, and in order to get a better view, we get up and wander towards the river, soon finding a soft patch of ground in the shade of a juniper tree. From there we can watch the climbers with ease. As time passes, the sun moves behind the western wall of the canyon, but the base of Angel's Landing still glows from light bouncing off the eastern cliffs. The view is mesmerizing—the warm breeze, energizing.

"We must have found another power spot," I tell Catherin.

She smiles and says, "Power spot or no, I'm getting hungry. Do you mind going back to the car and getting our lunch? Bring some water, and fetch the camera while you are at it."

I bring back a lunch of bread, turkey, cheese, and grapes, plus a gallon jug of water. I also bring a large bath towel for us to sit on.

Upon seeing my load, Catherin asks, "Did you remember the camera?"

"Um, no," I reply. "Of course not! They didn't call me Space in college for nothing."

I hand the lunch items to Catherin and turn around to retrieve the camera. On the way back I sneak behind the juniper tree, and jump in front to capture what turns out to be an endearing photo of a surprised Catherin, sitting on the towel in front of the tree, a loving, delightful smile on her face. Legs crossed, arms crossed, she sports her ever-present plain silver bracelet. Rosy cheeks and a newly tanned complexion make her look ten years younger. She seems to be right where she belongs, an earthy girl out in her element. Though she wears the same blue T-shirt as the day before, her mood is far different. That aura of sadness is nowhere to be found.

~ ~ ~

At three o'clock, we regretfully leave the canyon, with the long seven hour drive back to Phoenix awaiting. The familiar strains of *Green Fields* accompany us as we head east through the tunnels and out of the park. Lake Powell comes into view a few hours later, and since Catherin didn't have a chance to see it in the daytime on the way up, we decide to stop, making our way to the marina. As we venture down a catwalk that leads to where the boats are anchored, I see a small fishing boat. This triggers a memory.

"I was here few years ago with Alden and another friend from college," I say. "We rented a boat just like this one." I point to a four-teen-foot fishing boat bobbing in the waves. Seeing my reflection in the water, I reflect back to that time with my friends.

Catherin interrupts my thoughts. "My family had a boat when I was growing up," she says. "We used to go to the lakes quite often. I miss those days on the water."

She had mentioned her affinity for water to me before, but I had no idea the strength of that affinity. As much as I thought I knew her, we had only been together a short while. A big part of her was still a complete mystery.

I gaze out onto the lake, surveying distant rock formations jutting from the water.

"It's hard to appreciate the scale of this place," I say. "My friends and I found out the hard way. When we were at the counter renting that fourteen-foot fishing boat, I thought I overheard someone say it was fifteen miles to Rainbow Bridge—you know, the famous natural bridge?

"But it turned out to be a long ways, and only on the way back did we realize *how* long. As we sped towards the marina, I began wondering about the meaning of numbers we saw on the buoys lining the route. I studied a map we had brought along, and it finally dawned on me. Those buoys were mile markers, and near Rainbow Bridge we had passed buoy number fifty. In other words, Rainbow Bridge was *fifty* miles from the marina, not *fifteen*. Unbeknownst to us, we had embarked on a hundred-mile roundtrip adventure across the lake, in a small fishing boat."

"A hundred miles?" asks Catherin.

"I know it's hard to believe," I say, "but we had the sunburns to prove it."

I rub my arms in remembrance of that sunburn from long ago.

"We were *so* far off on the actual distance," I say, shaking my head. "Perception's sure a funny thing, isn't it?"

~ ~ ~

Heading south out of Lake Powell, we pass through a terrain of scrub grass and red sandy soil. Off to the west are teasing glimpses of scenic Marble Canyon, ringed by a rugged assortment of vermillion cliffs. Here, the Colorado River, after being temporarily stymied by Glen Canyon Dam, resumes its wild plunge through the Grand Canyon and on to the Gulf of Mexico. This area of northern Arizona is, to me, one of the most beautiful spots on earth, and although the weekend has been a long one, I feel invigorated by the landscape.

Having Catherin beside me certainly doesn't hurt, either. She works on her knitting while I drive, and we listen to a tape she gets to choose: an adaptation of the classic novel *Wuthering Heights*. It's spooky hearing the story of a ghost named Catherine, who knocks on the window of her bedroom, wanting in.

We enter a deep cutout in the surrounding vermillion-colored ridges and start descending the grade down Echo Cliffs, a ridge of upthrust caused by a major fault line. No sooner does this moment pass when a bird flies out of nowhere and thumps the windshield, falling onto the roadway. It's a wild dove. I have surely killed it.

Chapter 15.
Breaking Crayons

May 11–16, 1987

Daydreams are never far away for me. I'm easily distracted, and the silent movie playing outside my office window isn't helping. Desert quail hop down from the branches of a Palo Verde tree laden with the yellow blossoms of spring, scaring a rabbit that scampers from one cholla to the next. A roadrunner sneaks from behind a saguaro, and then after prancing a few steps, zooms out of view. Clinging to the side of another saguaro is a Gila Woodpecker.

I snap out of my daze and reach over to close the window blinds. I can't afford any distractions, not with a busy schedule coming up.

With bleary eyes I stare at the computer screen in a post-vacation hangover, and then yawn a big, wide, Monday morning yawn, trying to summon the energy for the tasks at hand. My first priority: to put finishing touches on a software demo I'm readying for a users' conference the company is hosting on Wednesday. And our band has two performances scheduled, one for a dinner party being held in conjunction with the same users' conference. What were Catherin and I thinking the past Friday, driving all night to go camping and hiking in Zion National Park for the weekend, only to have to rush back home late Sunday with a busy week awaiting?

The software is basically ready. I attribute my nervous exhaustion to the ever-present worry that the application will crash during the demo, in front of my boss and all our customers. This prompts me to work diligently the next two days, even though what I really want is to stay home and sleep.

After work on Wednesday I go directly to the party at my boss's house and wait for the rest of the band to trickle in, trying my best to mingle with the company guests, but never feeling entirely comfortable. I'll be glad when it's time for the music to start. Then I won't have to talk to anyone and can 'hide behind my fiddle.'

We set up by the swimming pool. The guests socialize around a cooler full of drinks, occasionally turning their attention to our music and politely clapping their approval. Despite the party not being an inspiring setting for playing our brand of music, Catherin displays her usual on-stage exuberance anyway.

She seems at ease in striking up conversation with the guests during dinner, and then afterwards when we play eight-ball on my boss's pool table. Catherin is wearing an attractive flowing white dress, and a light tan acquired from our camping trip gives her a youthful glow, adding to her appeal. The trip to Zion seems to have done her wonders. It has certainly brought us closer as a couple, and I see nothing but blue skies ahead.

Even so, I decide to stay home alone that night, sending Catherin off to her own place. I'm drained by all the socializing and need time by myself. Tired but still wound up, I have a bowl of cereal and reflect on my career. Completing the high-profile project and having a successful demo has nonetheless left me with little satisfaction. I keep thinking about the more potentially stimulating job at the Kitt Peak observatory—a missed opportunity. Too bad they had turned me down the first time. Too bad I had turned them down the second. But the timing had been wrong. After having just settled into my current job, it hadn't seemed appropriate to jump ship so quickly. But that was a year ago. Maybe it's time to reconsider.

~ ~ ~

The next evening our band plays at Roadrunner Park in north Phoenix—just a few miles north of Squaw Peak, the place where I had first encountered Catherin all those months before. After work, Catherin stops off at my place, and we travel to the park in my pick-up. Skirting around the northern flanks of Squaw Peak, through a pass called the Dreamy Draw, I drive silently, mulling over the possibility of changing jobs.

"You're awfully quiet tonight," says Catherin. "Is something the matter?"

I notice Catherin picking at the upholstery on the door of my truck, which makes me wonder if her question isn't really to herself.

"I was just dreaming," I say. "We *are* driving through the Dreamy Draw, after all."

I laugh at my own joke, but Catherin doesn't respond.

Early settlers of the Phoenix area once mined for mercury along the Dreamy Draw. Exposure to mercury vapor can cause, among other things, difficulties in talking and thinking clearly, giving the afflicted person the appearance of being dreamy. Hence the origin of the name.

I tell Catherin this brief history, and then remark, "Perhaps that's why I'm so spacey. I must have been exposed to too much mercury sometime in my life—and come to think of it, there is that Mercury rising in my chart."

Catherin chuckles at my clever astrological reference, but only half heartedly. She doesn't seem to be in the mood for jokes.

"Seriously, though," I continue. "I've been thinking of re-applying at Kitt Peak. My current job isn't cutting it. The mountain-programmer's job at the observatory would be a lot more fulfilling."

"It's good to see you begin to take charge of your life," she says, "and do the things you really want."

Catherin's positive response doesn't match her body language. She doesn't seem thrilled by my revelation, and she's distant as well. In my usual absent-mindedness—or should I say, dreaminess—I note this, but only in a detached way. I don't dwell on it further.

Our band sets up on a small stage at the center of Roadrunner Park, near a lake brimming with ducks and geese. Only a few onlookers besides our feathered friends are in the audience, and to add insult to injury, it is hot and stuffy, with no hint of wind to cool us off. I have to keep wiping the sweat off my face and the chinrest of my fiddle.

On the last selection of the night, I fail miserably in an attempt to play a tune that, although one of my favorites, is also my nemesis: *Blackberry Blossom.* I just can't play it the way I hear it in my mind— the way Mark O'Connor, fiddler extraordinaire, plays it. My fingers aren't fast enough, my intonation is off, and the bow bounces uncontrollably. Nope, I'm no Mark O'Connor. Not even close. I can just hear what Bubba and Mrs. Bubba would say about my performance, were they in the audience:

"Heh-heh-heh. Oot-oooo-weee-hooo! So you think you can play music!"

To top it off I'm starting to feel a little dizzy. Maybe it's the heat. Maybe that's why my playing is not up to par.

As we pack away our instruments, Catherin asks if I want to stay at her place that night. I say yes, and we climb into my pickup and depart for my apartment, where Catherin can retrieve her car, and I can follow in my truck.

Except for our recent trips and band outings, I hadn't seen much of Catherin since her new renters moved in. And when the two of us did spend time together, it was usually at my apartment. I don't know about her, but I suspect this was a subconscious choice for me, prodded only in part by wanting to be home so I could work on my computer. I felt uneasy around the two guys; most of that I attributed to my general discomfort of strangers, but was there more to it?

"One of my renters decided to move out," Catherin announces as we make our way south to my apartment in Tempe. "He came by the office today and turned in his keys."

"The Ethiopian?"

Catherin averts her eyes. "No, the other guy."

I wonder about this news. It seems out of the blue.

"You going to look for another renter?" I ask.

Catherin again picks at the upholstered door panel of my truck. "We'll see," she says.

The events of the past few months are beginning to overwhelm me; this latest news adding to the load. My admittedly lame response is avoidance, and I give the news no more thought.

~ ~ ~

Later that evening as we lie in bed, I reminisce with Catherin about our romantic weekend in Zion. The trip is beginning to take on legendary status in my mind.

"That was the best trip I've ever had," I say to Catherin. "And it was you that made it so." I brush the hair from her face and give her a heart-felt kiss.

Catherin buries her head into my chest, and a while later I think I hear a sob. I touch her cheeks. They are definitely wet.

"Is something the matter?" I ask.

I try to look in her eyes, but Catherin buries her head even further.

"Just when I think things are going well between us, you have one of these spells," I say, stroking her curly, dark hair. "Why the sadness?"

Catherin looks up, tears in her eyes. She wipes them away and tells me a story: "When I was little, my mother bought me a box of crayons. But then my friends came over and broke them before I got a chance to use them. I was hurt and angry. This happened several times. Finally, I got into a habit that whenever I was given a new box of crayons, I would immediately break them myself. That way I wouldn't get hurt if my friends came over, because the crayons were already broken."

I absent-mindedly comb my fingers through her hair, trying to understand her meaning.

"What crayons are being broken here?" I ask.

"You. Us. That we're going to part," she says softly.

I stop twirling her hair, untangling from our embrace. "What makes you say that?"

"Didn't you say you wanted to work at Kitt Peak?" asks Catherin. "That would involve you moving to Tucson. Where does that leave us?"

"Don't you think I would want us to be together somehow?" I ask. "We could work something out if it ever came to that. I wouldn't just go off and leave you. Besides, I haven't contacted them to see if they have any openings. I was just dreaming of the possibility."

Catherin moves to rest her head on my shoulder, and I stroke her hair and tell her that I love her. We eventually fall asleep—or at least, I know *I* do. A while later I wake for some reason, only to find Catherin watching me. She reaches over to give me a kiss.

"Thank you for being here," she says softly. "And for loving me." The patio door to her room is open, and a warm but cooling summer breeze filters in, mixing with dreams of Catherin that fill me the rest of the night.

~ ~ ~

The next morning we get ready for work, and as I put on dress pants and button my shirt, two words form in my head.

"Breaking Crayons," I say.

Catherin threads a belt onto her dress as she turns towards me, looking both puzzled and forlorn.

"Breaking Crayons," I repeat, tucking in my shirt, absent-mindedly leaving a portion hanging out. "You know—B and C?"

Catherin's face brightens with understanding, but only briefly. I had found the ultimate B and C word pair, more clever than any we had thought of before. How strange for us to invent such a game— a game that would later come into play with the special, intimate story Catherin had shared the previous night.

~ ~ ~

At work I feel exhausted and light-headed, and by noon my throat grows sore. I call Catherin to say I'm not feeling well, and ask her to come over and stay the night. During the course of the conversation Catherin mentions her household situation is changing, again. My attention isn't all there. I'm typing on the computer while holding the phone to my ear, using my shoulder for support.

"I've placed another ad in the paper," she says.

"For another renter? To replace the guy that just moved out?"

"Not exactly. I need to replace them both."

I stop typing so I can hold the phone properly in my hand and give Catherin my full attention.

"So the Ethiopian is moving out too?"

"He's going to leave soon. He says it's too far to school."

Something doesn't sound right. It's no more than ten miles to ASU. And if that was too far, he should have considered that before moving in.

"Are you sure that's all it is?" I ask.

"It's nothing … really," she says. "We'll talk later."

I shrug and hang up the phone, immediately returning back to my computer. Despite feeling run down, I become so distracted by programming—a common affliction of us software types—that I end up staying late at work. Big mistake. By the time I finish I'm really feeling out of it: dizzy, weak, and more spacey than usual.

Catherin has already made supper by the time I arrive at my apartment. Earlier she had gone to the store to buy a thermometer, and proceeds to take my temperature. It turns out I don't have a fever, and though I feel dizzy, I'm not sick to my stomach; just light-headed. I want nothing more than to lie down, but force myself to eat. Catherin has made chicken noodle soup. I sip slowly, stopping every few seconds to rest back in my chair. She watches intently with a concerned look on her face.

"Are you going to be okay?" she asks.

"It's just stress," I say, shrugging. "It's been a long week."

Catherin studies me from across the table. "I can see we're going to have to cut back on things."

Indeed, she does have us leading a whirlwind life, and it's too much for me. I need plenty of down-time. Catherin is just the opposite—always on the go, always ready for action. "Don't waste time!" is her motto.

"So what's been going on with your renters?" I ask after finishing the soup.

"We can talk about it later," she says. "You need to rest."

She ushers me to bed, but I'm not able to fall asleep. I glance around the room and realize what a pig sty it has become: socks and underwear everywhere, shirts lying in a heap. I was never one to keep things in pristine order, but this is ridiculous. After apologizing to Catherin about the mess, she in turn offers to help, and immediately goes into the bathroom and cleans the shower stall and toilet. She then proceeds to tidy the bedroom.

"I feel guilty you are doing this for me," I say, watching helplessly, feeling miserable. "It's my mess, my responsibility."

"It's no problem," she says, as she puts away clean clothes that had been piled on top of the dresser. "It's my lot in life."

"What do you mean?"

"Didn't I tell you about my astrological chart? It clearly indicates I'm to be of service to others."

"I see. How do you feel about that?"

Catherin sits down on the bed next to me. "In the past, I've thrived on helping others—hence the massage business. But there are times I grow tired of it."

"What about your own needs?" I ask. "Who is supposed to help you?"

Catherin sighs and gets up to continue her tasks. "My own considerations are secondary."

~ ~ ~

The next morning Catherin heads home to get work done around her own house. I stay at my place to try and fend off dizziness and low energy. But by four o'clock I'm getting lonely. I can't resist calling.

"How are you feeling?" Catherin asks over the phone.

"Better, but still light-headed. I miss you. Please come over and stay tonight."

"Are you sure I should? Don't you need more rest?"

I get the feeling that she very much wants to come over, but is pretending to give me a choice, as though it doesn't matter to her either way.

"I would really like you here," I say.

"I'll be there in half an hour."

She arrives on schedule, surprising me with her massage table, which she sets up in the living room. Once again I am the lucky beneficiary of an incredible massage.

Later that evening we go to lie down in the bedroom. For some reason, I have an impulse to turn on the TV next to the bed, only to see and hear the image and voice of Marvin, the Depressed Robot, as the TV warms up.

"Hey look, it's *Hitchhiker's Guide to the Galaxy*," I say, reaching over to turn up the volume. "How lucky can we get?"

"I didn't know there was a movie of that story," says Catherin. "I really enjoyed the audio tape we heard on our trip to Zion."

"I believe this is an episode of the TV series adapted from the book," I say.

We lie side by side and watch the show, our heads pointing towards the foot of the bed. I'm thrilled at this unexpected chance to watch *Hitchhiker's Guide*, but Catherin doesn't share my enthusiasm. From time to time I look over, only to see her lost in thought.

"You okay?" I ask as the show ends.

"It's nothing," she says, at first pausing. "Well, I admit I've been having trouble with the Ethiopian."

"The Ethiopian?"

"He's been making romantic advances," she blurts out. "That's why I've asked him to look for another place."

Stunned at her words, I reach over and turn off the TV. My heart begins to race as I lie back on the bed.

Catherin adds, "I'm glad you called to ask me over. I don't feel comfortable at home."

"What do you mean, you don't feel comfortable at home? How long has this been going on?"

"Ever since he moved in."

I can't believe what I'm hearing. Never once had Catherin said anything to me about this, though she had remarked right after he moved in that he seemed a little strange. But she had passed that off as just a side effect of his inarticulate command of English.

"When is he supposed to move out?" I ask.

"Well, I haven't told him yet," she replies. "But I thought by the end of the month."

"You haven't told him yet?"

"No," she admits, in a low, tentative voice. She picks at the quilted bed covering.

"He really should leave immediately," I say.

"I can't afford that," says Catherin. "I need the rent money."

I breathe a deep sigh. "How many times have we been over that? If you need help with your house payment, just ask. Your own considerations shouldn't be secondary."

We end the conversation on that note. I don't have the energy to press the issue further. My light-headedness seems to be worsening and the current revelations aren't helping. I know I haven't been giving Catherin's domestic situation enough attention. But I have to admit, even if I was feeling well, would I know how to handle things? Would I be able to go over to her house and command the Ethiopian to leave? I feel inadequate enough during peaceful interactions with others, let alone during confrontations.

Before tonight Catherin hadn't seemed concerned enough to clue me in on what was going on. She hadn't seemed concerned enough to take immediate corrective action of her own. Maybe it's not that serious.

With these thoughts, I push the situation aside. But life's railway is about to change directions, and neither of us are heeding the curves.

Chapter 16.
Saying Goodbye

Sunday Morning, May 17, 1987

Turning over towards the dark-haired, white mountain bike woman, I caress her warm sleepiness and lazily twirl her long, dark hair, feeling the fullness of the strands slip between my fingers.

"So, you're Catherin."

Catherin looks up from the pillow, a mixture of puzzlement and amusement in her eyes.

"Well, I sure hope I am."

I kiss her soft round cheeks, my lips brushing against the freckles on her face—freckles that for some reason, I had never noticed before. Catherin radiates with a glowing, youthful look. Her eyes shine with a curious combination of happiness and worry.

"So, you're Catherin."

"That's my name."

I have the strange feeling that I'm seeing Catherin for the first time—the hazy whirl of the past few months coming into sharp focus. Yes, she is really here, beside me. And she is mine. But with the words, "So, you're Catherin," it feels as though I'm also saying goodbye. Along with these paradoxical feelings comes a peculiar form of vertigo, and a bizarre dual perception that can only be described as 'simultaneous opposites.'

I have experienced this dual perception before. The first instance occurred during my teenage years. On one occasion, I was suffering in bed from a high fever, and had a sickening, nightmarish sensation that my hands were puffy and bony at the same time. In the months that followed, I started having dreams in which the scenes were somehow too fast and too slow—at the same time. I would wake up in a panic, with the too-fast, too-slow sensation still in force, affecting my perception of otherwise ordinary movements, giving everything a surreal, nightmarish quality. I once discovered that I could invoke this sensation by beating on a snare drum, at a tempo somewhere between one to two beats per second.

Over the years, the phenomenon has changed form, and seems to occur mostly when listening to music with a pair of headphones, in total darkness. In this new form, the opposites manifest as a 'too-big, too-small' sensation. I see the blackness of the inside of my head as being both infinitely big and infinitesimally small—expanding to the size of the universe and at the same time, converging to a point of singularity.

I have never heard of anyone else having these experiences, and no one seems to know what they are about. Now, this morning, I'm experiencing another form of simultaneous opposites, this time seeing Catherin as though for the first time—and as though for the last. My senses take on an exceptional, if confusing, clarity.

Catherin reaches for her guitar, which she had left by the side of the bed the night before. She sits up and begins to strum, singing:

> Here we go again
> I love you so again
> Once more it starts to end
> The moment it begins

She prompts me to sing harmony with her, but I still feel too weak to expend the effort. The song does bring back memories of hiking up to Emerald Pools in Zion Canyon, when I sang the refrain "He-ee-ere we go again," each time we rounded another switchback of the energy-robbing, sandy trail.

I immerse myself in the sweet, cozy sensations that Catherin's smooth, melodic singing coaxes from the morning air. A week ago our roles had been reversed, as we headed west towards Zion and through the park's tunnel entrance. It was then I had serenaded Catherin, as she rested half asleep, nuzzled against my shoulder.

"Do you remember the songs I was singing to you from the *Riders in the Sky*," I ask Catherin, "on our way to Zion? I have a tape of them we could play."

"Sure, if you want," she replies.

She leans her guitar against the wall and nestles back under the covers. I find the cassette and snap it into the tape machine on the night stand next to my bed.

I hadn't played that tape of the *Riders in the Sky* in a long while, even though at one time, it was one of my favorites. The reason I hadn't played it was because of a terrifying car accident that happened while listening to that very tape, the year before:

I had interviewed for the mountain-programming job at Kitt Peak, and had taken along my girlfriend at the time, Nancy. Afterwards, on the way back to Phoenix from Tucson, we decided to not take the freeway, but instead, drive up Highway 89 to Florence—a more scenic route, and much less traveled. Nancy drove at first, but as darkness came, she asked me to drive, for she didn't see well at night. I took over the wheel in Florence, and instead of continuing north to the eastern side of the Phoenix valley, I headed west back to the freeway. By doing this, we avoided a long trip through the city streets of Mesa on our way to my apartment in Tempe.

The route crossed through the Gila Indian Reservation, and soon we approached the reservation border. I had the tape of the *Riders in the Sky* playing, and was singing along while Nancy dozed beside me. I was excited over the prospect of working at Kitt Peak, and feeling happy that Nancy was there with me. Up ahead, though, I noticed a police car stopped on the left side of the road, lights flashing. I decided to slow down, thinking, *You never know what might be on the road.* I no more thought that, when there he was, a man in my headlights!

The man, a Native American, was crossing haphazardly from left to right, apparently oblivious to the fact that there was a car bearing down on him. I immediately swerved to the right and off the road towards the ditch, trying desperately to miss him. There was no time to think. There was also no time to avoid the impending hit, and I heard a sickening thump. The bottom went out of my stomach.

Oh my God. I just ran over someone! I've killed him for sure!

I slowed the car to a standstill and sat frozen in fear, hands still on the wheel, stunned as to what had just transpired.

Nancy had awakened as soon as she felt the car swerve.

"What's going on?" she asked, looking around for clues.

"We've been in an accident."

"But where's the other car?"

"There is no other car," I said. After a deep breath, I spoke again. "I think I hit someone."

A sickening look came over Nancy's face. "What do you mean, you hit someone? I don't see any vehicle except the patrol car over there."

"It wasn't a car that I hit. It was a pedestrian. I think I ran over him."

"Oh my God!"

Nancy covered her mouth in shock, and then leaned over to take my hands, searching for some way to soothe my terror, as well as her own. I was too shocked to feel anything. She soon noticed someone approaching the car. "Don't look now, but here comes a policeman."

I'm in deep trouble for sure, I thought. *I can just see the headlines: "White male runs over Indian on reservation."*

I heard a tap-tap-tap on the window beside me. I fumbled for the crank, and slowly rolled down the window, reluctantly waiting for my sentence, which I knew would be guilty as charged.

"Everything's okay," the policeman said, in a surprisingly friendly voice. "The man you hit is hurt, but he'll live."

That did little to alleviate the terrified look on my face.

"Don't worry," the policeman said. "I saw the whole thing. It wasn't your fault."

He stepped around to the back of the car and recorded my license plate number. Nancy got out and carefully walked back to the scene of the accident. I sat momentarily frozen in the front seat, trying to determine whether I should feel relieved by what the policeman said. Then I realized I couldn't let Nancy go back to the scene alone, so I climbed out of the car, and cautiously followed the policeman back towards what I thought would be a gruesome sight.

A few other officers had arrived and were tending to the pedestrian until the paramedics could get there. The man was lying on the ground, shaking mildly with shock, but didn't seem seriously hurt.

The police officer that I first spoke to told me he had found the man drunk outside a bar that was a few hundred yards up the road, conveniently located just outside the reservation border. Apparently, the man had gone up to the officer to ask for a ride home. But at the time, the officer was in the process of giving someone else a speeding ticket, and told the man to stand by the side of the road and wait. Being drunk, the man was confused, and proceeded to cross the road to stand on the *other* side. That's when my car happened to be there.

The paramedics finally arrived and we watched them tend to the victim, lifting arms and legs—checking for broken bones and internal injuries. He apparently had a broken leg, and was in some pain and mumbling gibberish.

The police officer worked on his report and showed me what he was writing down.

"After looking at your tire marks, I'd say you did the right thing by swerving," the officer said. "In fact, you saved the guy's life. It was good that you didn't try to use your brakes first, as any hesitation would have surely killed him."

So instead of running over the guy, I had merely clipped him with the left front fender of my car.

The officer made a few more notations on his report, and then said, "If I were you, I would avoid this road at night, particularly on the weekends. You'd be surprised how often this sort of thing happens."

Needless to say, I had never again taken that road across the Gila Indian Reservation, and until the present moment had never again listened to that *Riders in the Sky* tape.

I tell Catherin this story, and tell her I feel uneasy about playing the tape.

"Oh, that's just superstition," she says.

Outside on the Superstition Freeway, cars are speeding by, not more than a hundred yards from my apartment. Since moving in, I had gotten used to the whooshing sound of traffic, but for some reason, it annoys me now.

We listen to one side of the tape, dozing on and off in each other's arms, while I try, without success, to ward off dizziness. At nine o'clock Catherin climbs out of bed to get dressed.

"I have a business meeting with Larry this morning," she explains.

"At the shopping center?"

"No, over at Larry's. Would you like to come over and stay at my place today? You can rest there, and then we can have band practice later on."

"I don't know," I say, wearily. "I feel I'll get more rest here. Besides, I don't think I'm up for practicing today."

Catherin looks disappointed—more than not having me come to band practice calls for. "Well, Vincent gave me some living room chairs. Could you at least help me pick them up? They're at the shopping center."

My dizziness says no, but my voice says, "Sure. We can use my truck. You can drive it over to your house, and I'll come later in your car to help unload the chairs. Or perhaps Larry can deal with them."

I get dressed and we drive to the shopping center. I barely have the energy to help Catherin lift the chairs into the back of the pickup, but we manage.

On the way back to my apartment, we pass by a famous fast-food restaurant.

"Let's stop and get something to eat," says Catherin. "Chicken and egg biscuits are my favorite breakfast."

This came from the woman who routinely gulped down dozens of vitamins each day in the name of health and wellness.

"Whatever you'd like to do," I say with a perplexed tone.

After eating this unlikely breakfast and driving back to my apartment, we say goodbye and hug out in the parking lot. Catherin gives me the keys to her car.

"I'll call later and let you know if I feel like coming over for band practice," I tell her.

Catherin drives away in my pickup, and I move her car into my reserved parking space.

I try to lie down and rest, but my wiggly feet won't stay still. I push off the bed and shuffle out to the living room and boot my computer. I'm almost glad I'm staying home, for it gives me a chance to work on the astrology program I promised Catherin. I study several astronomy books, trying to figure out what equations I need. Astronomers of course don't recognize astrology as being a legitimate topic, so the books don't give many clues on what to do. And the astrology books, not being of a scientific bent, also yield few clues.

But this makes it more of a challenge, and soon I am absorbed in the task.

The rest of the morning flies by quickly. It's easy to see that someday a conflict will develop between us, because most programmers can spend hours, even days, in front of the computer, to the exclusion of everything else. I'm certainly no exception. Since meeting Catherin, I've battled this tendency, but playing in the band has helped keep it in check.

What I want most of all is for us to be together, and to end the constant traveling back and forth between her house and mine. I pause at the keyboard and day-dream about a more domestic life, with both of us at home; Catherin working on the sewing and knitting she likes to do and me working on the computer. When we need a break, we can practice music together. How nice it would be to spend quiet days like this, instead of scurrying about.

By two-thirty, the eye-strain from staring at the monitor and the mental effort needed to figure out astrological calculations conspire to make my dizziness worse. I decide to nap for a couple of hours and then see about heading over to Catherin's for band practice.

Superstitions notwithstanding, I play the other side of the *Riders in the Sky* tape, and soon drift off to sleep.

Chapter 17.
The Soul of Man Never Dies

Sunday afternoon, May 17, 1987

Riiiinnnngggg! Riiiinnnngggg! Somewhere out there a phone is ringing. After the third or fourth ring, I realize it is *my* phone. I grope for the receiver on the night stand next to my bed.

"Hello?" says my groggy voice into the phone.

"Bryan, is that you?"

"Catherin?"

"No, this isn't Catherin, it's Cecilia."

"Hi, Cecilia, what's up?"

My reasoning faculties, still a little dazed, slowly come into focus.

"Uh, I think Vincent wants to talk to you."

I try to guess what the phone call is about. I remember that Vincent is ready to buy a computer, and had asked previously if I would help him pick one out. But why is Cecilia handling the introductions? And why does she sound uncharacteristically hesitant?

Vincent is soon on the phone, and he gets right to the point. "Bryan, I'm afraid I have some very bad news. I don't know how to tell you this, but Catherin is dead."

"Dead?"

"She was killed in her home a few hours ago."

I lie there stunned. The smack from the cosmic two-by-four is severe.

Vincent sounds a lot like his brother Larry, who is known to play a practical joke or two. And I remember that Catherin met with Larry just this morning. A thought forms that yields a tiny thread of hope.

"Is this Larry?" I ask. "Is this some kind of joke?"

My voice cracks as I ask these questions. A bitter dryness forms in my throat when I hear the response from the other end.

"This is Vincent, and I assure you it's no joke."

Oh my God! This can't be happening!

"I'm really sorry," says Vincent.

His words clamp down like a cold, hard vise, squeezing out my old, comfortable view of the world. I don't know how to react to the new, horrible view. My heart pounds, and soon my mind starts concocting many dreadful scenarios, even though I try desperately to keep them from forming.

"Where—how—what happened? Did she fall and hit her head or something?"

"It was the Ethiopian," Vincent replies. "He shot her."

He shot her. Wham, wham, wham, strikes the cosmic two-by-four. With piercing, agonizing clarity, I remember the conversation with Catherin the night before, when we discussed the Ethiopian. What was I thinking earlier today? Why didn't I go over to her house? Why had I completely ignored her domestic situation?

"He's turned himself in," Vincent continues. "The police have blocked off the house and won't let anybody inside. We don't know anything else."

I'm glad Vincent has no more details. My mind spins with imagined sights and sounds of Catherin struggling and screaming. The blackness is darker than anything I have ever experienced.

Why, oh why, didn't I go over to her place like she wanted me to? Then none of this would have happened!

I'm in completely new territory, and don't know how to respond. No tears have formed. The only thoughts I have are the horrible ones that keep trying to surface, and I do my best to keep them at bay. I sit on the edge of the bed in shock, the phone still up to my ear.

Vincent breaks the silence. "I think you should come over to Larry's. We're waiting there for the police to finish their investigation at Catherin's. They may want to talk to you."

I tell Vincent I will be right over and hang up the phone. Machine-like, I put on clothes and hurry out the door. But tears aren't far behind. I can barely see by the time I make it to my reserved parking spot where I had parked Catherin's car earlier in the day. Fishing my pocket for car keys, I realize I don't have them. I rush back to the apartment, only to further realize at the door that I have no keys at all. I try the latch. Fortunately, I forgot to lock the door. Sometimes, it pays to be spacey.

Finding the keys, I rush back to the car. As I'm turning the ignition key, the full realization of the day's events suddenly washes over me. Just a few hours ago, we were standing at this very spot, hugging and saying goodbye, neither of us knowing that it was for the last time. I just couldn't believe it. How could she be alive one minute, and not the next?

The tears are so heavy I have trouble backing the car out of the parking space. What am I doing trying to drive down the freeway by myself, anyway? I come to my senses and re-park the car. Maybe Alden can take me over. I go back to the apartment and call him.

"Hey, Bryan, what's up?" answers Alden, in an innocent, cheerful tone.

How can he be so cheerful? Doesn't he know the world has just ended?

"Alden, I have some really bad news," I say mechanically. "Catherin is dead."

"What did you say?"

"She's dead!"

It takes a few moments before Alden can respond.

"Oh my God! What happened?"

"She was murdered," I say, my voice falling on that last word. I am now sobbing profusely.

"Murdered? … That's not possible! … Are you sure?"

"Vincent just called to tell me."

"Oh man! That can't be!" says Alden. "I can't believe this has happened!"

"Well, it has."

My crying is so intense it knocks the breath out of me. I eventually recover and take in a long breath.

"Will you take me over to her place?" I ask.

"I sure will," says Alden. "Just stay calm. I'll be right over."

As I wait for Alden to arrive, the pit in my stomach deepens. A new, agonizing reality seeps into my very being. The world takes on a surreal quality, colors changing to a yellowish-gray tint. I keep waiting for someone to change the channel, knowing full well that I'm stuck on this one.

I pace from room to room like a dazed bird, and at one point I enter the bedroom and sit on the bed as recent memories come pouring out. Just hours ago, we had been snuggling, right here. I re-member gazing into her eyes and saying, "So, you're Catherin." The odd sensation of simultaneously saying hello and goodbye now takes on a tragically prophetic nature.

I see Catherin's guitar leaning against the wall. She had forgot-ten to take it home. I can still hear her voice, clear and pure, as she sang and played that guitar, just this morning:

> Here we go again
> I love you so again
> Once more it starts to end
> The moment it begins

How uncanny those words seem now. And what of the *Riders in the Sky* tape that had come to take on superstitious qualities for me—qualities that Catherin dismissed? Was it a mistake to play that tape after all?

My thoughts come into focus. In a flash of insight, I recall a con-versation with Dr. Thomason, on our hike in the Superstitions—the day after my first date with Catherin. Dr. Thomason and I had been contemplating the metaphysics of what it meant to 'see.' I remem-ber telling him that even if there were a gargoyle standing next to a saguaro, we might not see it, because it wouldn't fit our expecta-tions—our ordinary view of the world.

Similarly, I didn't see Catherin's death coming. The thought of her dying suddenly was not in my world view. The idea was so for-eign to me that, like seeing a gargoyle, my mind blocked out the possibility.

It's not like there hadn't been warning signs. In fact, now that I think about it, the situation with Catherin's friend Michelle in San Diego was similar. Michelle seemed oblivious to the danger of living with a slightly off kilter guy who obviously had designs on her. And she seemed in no hurry to find a different living situation. She could have moved in with her boyfriend Tony, but she wasn't ready to. Just like I hadn't been ready to move in with Catherin.

In her optimism, Michelle had no concept that anything could go wrong. And what about me? How could I have been so oblivious to Catherin's situation?

~ ~ ~

Alden soon arrives with his girlfriend Kimberly. I'm surprised to see tears in their eyes, although in retrospect that seems pretty foolish. Still reeling, I sit in the back seat of Alden's car as we ride down the freeway. Overpasses and traffic signs whiz by, reminding me of riding with Catherin up the freeway towards Flagstaff, and the Utah canyons beyond. That had been only a week before, and Catherin had been so happy then. We had been so attuned to each other.

There it was, the word *had*.

It's the first time I really think of Catherin in the past tense—as someone who isn't coming back. A wave of uncontrollable sadness courses through me.

"She was my soul mate," I cry to Alden and Kimberly. "I've lost my soul mate!"

Kimberly turns around and tries to comfort me, holding my hand as best she can over the front seat. I think she knows there isn't anything that can make things right for me now. Only Catherin magically appearing alive would do that.

As we round the corner to Larry and Amy's, I can see Catherin's house down the street; the ugly pink apartments beyond that. Yellow police ribbons barricade Catherin's yard, a sight that slams me like an emotional tidal wave. On the freeway, I kept hoping I would get to Catherin's house and find her okay. The yellow ribbons say otherwise.

We enter Larry and Amy's house, where an oppressive gloom has settled in. Everyone waits for the police to finish their work down the street. People speak in despondent, low voices. And nobody will look at me directly, as though I'm a mortally wounded dog lying on the side of the road after being hit by a car. I soon lie down on the couch, being too dizzy to stand up. Unbeknownst to me, I had been breathing rapidly all the way to Gilbert. A knot forms in my stomach. My hands tingle. I'm hyperventilating, just like that time in Jeff's plane.

I try breathing with hands cupped over my face, and then ask for a paper sack—a trick I once learned to help control hyperventilation. Lying on the couch, I breathe into the paper sack, my eyes darting around the room. There is that stairway—the same stairway where Catherin and I had first played together, on New Year's Eve. And it was in this very room near this very couch that I had first kissed Catherin, in an uncharacteristic moment of impulse, right at the stroke of midnight. "Better watch what you're doing!" someone had cautioned Catherin. And on this very couch Catherin and I had rubbed shoulders, the electricity shooting between us. Memories like these are all I have left now.

The top of the paper sack becomes damp.

It's not possible Catherin is gone. It's just not.

I need to be alone. A place nearby comes to mind.

"I'm going over to the Magic Farm," I say to the crowd.

"The Magic Farm?" Vincent asks.

"It's a place not far from here—a secret place of Catherin's."

Vincent shakes his head. "I don't think that's a good idea, Bryan. You shouldn't be alone right now."

Everyone looks at me with the concern a parent might have for a child in need—a stubborn child at that.

"Well, I'm going, and that's that," I say.

Alden speaks up. "I can take you over there in my car."

I shrug. "Sure."

Alden drives me to the Magic Farm, and as soon as we step past the gates of the canal, the world becomes noticeably quieter. The old place seems to hold a spell that keeps it insulated from noisy traffic on the nearby street. Too bad it's not able to insulate me from everything else, too. And it's hot in the afternoon sun, making the awful events of the past few hours all that more unbearable.

Alden respectfully keeps his distance as I slowly cross the canal and head to the big cottonwood tree at the south end of the farm. I've spent many a peaceful hour there with Catherin. We used to gaze at the green fields while sitting under this tree—the green fields that are now rapidly disappearing. Bulldozers and earth movers have seen to that, and the first signs of houses are sprouting up in what was once an expanse of green grass, bringing to mind that song from Laurie Lewis:

> *Where are my green fields now?*
> *No, nowhere around*
> *So I'll steal away with my memories,*
> *And in green fields I'll lay me down*

I prop my back against the cottonwood tree, expecting the usual coo of doves above me. There is only silence now. I do become aware of a flock of peacocks prancing my direction, coming from behind the dilapidated water tank. The sight is startling, for the males are proudly showing off their iridescent purple feathers.

In all my previous visits to the Magic Farm, I had never seen this display of feathers. How odd the peacocks would choose this time. I have the sense that Catherin is involved somehow. Maybe the peacocks are bearing their own witness to Catherin, or perhaps they are sending a message from her, telling me that beauty and glory lies beyond.

Intuitively, I know one of these explanations is true. But my logical, scientific mind can't accept either one. The peacocks are just a coincidence, aren't they?

We return to Larry's house, but the prevailing gloom is too much. The next thing I know I'm walking down the sidewalk to Catherin's place. It's a sunny afternoon, with a few clouds to the west. The Palo Verde trees are fully dressed in their seasonal yellow bloom. But the promise of summer has been shattered irrevocably.

A police detective is out on the front lawn as I reach Catherin's yard. I stop on the other side of the yellow ribbon, and explain to the detective who I am.

"We'll be bringing *the body* out shortly," he says.

The body. How two small words can be so devastating.

"I know it'll be hard, but we need someone who knew Catherin to come inside and give us a positive identification," says the detective. "Do you suppose you could do that for us?"

I hesitate, not wanting to say no, but knowing I have to.

"I should warn you," the officer continues, "it's not a pretty sight."

I thought the pit in my stomach couldn't possibly sink lower. It does anyway. I want to remember Catherin the way she was when she was alive. I especially want to remember the way she had been exactly a week earlier, when she was sitting underneath a tree in Zion Canyon, flashing a delightful smile.

"I'm sorry," I tell the officer. "I don't think I can do it."

"I understand," he says. "Is there anyone over the other place that can?"

I tell the officer I will ask, and go back to Larry and Amy's. When Vincent hears of the situation, he replies, "I knew you probably wouldn't be able to make the identification, so I had planned on being the one. But could you walk down there with me?"

I say yes, and Arielle comes too, along with Alden and Kimberly. We form a small procession down the sidewalk, passing by neighbors standing out in their front yards, looking curious as to what is going on.

We wait outside Catherin's house, beyond the yellow ribbons, as Vincent goes inside with the police. Arielle turns to me with unusual news.

"I've been in contact with her," says Arielle.

I give her a confused look. "With who?"

"With Catherin. She says that she is fine. She has been trying to communicate with all of us, but apparently I'm the only one who has been able to notice."

I had almost forgotten. Arielle was a self-professed psychic. Not really believing, but wanting to, I ask, "What has she been saying?"

"She is not in any pain. Her spirit guides are taking care of her now. They pulled her out of her body as soon as they realized what was happening."

I'm not sure how to take Arielle's words. Does she really have the power to hear all of this, or is she making it all up, to make me feel better? Although I have always believed psychic powers are possible, I have never been in a situation where it matters whether they are or not. And what about these so-called spirit guides, supposedly pulling Catherin out of her body?

"So what exactly happened?" I ask Arielle. "Have the police said anything?"

"Her roommate had been making romantic advances," Arielle says. "And they had been arguing. Catherin had gone into her bathroom. He went back to his room and found his gun. He came up behind her, and when she turned around, he shot her multiple times. She didn't know it was coming. She died instantly."

Arielle's words are so painful that I try to find anything to hold on to, looking for any thread of comfort. There *is* some comfort in that it happened so quickly, but that's a small comfort indeed.

And is there life after death? Catherin and I had spent many hours discussing this very topic, but at the time it had seemed part of a game, an intellectual musing. I never thought I would have to personally deal with questions like it so soon in my life, for real.

I have to deal with them now. I'm forced to believe that *something* survives death. To think of us just dying, with no more memories, no thoughts, no nothing, well, it's too illogical, too unbearable.

What form does this continued existence take? I offer no conjectures—any that I have are just speculation. What matters is that we don't just *end*. I'm reminded of the gospel songs our band had been working on—one in particular. How uncanny for Catherin to take up singing these lyrics just weeks ago:

Where the Soul Never Dies

To Canaan's land I'm on my way
Where the soul of man never dies.
My darkest night will turn to day
Where the soul of man never dies.

   Dear friends there'll be no sad farewells
   There'll be no tear dimmed eyes.
   Where all is peace and joy and love
   And the soul of man never dies.

The roses bloom in there for me
Where the soul of man never dies.
And I will spend eternity
Where the soul of man never dies.

   Chorus

A love light beams across the foam
Where the soul of man never dies.
It shines to light the shores of home
Where the soul of man never dies.

   Chorus

   — William M. Golden, 1914

Vincent soon returns, his face a shade of green—a desolate look of despair and grief the likes of which I've never seen.

"This is the darkest hour of my life," he declares.

It is my darkest hour as well.

Soon they bring out Catherin, lying on a cot, underneath sheets of red linen. I try to ignore the reason they use red linen. When they push the cot through the doorway, the wheels catch on the threshold. I see the body underneath move and shake, just like a wiggling piece of meat.

My girlfriend, my soul mate, reduced to a piece of meat!

Now there is no doubt she is dead. The sickening, horrible thought burrows deep into my soul. A police officer wisely takes me aside and asks for my address and phone number. It's obvious he is trying to distract me, pulling me away from the gruesome scene. I don't resist.

Afterwards, we watch as they finish loading Catherin's body into an ambulance. I'm standing next to Arielle when she says, "Although Catherin has to go with her body now, her spirit will be back. She says she wants to spend a lot of time with you."

These words take my breath away momentarily. Tears soon follow. Trying to recover my composure, I tilt my head back and inhale deeply, only to see two aircraft in the sky, their jet streams crossing. One plane heads west, soon disappearing into the clouds. The other remains visible and heads off in a northwesterly direction. Instantly and intuitively, I understand the symbolism. The paths of Catherin and I had crossed, joining together for a brief time. The jet heading west is Catherin, about to disappear into the clouds and away from earthly view. The other jet is me, alone now in my journey through life, still in sight of, and still bound by, the green fields of Earth.

Many coincidences on this day, the darkest day of my life. First the simultaneous opposites, the songs, the *Riders in the Sky* tape, the peacocks, and now the crossing jets. What is going on?

The police finish their work and let us into the house. Vincent, Larry, and Amy go in with me. As I step through the front door, I feel something not unlike a blast of hot air. It's as if all the violent energies unleashed a few hours ago are rushing out the door, smacking me in the face. My body trembles at the impact.

The first sight to greet me as I enter Catherin's house is the picture of a white dove flying through the clouds. It seems so out of place now, its message of peace and spiritual tranquility canceled by the imagined sounds of screams and gunshots that seem to echo through the house.

Gunshots. Hadn't Catherin been unusually sensitive to the sound? I remember the gunshots in the distance during our time in Zion, as we hiked down from Angel's Landing. Catherin had been visibly shaken by the occurrence.

Catherin's turtle doves sit on their perches in the aviary. The birds are very subdued. Mr. Bubba, who is usually quite responsive to people, is now completely motionless. Did her birds sense what was happening when they heard the screams, the gunshots? Or were they simply stunned by the sounds?

An egg had hatched that weekend, and Mrs. Bubba soon flits back to the nest to tend to it.

We pass through the dining area and turn the corner, starting down the now silent hallway towards Catherin's bedroom—to ground zero—her master bathroom. Each step makes my skin crawl. A dark cloud seems to hover down that hallway. Am I really going there?

I've heard it is better to confront situations like this as soon as possible, rather than wait and let the fears and emotions fester—to desensitize sooner than later. But after a few more steps, there is no doubt it will have to be later. I turn around and immediately leave the house, rushing out to the sidewalk and back to Larry and Amy's.

Chapter 18.
Aftermath

People speak in low, somber voices in the gloom of Larry and Amy's living room. All afternoon I've been going in and out, never quite being settled. I go outside once again into the … sunshine? How can the sun still be shining?

I glance down the street towards Catherin's place. The afternoon shadows are getting longer, and the ambulance that took Catherin's body away under ominous sheets of red linen has long since departed. Long, fluffy strips, almost dissipated, are all that remain of the two crossing jet streams I saw when they rolled Catherin's body out on a stretcher. Although most of the police have left, a patrol car is still parked down the street, and yellow crime tape still surrounds the yard.

Sunshine or not, it's as gloomy out here as it is inside, so back inside I go. Vincent is talking on the phone with Catherin's parents about funeral arrangements, something too overwhelming for me to contemplate. Larry and Amy mention that Catherin hadn't seen or spoken to her parents in over a year. No one offers any explanation.

Speaking of parents, I should call my own mother. It's time to go back to my apartment. I pull out my truck keys, jangling them in my hand.

"See you guys later," I say to the crowd, heading towards the front door.

My pronouncement is met with a series of objections from just about everybody:

"Where are you going?"

"You're not going home are you?"

"We don't think you should be alone."

I turn to address them. "I'll be fine. Really."

"Why don't you stay at my apartment tonight?" Alden suggests. "I've got plenty of room."

"I'd rather be by myself."

But others concur that staying at Alden's is a better idea. It seems the group has ganged up on me.

I sigh. "Do I have a choice?"

"No," says Alden, with as much of a smile as he can manage, given the circumstances.

I give in. "Just let me go back to my apartment and get a fresh set of clothes, and then I'll head over to your place."

My truck is parked in the garage at Catherin's. I leave Larry and Amy's and make another trek down the sidewalk. Memories come pouring out—memories of walking this way with Catherin, an instrument in each hand, returning to her place after the New Year's Eve party. That now bittersweet view of the world is completely shattered. Gone is the hope and excitement of those times. Gone is the innocence. And gone is my naive view that nothing bad would ever happen to someone close to me.

A policeman stands guard outside Catherin's house. I tell him who I am and ask if it's okay to take my truck. He says fine, and opens the garage door for me.

I climb in the truck. Just hours ago, Catherin had driven it into the garage. Just hours ago, she had still been alive. With these thoughts it's hard to put together the right sequence of motions to start the motor and back out of the garage. Somehow I manage.

And somehow, I manage to negotiate traffic on the streets of Gilbert and Mesa. I choose not to take the freeway. On the streets, I can drive slower, and can take advantage of stop lights to rest and recover from any teary episode I might have.

It's too quiet in the cab of my truck. Something is missing. I look over to the passenger seat—Catherin's seat.

"I'd much rather sit next to you than my guitar," I hear her say in my memories. She had said this on our first date, after scooting over closer to me, strategically placing her guitar by the door instead of the middle.

Now there is just emptiness: on the seat, in my heart—and apparently, my gas tank. The low-fuel indicator on the dash has lit up. Looking at the fuel gauge, I see that I am indeed about out of gas. Of all the things to have to deal with now.

I pull in to the next gas station I see, and fill the tank in a daze, just going through the motions: twisting off the gas cap, lifting the pump handle, inserting the nozzle into the tank, and starting the gas flowing. It seems so trivial, so mechanical, so surreal.

Others are pumping gas too, and out on the busy street, cars are whizzing by—people going about their business as though everything is normal. And here I am, also acting as if everything is normal. But it's not. Someone has just died, and not just anyone, but the dearest person in the world to me. How *dare* the world go on?

Go on it will, regardless of how I feel about it. I will be pumping gas many more times in the future. How many more times will hurt so much? There isn't any choice in the matter. I'm going to have to live with Catherin's death, and that's that. Such an ironic twist of words, to live with death.

I blink my eyes, at first not realizing I just added another memory into my bank of eye-blinking memories. I have a feeling though, that the eye-blinking game will be replaced with the act of pumping gas. From now on, whenever I fill up at a station, this moment is sure to be nearby.

~ ~ ~

I dial my mom back in Nebraska. She answers hello.

"Mom?"

There is a short pause, and then she says, "Well, I'll be dammed if it isn't my son Bryan! My goodness. I just talked to you a few weeks ago on Mother's Day, but I'm always glad to hear your voice."

"Well, you won't be so glad after I tell you why I called," I say.

"Oh? What's up?"

"I have some bad news. I don't know if I told you about my new girlfriend, Catherin. I may have mentioned her when I called on Mother's Day."

"Yes, I remember you saying something about her."

"I'll just come out with it. She was killed today."

"Oh my God."

"It gets worse. She was shot by a renter living in her home."

"I can't believe I'm hearing this."

I give her the details, after which she says, "I'm so sorry for you, son. Is there anything I can do? Do you want me to come down?"

"Come down?" I ask. "You mean to Phoenix? I hadn't thought of that. I don't know if it's necessary."

"I want to help in any way I can."

"It's an awfully long drive down here, at least twenty hours. You'd have to fly."

"I've never flown in a plane before," Mom says. "But I suppose I can handle it. One of my sons is in need."

"Tell you what," I say. "I can arrange the airline tickets. But you'll probably have to drive to Denver to catch the plane. I'm betting it'll be too expensive to fly from western Nebraska."

"I'm sure I can manage to get to Denver. What about Catherin's parents? Do they live in Phoenix?"

"They're from Pennsylvania, near Pittsburgh. I don't know if they are coming or not. I know they've been contacted."

After hanging up, I book Mom a roundtrip flight from Denver to Phoenix. Often times, one can get reasonable fares between these two cities, even on short notice, and today was no exception.

I call Mom back to provide flight information and then gather up a change of clothes and head over to Alden's place. This time, I remember my keys, and remember to lock the door on the way out. And this time, the tears aren't flowing. I'm not sure they could anyway, as I don't think I have any tears left. But the rest of me is still a total mess.

Lying on the floor in a sleeping bag that night at Alden's place, I don't sleep at all. I keep twisting and turning. And this is not my ordinary fidgeting. No, it's the events of the day spinning around in my head. *If only I had gone over to Catherin's place earlier, like she had asked. If only, if only …*

~ ~ ~

I spend the next day at Alden's, and on Tuesday morning drive to the airport and wait at the gate for passengers arriving from Denver. I see Mom coming down the jetway, looking a bit wobbly. This is the first time she has flown on a jet, and with her health the way it is—a propensity for dizziness and having back problems to boot— she probably didn't enjoy the trip very much.

As soon as she sees me, she calls out with tears in her eyes, "There's my son."

She gives me a hug and asks how I'm doing, and then starts telling me about her first plane flight.

"I'm still a bit woozy from that landing," she says. "It was pretty bumpy over the mountains. I wasn't sure I was going to make it. But I don't feel as bad as I thought I would. I guess it was because the good Lord knew I had to be here for you."

During the drive home, Mom wants to know more about Catherin. I tell her the basics: That she was thirty-five, a leasing agent at a shopping center, and played guitar in our band.

"Did Catherin go to church?" Mom asks. "What religion was she?"

"To tell you the truth, I don't know," I say.

Our family was from the Midwest, mostly of German heritage, and as you might expect, we were raised Lutheran. My mom has attended church all of her life. Matters of religion are important to her. Apparently, they aren't as important to me. Maybe Catherin mentioned her religious background to me, which I've forgotten. I know I'm too self-absorbed and spacey to have raised a direct question about it.

"It's ironic that I don't know what Catherin's religion was," I say to Mom. "Because we spent a lot of time talking about metaphysics and spirituality."

"Metaphysics?" she asks. "What is that?"

"It's hard to define, for it means different things to different people. It's basically the philosophical study of being and knowing. For me personally, it's the study of spirituality, without any particular religious dogma. Catherin was spiritual in this sense. She was certainly searching for answers."

I don't tell Mom that Catherin was into astrology. I figure she would get the wrong idea.

"I always made it a point to take you kids to church when you were growing up," Mom says. "Do you go to church down here?"

"Not very often. I think the last time was on Easter a few years ago, at a Catholic service with a former girlfriend. I remember it being a moving service, and left me feeling serene. But I can't say I've been back."

"Why not?"

I shrug. "I don't care much for organized religion. I don't like the dogma. I believe there is more than one spiritual path, and that it's unique for each individual. Many organized religions want you to think otherwise."

"But you still believe in God, don't you?" Mom asks.

"That's a good question."

I struggle to assemble my thoughts on religion and spirituality into some sort of coherence. During the time I knew Catherin, I accumulated many new viewpoints and ideas to consider. I read books on Eastern philosophy and religion, on New Age thinking, and I recently loaned Catherin—and reread myself—a book called *The Road Less Traveled*, a mix of psychology and spirituality. I hadn't yet had time to sort it all out.

I give it a try and say to Mom, "I believe there is more to the world than just what our ordinary senses tell us. I believe there is an awareness, a power and an order to things in the universe. I guess you could call that God. But I don't think of God as a super-being overseeing all of us. I think we each have a bit of the universal divine spark inside us, and we're here in this life to rediscover and reconnect with that spark—to lose our sense of separation."

"Do you still consider yourself a Christian?"

I consider that for a moment. "It's hard to let go how you were brought up."

I then ramble through a stream-of-consciousness monologue about my thoughts and feelings on the subject:

"There are parts of the Christian faith that still resonate, like the fact that Jesus was an extraordinary being. But in my opinion he's been misinterpreted over the years by people who don't understand the meaning of his life here on Earth, and also by people who were and are purposely distorting his message, for their own personal and political agendas. I believe he was trying to show that we could *all* live within the spirit, having an awareness of a reality above and beyond the ordinary one we experience, while still occupying a physical body; that we could even transcend the constraints of our physical bodies. That's how I interpret being 'saved,' as some like to call it.

"But I'm disenchanted with the linear view of life that Christianity teaches: God creates you imperfectly—that is, with 'original sin'—and you get one chance in life to make it right. But is one lifetime always going to be enough? What about untimely deaths? Why leave all the unfinished business? What's the point?"

Mom nods her head while I'm speaking. It's hard to tell what she is thinking.

I continue: "The Eastern cyclical view seems more natural to me. You are born with lessons to learn, you live your life, and you try to grow by learning these lessons, which may take many lifetimes. The goal of these lessons is to lose your sense of separation from the whole. The main reason for living should be to come back to the whole, by your own free will and understanding, not by fear of being punished.

"I know one of the criticisms of the reincarnation view is the implication you are always bound by karma, and that with Christianity, the karmic cycle can be broken by the grace of God, or as some would say, by Jesus as mankind's savior. But from what I've been able to figure out, there's nothing in the reincarnation teachings that says the cycle of karma can't be broken by other means. It can—either by enlightenment, or by the karma of forgiveness. At least, that's how I've come to understand it."

I'm not sure what Mom thinks of my views. I'm not sure what I think of them either. They are certainly in flux. I try to put a more positive spin on things:

"It's funny," I continue. "We started playing gospel tunes in our band. Catherin seemed to enjoy them. I did too. I like the old melodies and overall feel of gospel songs. Perhaps it's nostalgia from all those Sundays you took us to church."

~ ~ ~

After arriving back at the apartment Mom asks what the plan is for the day.

"I'm sure you are tired from the plane trip," I say, "so why don't you rest? There's nothing planned till this evening. We're supposed to go over to Larry and Amy's house for supper."

"Larry and Amy's?"

"They were friends of Catherin. Her parents are arriving from Pittsburgh today, and will be there as well."

While Mom naps, I go to the local pharmacy to pick up photos from the trip to Zion that I had taken to get developed the day before. On the drive to the store, it occurs to me that Catherin's turtle doves are still over at her house. Larry and Amy had been feeding them, but no one is caring for them on a continuous basis. They need a new home, and what better place than mine? It would be like having part of Catherin with me, for she so loved her birds. But where would I keep them? I can't use their cage—their aviary. It's built into a wall of Catherin's house, in the living room.

Mom is still asleep when I arrive home, but later she shuffles out of the bedroom. She sees me and sees the clock on the wall and says, "Well, would you look at the time? It's already two."

"Do you suppose you could help me build a bird cage?" I ask.

"A bird cage?" she asks, filling a glass with water from the sink and taking some pills. "Good Lord, what do you need one for?"

"Catherin had birds—turtle doves. I figure I'll take care of them."

Mom thinks about that for a moment and says, "I suppose I could help you cobble a cage together. It'll give me a way to be useful."

Even though I have an engineering degree—mechanical no less—I'm not a hands-on kind of guy. Carpentry is not my forte. I'm more comfortable with equations and theories than with hammer and saw. Even so, I'm sure I could build a cage no problem, but I know Mom will enjoy the project too. We were a poor family when I was growing up, with just Mom to take care of us eight kids. Whenever something around the house needed fixing, Mom couldn't afford to hire anyone, so she learned to do it herself, whether it was painting, plumbing, laying down new tile, or even tearing out walls and building new ones.

We make plans for the bird cage, deciding to build it six feet in height, with four-by-fours for pillars, and plywood for top and bottom. Wrapped chicken wire would form the walls, and we would install a wood dowel as a perch. A screen door made from chicken wire would finish the design. I make out a list of supplies and head for the hardware store, while Mom stays home to rest.

I'm driving to the store when Catherin's singing comes to me, out of nowhere. I can hear her pure, clear, voice, just like she's right there. The thought that I will never hear her voice again—for real—hits home hard. She's gone. Forever. The thought is agonizing; the heartbreak, staggering. I start wailing—a deep, loud, long, soul-shattering wail, sounding not unlike the call of a wolf. It's the most anguish I have ever felt and its intensity knocks the breath out of me. I wonder later if other drivers heard those wails.

A few miles up the road, I happen upon an accident scene. There are several cars smashed, and someone on a stretcher is being loaded into an ambulance. In the past, whenever I encountered a scene like this, I would be unnerved, as most people would, but it would always feel distant and unreal, because it wasn't happening to me or others I knew personally. But now, the tragic scene strikes me with great emotion. The empathy I feel for the accident victims is overwhelming, even though they are complete strangers.

~ ~ ~

Later that evening we head over to Larry and Amy's for supper. I bring Catherin's guitar, which she had left over at my place on that fateful day. Catherin's parents, Herbert and Geraldine, have arrived from Pittsburgh, along with their other daughter Annette. I'm anxious to meet them, for I know virtually nothing about Catherin's family. When I enter the kitchen and catch sight of her sister, a shock runs through me. Catherin and her sister look so much alike. How uncanny it is to see someone having Catherin's appearance and mannerisms—but not quite. Though spooky, I like being around Annette. It's almost like having Catherin there; a small comfort, but I latch onto it anyway.

Most of the group is sitting at the kitchen table, talking about the upcoming funeral, which is to be held on Friday in Pittsburgh, with Catherin's body flown back beforehand. A memorial service is planned for those of us in Phoenix, on Sunday, a week later. Larry and Amy will host.

Thoughts whirl through my head: I wonder if I should go to the funeral. But what about the cost of tickets, having to fly on such short notice to Pittsburgh? Someone makes a comment about funerals being for the living, not the dead. Seems like an argument for not going. Besides, I'm not feeling the need to mourn Catherin by attending her funeral. The memorial here in Phoenix will suffice. But I'm not sure about this decision. It's hard to think straight right now.

I give copies of the pictures from the Zion camping trip to Catherin's parents. Two of the pictures I had taken of Catherin—sitting in the grass by the Virgin River, and also underneath the tree next to Angel's Landing—had turned out exceptionally well. Geraldine is very moved by them, and she cries for a long time as she stares at the pictures, while Herbert takes a glance and says nothing.

Catherin's parents are warm and friendly, making me wonder what reason Catherin had for not speaking to them for such a long time. When I ask Geraldine about this, she doesn't have much of an answer. She does tell me a few things, though:

"When Catherin was a child, she was cheerful and happy. She was a special little girl, very pretty and sunny. Something happened when she became a teenager. She changed, and became morose and sullen, more so than most teenagers. She became an angry young lady, and has been a problem ever since. We've never understood it."

I consider pressing for more details, but it doesn't seem like the time or place, and then, after further thought, I decide it isn't necessary to know. Nothing will be changed by it.

Geraldine is sporting a piece of jewelry on her arm—that silver bracelet of Catherin's. Her mom apparently found it with her daughter's things and had decided to wear it. Seeing that bracelet brings another wave of emotion. Catherin was down to earth when it came to fashion. She rarely wore much jewelry, but she seemed to treasure that simple bracelet. Now it appears her mom does as well.

What material things of Catherin's will I treasure? I immediately think of her guitar and politely ask Geraldine about it, explaining that with Catherin's guitar, a part of her would always be with me. Maybe she would guide my hands whenever I played it. After hearing this, Geraldine graciously says I can keep it.

~ ~ ~

In the early morning hours, Catherin steps up the sidewalk to my apartment, wearing shorts and her favorite blue T-shirt—the same clothes she wore in the pictures from Zion, the ones I will always remember her in. She knocks on the door, which I open to greet her, and we happily embrace. *Where have you been?* I ask. I feel so relieved. She wasn't dead after all. It had all been a bad dream.

Then I wake up.

~ ~ ~

Mom spends the next day helping me construct the bird cage for Catherin's turtle doves. Other friends come over to help as well. Building the cage keeps my mind off things, acting as a form of therapy. We hammer and saw and yak out on the patio. I'm sure the neighbors wonder what we are up to.

When the cage is finished, Larry and Amy go to Catherin's place for me and retrieve Bubba and Mrs. Bubba—and a little fledgling that just hatched. At first, I keep the doves in their cage out on the patio, but after only one night, neighbors complain and I have to move the bird cage indoors. I guess the neighbors don't like hearing the single repertoire of my newly acquired doves:

"Heh-heh-heh. Oot-oooo-weee-hooo! Oot-oooo-weee-hooo!"

~ ~ ~

On Thursday afternoon I get a call from my former fiddle teacher, Jessie. Before I can say anything, she begins telling me about a bar where her band is playing that weekend—a place called the *Salt River Saloon*. She invites me to come listen.

"How's *your* band going?" she asks, after giving directions to where she's playing.

"I guess you haven't heard," I reply. "I have some bad news. My girlfriend Catherin was killed last weekend."

After her initial shock of hearing this news, I give Jessie a brief summary of the events.

"I am so, so sorry," she says, once I've finished. "Why didn't you say something earlier? Are you okay?"

"About as well as to be expected."

"Say, I've got some free time this afternoon," she tells me. "Why don't you come over? I want to hear more about what happened. And it'll be good to see you—like old times. Bring your fiddle if you feel up to it."

I hadn't seen Jessie in a while, and missed the days of going to her place for lessons. She had aspirations of becoming a successful country musician, and I admired her for taking chances and striking out on her own. She served as an important and ongoing inspiration for my own fiddle playing. So I didn't hesitate to take up her offer.

I navigate my way through the streets of east-central Phoenix, looking for and finding a gravel driveway that leads to a small, one bedroom farm house surrounded by trees; almost isolated, except for two houses circumscribing the same graveled yard, and except for the chickens, pigs, and billy goat or two that also serve as neighbors. As with the Magic Farm, it's easy to imagine you are out in the country at Jessie's place.

Jessie greets me on the sidewalk, her long, black hair pulled back into a loose pony tail, a look of concern on her face. She gives me a hug and holds my hand as we walk up the steps into the house. For the next few hours I fill in the details of my time with Catherin. I tell Jessie about the trip to Zion National Park, and the discovery of the music of Laurie Lewis. We play tunes, trading ones I had learned in my band for ones she'd been playing in hers, and then we play tunes she had taught me back in the day when I was her student. One such tune came to mind for Jessie, a tune I had always struggled with.

"Why don't you try playing *Blackberry Blossom* for me?" she asks.

The mention of that tune almost brings tears to my eyes. My voice does crack a little when I reply, "You know something Jessie? I believe *Blackberry Blossom* was the last fiddle tune I ever played with Catherin. Our band had a performance at a park in north Phoenix a week ago, and we ended the night with *Blackberry Blossom.*"

When Jessie hears Catherin's name, her brow furrows in its unique, endearing way. It's a classic Jessie look.

"After watching you today," she says, "I'm struck with how well you seem to be handling things. I can't imagine what you are going through."

I shrug and settle back in my chair. "I've always been a laid-back person. I guess that hasn't changed."

"Most people would be completely devastated and dysfunctional, but not you. You seem to have a lot of inner strength. I really admire that."

"Thanks for the compliment," I say, head bowing in humbleness. "I hope I'm worthy. It may appear I'm handling her death well, but I wonder if I'm still in shock."

"Aren't you angry at the man that killed her?"

"To be honest, I don't know. I don't dwell on it. There's nothing that can be changed by it. I can only try and move on."

"Seems like a good attitude to have."

We're silent for a moment, and then I take a deep breath and say, "I guess it's time for *Blackberry Blossom*. Let's play it in memory of Catherin."

"Okay," says Jessie. "I'll back you on guitar."

I hold back tears as I pick up the fiddle. So wanting to impress my former teacher, I'm very nervous. My bow is unsteady, my fingers fumble, and I miss way too many notes. I scrunch my nose whenever I make a mistake. Strumming her guitar, Jessie watches with seeming amusement when I get things right—and when I get things wrong.

The tune thankfully ends.

"That was terrible," I say.

Jessie laughs as she puts her guitar down. "It wasn't that bad. I'm sure it's just nerves."

We move to the kitchen and Jessie hands me a bottle of water out of the fridge. While taking a sip, I notice a poster on the kitchen wall. It's a familiar series of poems, about the meaning of life, lost love, and destiny. I don't recall where I had seen these poems before—perhaps in a high school year book. But I know right away what to do with them. I need something to say at Catherin's memorial, and they will do quite nicely. Jessie lets me borrow the poster so I can make a copy.

A certain tranquility has always surrounded Jessie's house, and playing tunes with her that afternoon was no exception, being very soothing to my soul. For the first time since Catherin's death, I almost feel normal.

~ ~ ~

That Friday, on the morning of Catherin's funeral, I make a journey to the Magic Farm. I find our favorite cottonwood tree and sit in silence as best I can, thinking about Catherin as I knew her: so full of life, energy, and talent, yet struggling with problems that will probably always remain a mystery. She had been making efforts to take control of these problems, and seemed to be gaining back the happiness her parents said was her natural state as a child. In my view, that progress was the important part.

My thoughts roam thousands of miles away to a small town in western Pennsylvania, where Catherin's funeral is being held, probably this very moment. I fashion a memorial of sorts at the cotton-wood tree, arranging pictures from the Zion trip around its base. If Catherin's spirit were to come back to the Phoenix valley, I suspect it would be to this farm and this tree, and these pictures would be a reminder of her last vacation on this green Earth—our special trip to Zion National Park.

My private memorial service is not as peaceful as I would like. Bulldozers are tearing up what's left of the fields west of the farm. Hammers are pounding away on the two-by-fours of the first new houses going up. On top of that, the sun is bearing down and it's getting downright hot.

I watch the bulldozers with sadness. Green fields, disappearing. The situation brings to mind that song by Laurie Lewis—the theme song on our trip to Zion. Another song comes to mind too, the song I had started a few months ago, about a farm, this very farm I'm now visiting—the Magic Farm.

I never had finished that song, I now realize. Perhaps it's time to do so. I go back to the truck and fetch a pen and notepad. Despite the noise and heat, I manage to come up with more verses to the *Magic Farm*, scribbling them down on the notepad, with sweat dripping down my face. I rip off the finished sheets, and fold and tuck them into my pocket.

Afterwards I head to the Gilbert police station. Earlier in the day they had called and asked me to come by and fill out a statement about Catherin's death. I handle the matter with one of the police detectives. When we finish up, the detective says he's going over to Catherin's house to do some further investigation, and asks if I want to come too. I follow in my truck.

Vincent, Larry, and Amy arrive just as we pull up to the house. Apparently, they had been told the police were stopping by. We enter the house and thankfully, the horrible wave of psychic energy has dissipated. But bittersweet memories greet me at every turn and imagined terrors keep banging on the cellar door of my mind. Keeping those fears at bay, I bravely follow the group into Catherin's bedroom, and then into the bathroom where she had been gunned down. Chills spread down my spine. The air here is still very heavy with that horrible energy.

To my surprise I find a book on the floor. It's the *Road Less Traveled*, the book I had loaned Catherin a few weeks earlier—the one about spiritual growth, grace, and love. I turn the book over and receive a shock when I find dried bloodstains on the cover. A sickening, maddening feeling courses through me. What terrible irony that a book on love and grace would be witness to such violence.

I drop the book and hurry back to the living room, not wanting to spend any more time in the bathroom. Vincent and the detective follow close behind.

"What will happen to the guy?" Vincent asks the detective as we get ready to leave. "How much time will he serve?"

"Well, I hate to tell you this," the officer begins, "but not as much as you might think. In my opinion, the justice system is pretty screwed up. He'll probably be charged with second degree murder. In cases like this, about all you can hope for is a sentence of twenty years."

Twenty years—just twenty years traded for someone's life! Catherin was thirty-five when she was killed. She still had a good fifty years left, I reckon, and those were years we might have spent together. It's hard to imagine forgiving the person who took this possibility away.

As you forgive, so will you be forgiven. These famous words come to me now. Perhaps I need to read the *Road Less Traveled* again—just not the blood-stained copy left in the bathroom.

~ ~ ~

It's Saturday morning. I drive my mom to the airport for her flight back to Nebraska. It's too bad she can't stay for another week and attend Catherin's memorial, but I had purchased her non-refundable tickets before I knew the schedule.

Back at my apartment, I'm truly alone for the first time since Catherin's passing. My friends may worry about me, but I know I'll be okay. I won't be going off on some kind of angry rampage—that's simply not in my nature. And somehow, I know I won't be having any nightmares.

I don't. In fact, I have no dreams at all. This saddens me, for I fervently wish for Catherin to come to me again in my dreams. She had once, a few nights ago. Why hadn't she since?

Chapter 19.
Burning Candles in the Night

May 31, 1987

Haunting, ethereal music drifts into the living room—a recording of dreamy space music composed with Lyricon wind synthesizers, guitar, and flute—which puts me into a relaxed, meditative state. Eyes closed, I sit with memories of Catherin, trying to visualize her shining brown eyes. But it's getting harder by the day to recall her face, and her pure, clear voice is growing fainter.

I can't believe you're gone, I say to Catherin in my thoughts. *I just can't.*

A tingling develops at the crown of my head, coursing down my back. Someone taps my shoulder.

Catherin, is that you? I ask in my thoughts.

I open my eyes and turn my head. It's Arielle.

"You do know that Catherin is here with you, don't you?" she says.

I'm taken aback by the coincidence of these words. More goose bumps form.

Arielle continues, "Catherin has been in touch with me, and says she is happy and surprised that so many people have shown up today."

It's Sunday, the day of Catherin's memorial, two weeks after her passing. When I had first arrived, I attempted to be sociable, trying my best to contribute in conversations. But this isn't a natural state for me, so I had settled into a recliner in the living room, and it was after I sat down and closed my eyes that Arielle tapped me on the shoulder.

I don't know what to make of Arielle's unsettling and extraordinary comments. The tingling I felt was just nerves, wasn't it? But a part of me, that non-skeptical, gargoyle-standing-by-the-saguaro part, isn't so sure.

Vincent steps into the room and says, "I think everybody has arrived, so we should get started."

We gather in the living room for a short informal ceremony. I replace the cassette in the tape player with a recording of a particular tune that had been running through my head all morning. It's the long, slow, poignant version of *Pachelbel's Canon* I had introduced Catherin to some months ago—a particularly emotional rendition on the violin that eloquently expresses the joys and tragedies of life. On Valentine's Day, Catherin had subsequently presented me with a tape of alternate versions of this classical work, as we rode up the freeway north of Tucson, the full moon rising. Such romantic memories, now bittersweet.

I read the series of poems on life, love, and destiny that Jessie had lent me. Never having been comfortable speaking in public, on this day I have little difficulty. Any stage fright I have seems insignificant compared to Catherin's death.

After my short eulogy, others give theirs. We stand quietly as the sweet strains of a violin fade slowly away, ending *Pachelbel's Canon* on a single note. *Just like the fading away of life*, I say to myself. I tremble at the symbolism, and have to leave the room to regain my composure. I find a seat at a small table in the adjoining room. On the table are mementos of Catherin, including two photos from our trip to Zion National Park.

Through tears, I stare at the photos, one which reveals Catherin's unexplained underlying sadness; the other, her newly found delightful smile. I want to believe the latter photo represents the new Catherin, the real Catherin. She would not have wanted all this sadness. I rejoin the others in the living room and clear my throat to get their attention.

"Catherin had a favorite saying," I tell the group. "'Don't waste time.' It was almost like she knew she didn't have much time left. Since I'd known her, whenever she figured out what she wanted to do, she went for it without hesitating—like the way she started *Dusty River*. It only took her a few short weeks to organize the band and she kept us all in line, making sure we practiced regularly. We didn't call her the boss lady for nothing. I'm sure she would want us to continue playing, so in the words of a true bluegrass player ... let's pick!"

On that cue, members of the band disperse to gather instruments. I had stashed my fiddle upstairs in the spare bedroom, and climb the stairs to retrieve it. Catherin's guitar is there too, sitting on the floor next to my instrument. I grab the fiddle and start out the door before I realize I'm leaving Catherin's guitar behind, all alone. I can't believe I'm doing that. I turn around and pick up her guitar to carry downstairs too. As the band sets up I take the guitar out of its case and place it upright on a chair, in an honorary position amongst the circle of musicians.

We tune our instruments. I test my fiddle's tuning by trying a few double stops—bowing two strings simultaneously—listening for the perfect fifth intervals that indicate the proper tuning of a violin. Perfect fifths are what I hear.

"Hey, my fiddle is ready to go," I say to the other band members.

Darrell cross-checks a few notes with me on his instrument, and says with amazement, "So is my mandolin."

I hear Dwight testing his bass and turn to him to say, "You're bass sounds good to me."

Pete plucks the strings of his banjo, and then checks his Dobro. Usually, these instruments are the source of many tuning problems, but not today.

"I can't believe it," says Pete. "My instruments are in tune as well."

We play all the bluegrass songs in our repertoire and then transition to gospel tunes. With polished chops and tight arrangements, the whole band is on form. My fiddling is crisper than usual and my intonation more accurate. I am finally getting the knack for playing in the bluegrass style, it seems.

Did Catherin have something to do with the tuning of our instruments and our inspired playing? I like to think so.

~ ~ ~

"You must be Bryan," says a woman who walks up to me later in the afternoon. "I'm Janet, an old friend of Catherin's."

I look at her without recognition.

"You wouldn't know me," she says. "I knew Catherin from long ago. I was shocked to find out what happened."

Janet had found out the hard way—as if there is an easy way. She had read it in the paper, she tells me. Then she says, "Amy has candles and suggests we go down to Catherin's house to light them in memorial. Would you like to come?"

I say yes and join Janet and Amy down the sidewalk. Tagging along also is Annette, who had come back from Pittsburgh to finish sorting through Catherin's things, and to attend the memorial.

I use my key to open the door and we step inside. The place is deathly silent and sadly empty. Once it was so full of life, so full of Catherin. Now, it's just floors no longer walked; doors no longer opened. Bubba and Mrs. Bubba aren't even there to greet us, living now in their hand-built cage back at my place. I follow behind the others as they explore, rounding the corner to the hallway towards Catherin's bedroom. It's still hard for me to go back there. I stop half-way down and turn into the spare bedroom—the Ethiopian's room.

A photo of him sits on the dresser. I quickly divert my eyes as soon as I realize who I'm looking at. I sure don't want to remember the face of the person who so brutally ended Catherin's life. As my eyes turn away, another picture comes into view. Staring back from the wall is the beatific countenance of Jesus, which had born witness to the violence just a week before. What was the Ethiopian thinking when he came back into this room, and in a fit of rage, retrieved his gun? Did he not see this picture of Jesus on the wall? Exactly what was his brand of Christianity telling him to do—hunt Catherin down and empty the contents of his gun into her?

I glance sideways at the picture of the Ethiopian on the dresser, and in a fit of righteous anger, knock it to the floor, swearing under my breath.

This is all too much. I can't stay here any longer. I find the others, and ask if they are ready to leave. I lock the door behind us, and Janet and Annette light candles on a ledge by the steps. We stand in silence. I'm calmer now, lost in memories, staring at the front of the house in the fading sunset as the candles create a flicker of light and shadow across the closed front door. Never again will that door open to have Catherin standing there, greeting me from a long day at work. Never again will I feel her warm embrace.

We leave the burning candles behind and walk solemnly back to Larry and Amy's place. Afterwards Amy turns to me with a question.

"Bryan, could you tell me how far it is to the farm you mentioned to us before, Catherin's favorite place?"

"You mean the Magic Farm?"

"Yes," says Amy. "I was thinking we could take the rest of the candles down there. Vincent says he has torches as well. We could form a procession."

"That's a good idea," I say. "The farm is only a mile away."

Amy organizes the group. She and Vincent hand out torches that are soon lit. But to my consternation, everyone looks to me as the de facto leader of the procession, motioning me to the front. Me, the leader? Catherin had told me that as a Leo I should feel natural in that role, but I never had at any point in my life. I take a deep breath and summon my lion courage. This is Catherin's memorial, and that changes everything.

I try my best to act as leader when we march through the streets of the neighborhood, turning south to the canal and then east to the Magic Farm. My shoes crunch along the graveled canal path, and my torch flares up periodically, spooking me a couple of times. I wonder if Catherin has anything to do with this. Perhaps it's her way of getting attention.

By the time we reach the farm, our torches have played out. We stand in the darkening twilight, looking west across the fence towards the water tower. Several peacocks are perched in silhouette, just as they always are this time of day.

Amy arranges and lights candles on top of a concrete culvert near the canal while Vincent and the rest of us watch. The candle light attracts unwanted attention, for a Hispanic-looking woman soon comes out of the farmhouse.

"Hey! What are you doing there?" she yells, rushing over to the fence. "Are you trying to burn the place down?"

"Sorry," says Vincent. "We didn't mean to disturb anyone. We're here to light candles in memorial to a friend of ours that just passed away."

"This was a special place to my late girlfriend," I explain. "She called it the Magic Farm. We used to come here frequently, and loved to watch the animals as we passed by on the canal, especially the peacocks."

"I see," says the woman, calming down. "I'm sorry for your loss, but please understand, we've had problems with vandalism lately. We don't know how much longer we can keep the peacocks. Several have been hurt by kids throwing rocks at them. The owner isn't happy about all this trouble, and is itching to sell this place anyway."

"I often see an old man out on the porch. Is he the owner, may I ask?"

"He's my uncle, who lives here with me. He has been on this farm most of his life, but doesn't own the place. We're trying to convince the owner to let us keep living here, but I don't know how long that will last."

I feel sad for the old place. Its days are surely numbered. The neighboring properties are sporting new housing developments, and bulldozers stand poised not far from the farm. That reminds me. Earlier in the day, I had made a copy of the recently finished lyrics to the *Magic Farm* song, to bring to the memorial and show to others. I pull the folded sheets from my front shirt pocket.

"I wrote a song about this farm," I tell the woman, handing her the sheets. "Perhaps you and your uncle would like to read the lyrics. Good luck on keeping this place."

"Thank you," she says, taking the lyrics. "You may stay here as long as you like, but do us a favor. Please don't leave any candles lit."

She disappears back into the farmhouse.

We honor her wishes and make sure the candles are blown out, and then take them with us. I fire up another torch, however, to light the way back down the canal. A few others do likewise. I'm last to leave, and glance back from time to time to make sure the Magic Farm is still there. I half expect it to disappear, much like Avalon had disappeared in the *Mists of Avalon* novel.

Memories of Catherin walk with me, west along the canal and underneath the power lines. "I can feel the vibrations of your spirit," she had once told me, as we stood beneath these very power lines. How I wish I could feel her spirit now.

When I reach the end of the canal, I stick the torch into the ground to let it burn out. Several others had done the same, and the torches stand as final witnesses to the tragic events of the past week. They also stand as final guards to the Magic Farm. I know the torches will soon burn out, and will not be able to guard the Magic Farm for long.

~ ~ ~

I'm back home now, alone. Though weary and emotionally wrought from a day of mourning, I have the urge to play Catherin's guitar. I open the case and pull out the instrument, holding it lovingly in my hands. It feels sad and strange to think that Catherin's hands had once held this neck, and strummed these strings.

I play a few instrumentals, finger-pick style, rambling through notes and chords. Though I'd played Catherin's guitar a few times, it seems to have a nice ring to it now, a resonance I don't remember it having before—almost like Catherin's spirit joining in …

I start playing a few fiddle tunes that I'd been practicing on guitar, but for that I really need a pick. I rummage through the case looking for one, and while doing so I find papers inside, mostly notes Catherin had made during band practices. But along with these notes is something else. Scrawled on a sheet of paper are the lyrics to the *Magic Farm* Catherin had recorded back in February, when I had played chords and sang words that came by free association. I had completely forgotten about these older lyrics when I finished the song the past Friday. One particular line sends me reeling:

Burning candles in the night

My God! How could I have forgotten this? Both Catherin and I had remarked at the time how spooky these words were, and how odd it was for me to come up with them. And now they have come true. I had felt a sense of loss when I blurted out those words back in February. Mercy would have it that I didn't know then, what that sense of loss was really for.

Another round of sadness washes over me. *She just can't be gone,* I say to myself. *She just can't.* I'm no longer in the mood to play guitar. I pack it away and get ready for bed. There, I toss and turn, wondering whether Catherin is still around somehow, as Arielle claims. Can she see me? Is she trying to communicate?

"Catherin, if you're still here, show me a sign. Give me some proof." I speak the words out loud and close my eyes to wait for sleep.

The next morning I rise and prepare for work, disappointed that no dreams of her have come in the night, and disappointed that no signs have presented themselves either. I grab a clean pair of pants from my dresser. Something falls out with them. It's a small, fuzzy wad of paper—like something you might find in the pocket of laundered jeans. Just as I'm about to toss the paper in the trash, I notice something odd. Printed on the paper's surface is one word:

"Proof."

Chapter 20.

These Tears Are Real

Sitting on the edge of the bed, I stare with disbelief at the wad of paper in my hand, the word "Proof" staring back. What to make of this? Was it just a coincidence that last night I had asked Catherin for a sign, for proof of her existence? And what to make of the candle lighting ceremony on the front steps of her house, and the torch-lit procession down to the Magic Farm? Had it been a premonition when I sang the words "burning candles in the night," a few months before?

The surreal events of the previous day swirl in my mind and leave me shaken. I'm in no condition to go into work. How can I concentrate on the mundane details of a job? I call in to say I'm taking the day off.

It turns out I'm in no condition to stay home either. I pace around the apartment, unsettled. I try walking the apartment grounds, following a circuit of sidewalks I sometimes use when I'm restless and need to think. I try going for a swim. Nothing works. I need to be around others that know what I'm going through. Someone like Catherin's sister Annette, it occurs to me. I believe she's still in town, so I call Larry and Amy's. Annette is at Catherin's house packing, they say. I decide to head over and help out.

~~~

Someone is saying hello to me from Catherin's sitting room, as I stand in the doorway. Someone whose voice and appearance are just enough like Catherin's that I do a double-take. It's Annette, of course. Their sisterly connection is definitely there: the same fair complexion, the same dark hair, the same speech patterns. It's both unnerving and comforting—another form of simultaneous opposites.

Catherin's things are strewn about in the sitting room as Annette sorts through them: knitting yarn, material, patterns, needles,
thread, books, notes, sheets of music, old guitar straps, and lots of
cassette tapes, some labeled, many not. What is it like, I wonder, to
have all of your personal things out on display, when you don't have
the ability to tidy them up?

I sort through Catherin's cassettes and find a few I'd like to keep,
including ones that appear to be interviews with her astrologer. I ask
Annette if I can have them, and she says yes.

Inside another box I find folders containing typed lyrics of songs
that Catherin had written. I hadn't seen these before, although come
to think of it, she had once mentioned them in passing. After reading through these lyrics, I'm amazed and saddened. Such song writing talent, now cut short. But I get the feeling Catherin would have
just as soon forgotten these songs, and the times they represented.

And what dark times these must have been. For the first time, I
see a glimpse of her innermost thoughts, her innermost turmoil, her
struggles to be free. I still don't know what her problems were, but
revealed was someone taking steps to be rid of them.

As depressed as it sounds like Catherin had been in the past, in
the last few weeks I knew her, she seemed happy. Not that everything was all roses, but she seemed more in control of herself. She
had found me, and I had found her. More importantly, Catherin had
found herself. Her delightful smile underneath the tree near Angel's
Landing in Zion National Park was the new Catherin, happy and
contented with life. I gathered from what her mother had said that
this was also the original Catherin, before whatever troubles had
befallen her.

I show the lyrics to Annette and ask, "Can I have these?"

Annette takes a quick glance and pauses without comment. I
think she is too overwhelmed to take in all they represent.

"I guess you can keep them," she finally says, "if you'll make copies for me. There are other things of Catherin's out in the garage that
you can look through. If you find anything else you'd like to have, let
me know."

"Thanks," I say.

I collect Catherin's songs into a spare folder. My tears are very
real when I realize I'll never hear the melodies to these lyrics:

These Tears Are Real

OK, it's time to face it
And stop running from yourself
OK, it's time to make it
Put bad habits on the shelf

Oh, the paranoia darkly looms
But it's only me who's out to get me
Oh, the tears cried at the moon
It's only me who can save me

> *Sing your heart out, these tears are real*
> *Show the world, just how you feel*
> *Sing your heart out, these tears are mine*
> *They were cried, for all mankind*

Now take a look inside
And see what you've become
There's a light and a dark side
Been that way since you were young

Ah, the sides both are strong
See they're tearing you apart
You'll find the answer in a song
But only when it's from the heart
Only when it's from the heart

> *Chorus*

OK, now that you've faced it
Stopped running from yourself
OK, now that you've made it
Put bad habits on the shelf

Now the songs flow easily
And they're coming from the heart
Now the love flows freely
Always been there from the start

> *I'm singing my heart out, those tears were real*
> *I show the world just how I feel*
> *Sing your heart out, your tears are mine*
> *(… 'I need a line!' she had written here …)*

> *— Catherin Delaney, 1984*

A Song for Myself

Let me out, a prisoner held
Within my soul, a lonely cell

Let me out, the sentence served
My term is up, the lesson learned

> *I'm bursting forth*
> *I'm bursting out*
> *So much to feel*
> *Pain? I'll do without*

> *I'm bursting out*
> *I'm bursting free*
> *One last chance*
> *His love to be*

I speak to myself from within
Allow the release of me from sin

They're bitter sweet—the tears I shed
It was sad yet lonely the road I tread

> *Chorus*

I'll face the pain, I'll face the fear
To be with the one, that I hold dear

I loved you then, I love you now
We'll be together, in a little while

> *Chorus*

I'll write my poems, till the tears begin
Then I'll get, to the core within

I'll sing my songs, till they're reconciled
The pains and sorrows, and heartaches mild

— Catherin Delaney, 1984

Let the Loving One Be

Why were you so angry
Why were you so sad?
Why did you feel as though
You would soon go mad?

It's time to leave that all behind
And to yourself be true and kind
And stop the battle to be free

    Be strong, control yourself
    Be strong, the power's there
    Be strong, let the loving one be

Why were you so lonely
Why were you so blue?
Why did you refuse to see
The answer lay within you?

Years of hiding your true self
Delayed the friendships and the wealth
And played havoc with your health

    Be strong, and be revealed
    Be strong, let past hurts heal
    Be strong, let the loving one be

Why were you a stranger
Why were you confused
Why did you ignore yourself
And let yourself be used

Sometimes in order to change
Your life you need to rearrange
And let the lifetime heartaches mend

    Be strong, you're older now
    Be strong, you're bolder now
    Be strong, let the loving one be

— *Catherin Delaney, 1984*

I go out to the garage to see what else I can find. I discover Catherin's camouflaged hip-pack, the one we had used on our first hike together in the Superstitions. I set it aside with a few other things, and then something in a box catches my eye. It's the framed picture showing a white dove flying through the clouds—the picture that had hung on the wall in the dining room. I can still remember sitting underneath it the first time I was in Catherin's house on New Year's Eve.

With excitement, I rush back into the kitchen where Annette is packing.

"Could I have this?" I ask, showing her the picture.

Annette takes a look and shakes her head. "No, I was going to keep that. The stuff in the box where that came from are things that were for me. Sorry, I forgot to mention that."

"Oh, I see."

Annette probably sees sadness and disappointment on my face. But she apparently misinterprets my reaction and doesn't understand the reason.

"I'm really sorry about what happened," says Annette, tears forming in her eyes. "You know I'll miss her too." She gives me a consoling hug, which feels very strange coming from a woman who looks and acts so much like Catherin herself.

There is weariness in Annette's eyes, a weariness that's a mixture of sadness, disbelief, and resignation. I had only known Catherin a few months. What is it like to lose a sister you've known all of your life?

Annette makes no subsequent offer to give me the picture. I don't press the issue. She is Catherin's sister after all, and has every right to Catherin's things. I take the picture to the garage and place it back in the box.

Annette moves to the rear of the house and into Catherin's closet in the master bedroom, where she begins packing Catherin's clothes. I follow to help. One by one, out come the dresses, skirts, and blouses that Catherin had worn, triggering a corresponding succession of memories: That one was the country-style outfit she had worn the first night we met at the Christmas party … that was the black dress she wore on New Year's Eve … that ugly pinkish purple dress was one she wore all of the time. It must have been her favorite. I never really liked it. The dress reminds me of the ugly pink apartments down the street. But that doesn't stop the memories of her wearing it from being bittersweet.

The closet is right next to the bathroom—the bathroom where unspeakable acts had occurred. And what about this closet? The police had told me they found a gun here, apparently Catherin's. I try to picture her with a gun and cannot. I don't understand why people feel the need to keep a gun in the house. Why live in fear like that? Does it really make you safer? Her gun had been of little use, hadn't it? She had absolutely no time to retrieve it, even if she had thought of it. And if her killer hadn't kept his own gun, might this whole tragedy been avoided in the first place?

My back is turned away from the master bathroom. An icy dread emanates from there: lingering effects of past violence that creep across the floor and tingle up my spine.

"It's time for me to go," I say to Annette with an involuntary shiver. "I don't think I can handle this anymore."

Annette looks up from sorting a pile of clothes. "I understand," she says. "I'm glad you came over even for a short while. It's really hard to go through this by myself."

"How long are you planning to stay in Phoenix?" I ask.

"I leave tomorrow."

"Well, I'm glad I got to meet you," I say. "Wish it were under different circumstances."

I receive one last mutually consoling hug from this woman who looks so much like the dark-haired, white mountain bike woman, and we say goodbye.

I take the belongings of Catherin I had chosen, but sadly, not the picture of the white dove, flying through the clouds.

~ ~ ~

In many ways, *Dusty River* was Catherin's band. She was the leader and main motivator—the 'boss lady.' It just wouldn't be the same without her. That's what we'uns guys concur at the next band meeting. The general consensus is to break up the band, and move on to other things—but not before one last performance, dedicated to Catherin, at the place it had all started: the coffeehouse. I make arrangements with the owner and we are penciled in to play the following Saturday.

There is one problem, though. What are we going to do without our main vocalist? Darrell is a good singer, but many of the band's songs centered around Catherin's vocal abilities. Who can take her place? Who will sing her harmonies?

I remember Catherin prompting me, somewhat unsuccessfully, to sing harmonies with her. There had only been one song that we sang together in public: *Columbus Stockade Blues*. The first time we had attempted that feat was on a cold and windy day in March at a park in central Phoenix. And someone else had been there, as I recall. Someone who had been taking voice lessons, and being Catherin's neighbor, often frequented our band practices: Cecilia.

We invite Cecilia to band rehearsal a few days later, and she does her best to recreate the melodies and harmonies that Catherin used to sing. But it's not the same, and that makes me sad, especially when we rehearse the harmonies on *Columbus Stockade Blues*. I know the comparisons between Cecilia's singing and Catherin's singing aren't fair, but I can't help making them. I'm starting to place Catherin on a pedestal in my mind, in a museum where only her talents, good looks, and newly found cheerfulness are presented. Her faults rest unnoticed in a hidden corner of this museum.

~ ~ ~

Saturday night comes. I drive to the coffeehouse and park under the grove of cottonwood trees. It wasn't that long ago that Catherin and I had been sitting in her car at this very spot, 'not seeing each other.' And back then, with the moon shining brightly through the trees, I had tried to convince her that "there ain't no moon in my Gemini," denying any ambivalence in feelings toward her.

There's no moon at all in the sky tonight, and one thing is for sure: I no longer have ambivalent feelings about Catherin, or whether I should have moved in with her, for whatever good that does now.

Before our band performs, I play a few songs in a solo tribute to Catherin. I choose my *Superstitions* song, the one I had sang to Catherin on the night we fell in love, and follow with the recently finished *Magic Farm* song.

I'm not the world's greatest singer, having limited range. Even so, I sing better than I ever have. I think using Catherin's guitar—the same guitar she strummed many times on this very stage—has something to do with it. And I swear her guitar now has an extra resonance, not unlike the haunting, sympathetic strings of a Norwegian hardingfele—haunting being the operative word.

~ ~ ~

I sleep late into the following afternoon. Memories of Catherin wake with me, as they often do these days. Rather than get up right away, I languish in bed, reliving those memories, trying in vain to make them real again.

That is basically all I do any more—that and listen to the tape of Laurie Lewis that had been the theme music on our Zion trip. The memories become ever more poignant as the days pass, and my sentimental feelings are augmented by the music as I indulge in heartbreak and self-pity under the influence of a moaning pedal steel and sweet and lyrical fiddling. Indeed, the memories of Catherin and the music on that tape are beginning to merge as one.

Rising out of bed, I fix supper. Tomorrow starts another work week; can I really face that? Work hadn't been very satisfying lately, and Catherin's death made it seem all the more irrelevant. A day off here or there isn't enough time to find my bearings. I need a couple of weeks, maybe more. And when I find said bearings, will I want the same job?

Chapter 21.
Nothing to Fear

Early June, 1987

Monday morning brings the blues. So does Tuesday, and Wednesday. Spending the days watching rabbits scamper around the chollas out the office window fails to lift my spirits. All it's doing is adding more distraction to my already distracted thoughts. The last thing on my mind is work.

I need to take action and ask for extended time off. I go to my boss's office with that purpose in mind, only to find he is out for a few hours. In the interim, I chat with a co-worker about my intentions and muse about other opportunities.

"What do you have in mind?" my co-worker asks.

"Well, I could reapply at Kitt Peak," I say. "But that would require moving to Tucson. So I don't really know."

"I'd hate to see you leave us," says my co-worker. "But if you want another job here in the valley, I know a company looking for a programmer. Do you know COBOL?"

I scrunch up my nose at the mention of COBOL. One of the earliest programming languages, COBOL is intended for business software on large mainframe computers—exactly the kind of programming I didn't like: the IBM-style, white shirt, black tie kind I envisioned when first learning I had to take computer classes in college.

"I'd *never* take a job that involves COBOL," I say to my co-worker. "Not my cup of tea."

"Okay, whatever," he says, shrugging. "Just thought I'd mention it to you."

"Thanks anyway," I say.

Later my boss Dean returns to his office. I knock on his door and he yells for me to come in. I sit across from him at his desk and announce my desire for time off.

"I perfectly understand your situation," he says. "It's hard to imagine what you must be going through. You certainly should take time off. How much are you talking about?"

"I don't know, at least several weeks, maybe a few months."

I wonder what he will say to that last suggestion. I surprise myself for even voicing it.

"A few months?" he asks. "You realize we can't afford to have you gone that long. That much time off might not be the best thing for you, anyway. I'd hate to see you lying around, wallowing in self-pity. Why not take off a week or two, or work part-time for a while?"

"Working part-time might be a good idea," I say. "But to be honest, I don't think the projects you have lined up for me are all that satisfying. I'm not sure this job is leading anywhere I want to go."

Dean leans over his desk. "Well, *that's* disappointing to hear. I specifically hired you to take over the programming that I myself have been doing. You don't want to do that anymore?"

"I'm not sure. I was thinking of re-applying for a job at Kitt Peak. Also, some friends are thinking of striking out on their own. That's beginning to appeal."

At this statement, Dean gets out of his chair and goes to stand by the window, looking out. "So you'd rather work for yourself?"

"Someday ... maybe now."

I can hardly believe this turn in the conversation. I am basically telling my boss I want to quit. I didn't expect that to happen so soon. Unwittingly, I seem to be following Catherin's advice: "Don't waste time!"

Dean returns to his desk, his face a shade of red. He smacks his fist down. "For Christ sakes! I can't believe this! That's what the last employee did. I spend time and money training him, and boom—he's out the door and off working for himself."

I hadn't seen this angrier side of my boss before. I'm taken aback, and realize here is another reason for leaving. Dean recomposes himself and sits back down. I remain passive. In my state of mind, with Catherin's death so close to my thoughts, there isn't much I'm afraid of.

"So are you really thinking of quitting?" Dean asks.

"Now that we've talked about it, yes. How about I give my two-week's notice today."

Dean shows initial shock, and then shrugs. "If that's what you want."

As he rises from his desk and shows me the door, Dean turns around and says, "You know, you can go off and work for yourself, but if you want my opinion, you are not being realistic. You are giving up a good stable job that's yours for the taking. I think someday, a two-by-four is going to come whack you on the head to let you know what a mistake you've made."

He says these words rather forcefully. I am shocked by the apparent anger he feels over my aspirations to work for myself. After all, he had started *his* own company. Why not me?

And what's this about a two-by-four? That wouldn't be the proverbial *cosmic* two-by-four would it? It's hard to imagine it could whack me any harder than it already has.

~ ~ ~

I spend my newly-found time off doing just what Dean was admonishing me not to do—wallowing in heartbreak and despair, pining away for a Catherin I could no longer have, and listening to the bluegrass album of Laurie Lewis. I listen only to that album. No other music will do.

I while away the hours trying to remember every detail about Catherin and our time together. I start a journal on my computer, thinking someday I will write a story about what happened. Despite this recapitulation, Catherin's face is fading from my vision. Frustrating though this is, at least I can look at the photos I have of her, even if they are frozen in time. The two photos from Zion see many tears. Good thing they are encased in clear plastic holders.

Also fading from my mind is Catherin's singing. I can still hear her, but I have to be in a quiet place, such as when I go hiking the following week with friends up in the Four Peaks Wilderness just east of Phoenix—the same area I had pointed out to Catherin only a few weeks before. During the hike, I lag behind the others on the steep, rocky trail, and stop to rest on a boulder. The day becomes still and my breath quiets. Catherin's singing comes to me—as though waiting for me to be still and listen.

~ ~ ~

Between bouts of self-pity and despair, I realize I *do* have to get on with my life. I hadn't really planned on quitting my job so soon. No other job prospects are in sight, and I have little money in savings. The thought makes me laugh. I never was one to plan things very well.

Even though I had told my now former boss I wanted to work for myself, I hadn't a clue how to go about it. I try applying for a job at Kitt Peak, but they have no immediate openings. So I turn my sights elsewhere.

I would love doing research, something that utilizes my training in artificial intelligence—something out of the ordinary. My former advisor at Arizona State comes to mind. He's always trying to get me to come back to school. I decide to phone him.

"It's funny you should call," he says after answering. "I was just talking about you."

"Should my ears be burning?" I ask.

"Quite the contrary. Somebody is looking for a programmer with your exact background. I mentioned you as a possibility."

"That's amazing," I say. "I was just calling about any work you might have at ASU. Research opportunities perhaps."

"Well, I don't have anything," he says. "But the guy I just talked to works for a small company in town. He could really use someone like you."

My advisor gives me the guy's phone number and says his name is Ray.

I interview with Ray the following week. He's an unusual guy: a member of the Karuk Indian Tribe, from southern Oregon. In talking with him, I find his views and mannerisms unconventional to say the least. Very smart, though—if a touch on the crazy side. But that's good. I had always told my friends I wanted to work for somebody smarter than me. The crazy part would just make it more interesting.

In Ray's description of the position, I see it's something I'm perfectly suited for, and is closely related to the subject I had researched for my master's thesis: using artificial intelligence techniques to analyze other computer programs. A large part of the job would be looking for patterns, something that has always intrigued me. What gargoyles might I find lurking in all that code?

As great as the job sounds, there is one catch. The programs to be analyzed are written in COBOL, even though I'd be using a different language to do analysis with. That's right, COBOL. Hadn't I told my former co-worker that I'd *never* work with COBOL? I should have known that by using the word *never*, it was almost a guarantee that I'd be doing just what I said I wouldn't.

Even so, it was the kind of job I had in mind when I finished graduate school. But never in my wildest dreams did I think such an opportunity existed in Phoenix. It wasn't in my realm of 'things that are possible,' and because of that, I hadn't looked for it. And here it was, popping out of nowhere.

I accept the job on one condition. I tell Ray my personal situation, and request six weeks to sort things out before starting work. He counters by saying I need to start within a month, but as a compromise, I can work part-time at first.

Now that my time off includes the security of a new job awaiting me, I can truly rest and reflect on my new direction in life—or so I think. As it happens, summer proves to be a busy time.

~ ~ ~

One day I get a call from Robyn, another fiddle player from the contra dance scene. I had gotten to know her better after Catherin's passing. She had been making it a point to check up on me, and we had played music together on occasion.

"Why don't you come over tomorrow and play some tunes?" asks Robyn. "Around five? Scooter has a new fiddle bow he'd like you to try. I'll fix supper as well."

"You make it hard to pass up," I say. "I'll be there."

Robyn was an art teacher, and besides playing guitar, fiddle, and piano, she liked to do pencil drawings and watercolors. She had her own pottery wheel and kiln out on the patio of her small duplex. Her friend Scooter was an old coot who played mostly southern old-timey fiddle tunes, and liked to do woodworking. He made his own fiddle bows, and from time to time I would try out his latest creations.

I arrive at Robyn's the next afternoon and knock on her screen door. The main door is open and I can see through the kitchen and out the open back door.

"I'm here on the patio," I hear Robyn yell.

I circle around the side of the house and crunch down the gravel walkway that leads to the back, where I find Robyn attending to pots she is getting ready to fire. She puts the pots down and comes over to give me a hug.

"It's good to see you, Bryan."

Robyn was an attractive, down to earth woman, with a light complexion and dark hair like Catherin's, but curlier. Since the time I first met Robyn, I had felt a strong connection with her, like we were old friends that had always known each other.

"Have a seat," offers Robyn, "and I'll make tea. I'll put soup on for supper as well."

She goes into the house while I relax in a rustic wooden chair, probably one that Scooter had made or restored. A warm but pleasant breeze drifts by, causing numerous wind chimes to tinkle and swirl. A dove coos off in the distance. Much like Jessie's place—and the Magic Farm—Robyn's home is an oasis of peace and tranquility, also situated not far from busy city streets. In fact, a towering twenty story office complex looms only blocks away.

Robyn returns with tea in speckled blue ceramic cups of her own creation. She sits next to me and hands me a cup.

"Where's Scooter?" I ask.

Robyn puts down her tea and waves a hand in dismissal. "Oh, he left this morning for North Carolina."

"North Carolina?"

"Yes," she says, with an annoyed look on her face. "He went to visit his son."

"How long is he going to be gone?"

"He wouldn't say. Maybe all summer. Says he wants to go to some festivals back there. He talked about the fiddle festival in Galax, Virginia. It's in August I think."

"But without you? All summer?"

Robyn doesn't look happy. She takes a quick sip of tea and replies, "Enough about me, what about you? How are you holding up?"

"I'm hanging in there. Not much I can do but go on." With that note I pause to take a sip from my cup. "Say, did I tell you I found a new job? It's another programming position. I start in July."

"A new job? I didn't know you quit the last one!"

"Yeah. And then I found a new one, just like that."

"Good for you," says Robyn.

"I quit the old one cold turkey. No backup plan."

"My goodness, weren't you afraid of not finding another job?"

"Not really," I say. "I'm sure Catherin's death had something to do with that. It made me realize how much time a person can waste. I wasn't happy at my last job, but if Catherin hadn't died, I probably would have worked there longer than I should have, too afraid to make the necessary changes."

"I'm struck by how calm you are about all this," says Robyn. "You seem to be handling things well."

"That's what another friend said. But I'm not so sure. You always hear that making abrupt changes in your life—like changing jobs or moving to another town—is a common reaction to grief, and not always a good one. Am I acting irrationally?"

"You can never know these things," says Robyn.

"What's amazing is how the new job fell into my lap," I say. "It's more in line with what I did for my master's thesis. I'll be analyzing other computer programs."

"I don't know how you can work on computers," says Robyn. "Seems so cold and rigid—so uncreative."

And Robyn is anything but cold, rigid, or uncreative. Scattered around her patio are stacks of cups, pots, and plates that she has made with her own hands. Strands of shiny beads and other trinkets adorn her kitchen window. Hanging from every vantage point are mobiles and wind chimes, handmade from glass, metal, and wood.

But software is handmade, too.

"People have so many misconceptions when it comes to programming," I tell Robyn. "I even used to. But writing software can be very creative—as creative as painting watercolors, or making pots. I treat it as an art form. It's just a different medium than what you are used to."

"I suppose so," replies Robyn. "Speaking of art, have you been playing your fiddle much?"

I shake my head no. "Just with you and Scooter. I know I should keep up the practice, but I don't feel motivated."

"Let me check on supper," says Robyn, rising to go into the house. She returns a short while later with an idea. "I know just the thing for you. Have you ever been to Port Townsend?"

"Port Townsend?"

"It's a town northwest of Seattle, on the Olympic Peninsula. They host the *American Fiddle Tunes Festival* the first week of July. I'm thinking of going. Why don't you come too? It would do you good."

A fiddle festival, in the Northwest, with Robyn? That has intriguing possibilities. But I have other plans that might get in the way.

"I'm supposed to go to the *Telluride Bluegrass Festival* next week," I say. "I already have tickets. When did you say the Port Townsend festival was?"

"First week of July," she says. "You'd have time for both."

"I really should go to Telluride," I say. "Catherin had purchased those tickets before she died. We were supposed to go together …"

My voice drops off on that last statement. My eyes moisten.

Robyn frowns and reaches over to comfort me, patting my shoulder.

"I know it must be hard," she says. "It's hard for me with Scooter gone."

"He's not going to Port Townsend with you?"

"I don't know. At first he said he would, and then he just ups and takes off, without saying when he'll be back."

"But at least you know he *can* come back," I say. "I have no such hope with Catherin."

Robyn doesn't seem to know what to say to that.

"The soup is probably ready," she says, rising again. "I'll bring the bowls out here. Meanwhile, think about my offer."

I'm going to the Telluride festival, no matter what. But Port Townsend too? Can I afford it? Then again, why worry about it?

Robyn comes back with soup, along with homemade bread. We dine quietly and engage in occasional small talk, enjoying each other's company. Wind chimes tinkle and whirl.

"So what do you think?" asks Robyn after we finish. "Will you go to Port Townsend with me?"

"What day were you planning on leaving?"

"I can't make it for the whole week of the festival," Robyn says. "I plan on flying to Seattle mid-week and then taking the ferry and bus to Port Townsend. Would that work for you?"

"Perhaps," I muse. "Yes, it could work. I'm going to Telluride for sure. Catherin would have wanted it that way. But why not Port Townsend too?"

~ ~ ~

The following day Alden calls me with another opportunity, asking if I'd like to go to an AI conference with him and Dr. Thomason.

"It's the third week of July, in Seattle," Alden says. "The three of us could stay at the same hotel and share a rental car."

"Seattle?" I reply. "That's funny, for I'm already going to be there the first week of July."

"Really?" asks Alden. "What for?"

"There's a fiddle festival up in that direction, in a town called Port Townsend."

"Well, there you go," says Alden. "You can do both. Be the first person to go to an AI conference *and* a fiddle festival!"

I laugh. "Why not? I have to start work the second week of July, but maybe my boss will let me take the following week off. I'm only going to be working part-time at first anyway."

We go over the particulars, and it dawns on me what I'm signing up for. In the next few weeks, I will be in Telluride, then Port Townsend via Seattle, and then Seattle again. Somehow in between I'm supposed to start a new job in Phoenix. One thing is for sure, I won't have a lot of time to lie around and mope.

~ ~ ~

She sits lovingly on my lap, wearing her favorite blue T-shirt. I'm so glad to see her, and tell her over and over that I love her. Her face has a look of serenity, but tinged with sadness, and then the scene shifts slightly and she now seems frustrated, almost angry. Catherin asks me where the pictures are. I can't figure out what she is talking about. What pictures? Then I remember the ones I had placed around the cottonwood tree at the Magic Farm, the day of her funeral. Those pictures? Have they blown away in the wind?

The scene shifts again. Catherin is lying next to me. I can feel her physical presence. She is whispering in my ear, trying to tell me something. But it's in a language I can't understand. It reminds me of my conversations with the thunderheads at Roosevelt Lake, that summer evening, long ago.

"Don't forget the perfume?" I ask, trying to parse the words. "That doesn't make any sense."

Catherin repeats the message several times. I try to understand but cannot. Vibrations start in the back of my head. These vibrations aren't unfamiliar to me; I've experienced them before. They usually occur in that nether world between being asleep and being awake. And somehow, a part of me knows I'm not really awake.

Scientists say these vibrations are the result of the brain shutting down muscle control, in a form of paralysis, readying the body for sleep. Things go haywire when you don't actually go to sleep. You are still aware of your surroundings, but if you try to move, you are shocked to find you can't. That's when the tremors start.

Others who aren't so averse to more esoteric explanations might say I'm having the start of an out-of-body experience, where the soul leaves the body and moves around in the astral plane. I've never had a full-fledged out-of-body experience before, but I have the intuition I've come close a few times. Nothing I can say conclusively, just a feeling.

I'm having those feelings now. These vibrations used to frighten me, for they often come with vivid images and intense, almost violent emotions, like sparks going off—as though something is about to snap. But now, I want them to last. I somehow know that being in this state is a way to stay in contact with Catherin, something I desperately want to do.

No sooner am I aware of these vibrations, they stop. I can't get them to come back. The dream fades, and I wake up elated, sad, unnerved.

Chapter 22.
No One to Cry To

Route 666, deep in the heart of Navajo country, is not a good place for your vehicle to break down. This is especially true during the heat of summer. That's why the squeaking noise coming from my truck has me worried. Gallup, New Mexico, is thirty miles back; Shiprock a 'mere' sixty miles up the road—the closest thing to civilization in the direction I'm going, and it's not much.

Pulsating sounds of drumming and chanting blare from the radio. I had tuned to a Navajo station after leaving Gallup, something I always do when in this territory—just for fun and novelty. But the drums and chants, which had masked the squeaking noise at first, are now adding to my trepidation. The last time this white man was on a reservation, things hadn't turned out so well.

I turn off the radio and slow down to pull off the road, rolling to a stop. The squeaking noise stops too. I kill the engine. Sitting uneasily for a moment, I take a deep breath and climb out of the pickup to look for the source of trouble.

No clues are found when I inspect the wheels and search under the hood. The belts are tight, showing only moderate signs of wear. No pulleys seem out of kilter and all fluid levels are normal. If I turn the engine back on, I surmise, maybe the sound will return. I straighten up, only to bang my head on the hood, causing me to swear under my breath and rub a sore head while I return to the cab and start the engine. Back under the hood, I listen for any abnormal sounds. But everything seems fine.

Avoiding the hood this time, I straighten up again and survey the situation: nothing but hot desolation for miles around. You know, I could have made this trip to the *Telluride Bluegrass Festival* with Darrell, for he had offered to give me a ride, but noooo! I just had to go it alone.

Turning down Darrell seemed like a good idea at the time. He had wanted to take side trips on the way to Colorado: camping at the Grand Canyon and Canyon de Chelly—both excellent places to visit. But the thought of spending quiet days in the outdoors without female companionship, and in particular, without Catherin, was too much to bear. I was sure all I would think about was that special weekend in Zion.

So I had determined the best way to travel was by myself. That would give me time to reflect on all that's happened. I wouldn't be under pressure to act normal. I could cry if I wanted to.

I slam the hood shut and climb back in the pickup, turning off the engine again to ponder my situation. Without the A/C on, a stifling heat spreads through the cab. It's time to act, but what to do? Should I press further along this desolate highway, with no prospect of a decent sized town for many miles, or go back to Gallup and find a service station?

"Ain't no moon in my Gemini," I once said to Catherin, underneath the moon outside the coffeehouse, denying my inability to make decisions. Back then it had been about moving in with her. She might still be alive, had I just gone for it.

I decide to go for it now—just move on down the road, see what happens. I turn the key and start the motor. So far, so good—no worrisome noise. I put the truck in gear and start down the highway. But to my consternation, the noise comes back, rising in frequency the faster I drive. This time though, I can tell the sound is coming from the dash. Of course—it is nothing more than the speedometer cable. I should have thought of that earlier.

This source of noise is mostly harmless, I think. But I still feel uneasy. Though I have always been lucky in life, I certainly hold no claim to that now. I drive along in tense silence and then start humming a tune to ease my apprehension.

A few minutes go by before I realize the tune I'm humming: it's the old western classic, *No One to Cry To*—a song Catherin had wanted to incorporate into our band's repertoire. She had prompted me to sing the harmony part, but I never practiced it much. How ironic for me to be humming the melody now.

Catherin's singing soon comes to the fore; her own rendition of *No One to Cry To* reverberating through the lonely, sentimental places of my soul. Those reverberations, once strong and clear in my mind, have grown ever fainter.

I once heard it said that when someone dies, it's like the fading, reverberating tones of a bell. The tones represent the way a person affects the world during life—wave upon wave of interaction. These tones are the song the person's soul sings into the world. And when that person dies, the song begins to fade, just like the shimmering tones of a bell after being struck. Just like Catherin's singing now.

With tears I turn to look at the empty passenger seat of my pickup, where Catherin should have been. There had been so much promise. Telluride was supposed to have been such a wonderful time. How could all of this have happened?

As I turn my teary gaze back to the road, something flickers in my peripheral vision, causing me to glance out the left window. A white dove is flying beside my pickup. It stays with me for a short distance and then veers off towards the west, with the harsh, burnt-looking mountains on the horizon providing a simmering, desolate backdrop.

What is a white dove doing out here in the middle of the desert, on a hot summer day? It sure has picked an opportune moment to fly by, right at a very low point in my feelings. Is Catherin somehow involved with this? Is she giving me a sign, like the wad of paper with the word "Proof" printed on it? Or is the dove Catherin's spirit flying beside me, reminding me that I'm not really alone?

Whatever the case, I feel my own spirit lift like a dove's wings on the wind, and I drive with a bit more enthusiasm towards Colorado.

~ ~ ~

I climb out of the pickup, arching my back and stretching my legs. It has taken ten hours to reach the town of Telluride. Except for the speedometer cable incident and one gas break, I have driven non-stop, much of the time in scorching desert summer heat. But at nine thousand feet, the streets of Telluride are rather chilly, and the late afternoon sun provides little warmth, blocked by mountains far to the west. I don my jacket and start down the street past rows of Victorian-style houses.

Telluride used to be a small mining town, but now relies mostly on skiing and tourism. Festivals like this one, with ten thousand concert-goers, are what keep towns like Telluride alive during the summer, after the revenues from skiing melt with the spring runoff.

Tall, majestic mountains guard the town on three sides; only the west entrance provides easy access to the valley. At the east end, a steep jeep trail makes its way up a winding, narrow incline, towards a waterfall known as Bridal Veil Falls. Just before the trail begins is the town park, where the bluegrass festival is being held. I have luckily parked my truck only a few blocks from the festival grounds, and part of the crowd of ten thousand is milling around in the streets.

I'll never find Darrell in all this, I say to myself, taking a few steps down the street—only to have someone walk up and say, "It's about time you showed up."

"Well, I'll be damned," I say, after recognizing Darrell with his crew cut and thick, black, square-rimmed glasses. "I was just looking for you."

"Well, you found me," he says, laughing. "How long you been here?"

"I just pulled in. With this huge crowd, I'm surprised I found a place to park."

"And right near my truck, no less," says Darrell, pointing out his camper a few spaces down.

I laugh. "That's amazing. Guess I didn't see your Arizona plates. Did you get a hotel room as planned?"

"Yes, but I wasn't sure you were actually coming, so I only registered myself at the hotel. Saved a few bucks that way. Hope you don't mind not having a key."

"Shouldn't be a problem," I say.

~ ~ ~

The weather for the festival is perfect, with sunny days and crystal clear nights. Accompanying the perfect weather and incredible views is the most amazing outdoor sound system I have ever heard. No matter where you sit, the sound has a clarity that matches the clear mountain air, virtually free of echoey muddiness. The sound quality is rivaled only by the quality of the main acts lined up for this festival. Many top-name bluegrass stars are headlined: New Grass Revival, Tony Rice, Sam Bush, Doc Watson, and my favorites— Tim O'Brien, his band *Hot Rize*, and fiddler extraordinaire, Mark

O'Connor. Their collective talents lead to many inspirational performances.

All of this is tempered, however, by the loss of Catherin. What bittersweet fate would have it that she couldn't be here to share the incredible music, scenery, and weather.

During the festival a series of workshops are held. I attend one hosted by none other than the *Riders in the Sky*, and am fortunate to find a seat in their packed workshop. Entertainers par excellence, they put on a humorous and informative show. During the workshop, I even have the opportunity to ask them a question about fiddle bowing styles.

It's strange how their music seems wrapped up in the tragic events of my life. First the almost fatal car accident on the Gila Indian Reservation, and then Catherin's death. During both times I had been listening to the *Riders in the Sky*. It's all just coincidence, right?

~ ~ ~

On stage, Tony Rice, master bluegrass guitar picker, is cranking out notes in rapid succession, never once making a mistake—at least none my ears can detect. The sun feels hot on my shoulders, but it's nothing like the summer heat of Arizona. Nevertheless, skin can burn quickly at this altitude, so I apply another coat of sun block. I'm sitting by myself, watching bands play and enjoying the beautiful scenery of the San Juan Mountains surrounding the festival grounds.

With a large afternoon crowd in attendance, a constant stream of people go up and down the aisles. Most are paired in couples; each woman holding on to her man. It seems everyone has someone special of their own. Everyone except me.

Is this the way it's going to be, I wonder? A few brief moments in the sunny climes of female companionship and then back to the interminable gray skies of loneliness? When I found Catherin, I felt certain my lonely, gray, and cloudy days were over. Boy had I been wrong.

Just as I think this, two friendly looking gals take seats in front of me. One is a tall blonde; the other, shorter and brunette. I keep my eye on them while several bands play, and observe that no one else comes to sit with them. From time to time, they turn sideways, chatting with each other, and the blonde occasionally steals glances in my direction.

At one point, the brunette leaves, and the blonde turns completely around, apparently wanting someone else to talk to.

"Have you been to this festival before?" she asks.

I stumble for a moment—but only for a moment.

"This is my first time," I say.

"We come here every year we can," she says. "Where are you from?"

"Phoenix."

"Wow, you came all the way from Phoenix?"

I nod yes. "And you?"

"We're from Fort Collins … north of Denver?"

"Yes, I know where Fort Collins is."

"I see," says the blonde. "A world traveler."

I laugh. "Not exactly. I grew up in western Nebraska, so I know the towns of eastern Colorado quite well."

"My name is Jean by the way," she says, offering her hand.

"Bryan," I say, reciprocating.

"You here by yourself?" asks Jean.

"Yes and no. A friend is here too."

Jean flashes a look of puzzlement.

"We drove up separately," I say. "He's attending a mandolin workshop right now. We used to be in a bluegrass band together."

Jean's face brightens. "You're musicians?"

"In theory," I say with a smile. "I play fiddle."

"A fiddle player," says Jean, eyes widening with interest. "So you don't have a band anymore? What happened?"

Oh-oh. Now I've done it. Now I'll have to explain why our band broke up—that it was due to Catherin's passing. It's not that I don't want to talk about her; I very much do. It's a way of keeping part of her alive. But telling her story will invariably bring sympathy. However well-intentioned, I'm growing weary of such sympathy—and its accompanying gloominess. Still, bringing up Catherin is one way to keep the conversation going.

"It's a long story," I say to Jean. "The leader of our band passed away last month."

"I'm so sorry," she says.

"She was my girlfriend, you see."

"That's so awful!"

Jean reaches out to touch my shoulder in sympathy, her hand lingering. A gloomy conversation follows, as expected, but I try to switch to lighter topics. I get my chance when another band takes the stage. It just happens to be *Hot Rize*.

"Are you enjoying the music?" I ask Jean.

"Yes," she says. "*Hot Rize* is my favorite band."

"No kidding," I say. "They are mine too."

"I like them because they are from my neck of the woods," says Jean. "From a town near Fort Collins."

At that moment, the brunette returns and sits down. Jean introduces her as Joan.

I shake Joan's hand and say to them both, "Jean and Joan ... You're not sisters are you?"

They laugh and say no, and then Jean asks, "Will your friend be joining you?"

"Anytime now."

"Well, when he arrives, why don't the two of you sit with us?"

"Sure," I say, moving up to their row. "Thanks."

Just like that, I have picked up not one woman, but two. Or did they pick me up? Either way, it seems my luck is changing.

Darrell appears a short while later. Introductions are made and we settle into chairs next to the two women. At one point Darrell glances over to me, his face a look of gratefulness.

Later on, Jean and Joan leave to get something to eat—assuring us they will be back.

"Good job in finding us gals to hang with," says Darrell after they're gone.

"Well, you owe me," I say, in a teasing voice.

We spend the rest of the day—and most of the next—with Jean and Joan. As the festival wears on, I can tell Jean is attracted to me, and by the closing concert on Saturday night she manages to move quite close, holding my arm and snuggling up against me as protection from the increasingly chilly air.

Darrell keeps two army blankets in his camper, he tells us, which he subsequently fetches. I do the math: two blankets and four people. We'll have to pair off into couples. How convenient. I pair-off with Jean, and Darrell with Joan. Jean huddles close underneath the blanket, and soon has her arms completely around me.

Jean's embrace feels bittersweet and awkward. I had grown so used to Catherin's touch. Jean's touch is foreign, and somehow lacking. Even though she has decent looks and seems like a nice gal, I don't feel a strong attraction to her. She is no match for Catherin. No woman could be, for by this time, Catherin has taken on legendary status in my mind. The lamentable irony is not lost on me that when we were together, I often compared her to other women—you know, the 'pasture is greener on the other side' syndrome. Moon in Gemini indeed.

The awkwardness of Jean's arms around me is countered by a most incredible concert. It's an 'All-star Jam' with all the top stars on stage at once, including my favorites, Tim O'Brien and Mark O'Connor. We are lucky to have seats fairly close to the front, and enjoy a dazzling performance. We hear a blizzard of notes, each impeccably timed and impeccably played.

When the concert ends, the four of us ramble downtown to check out the nightlife of Telluride. After a few drinks at a bar, Joan announces she is tired, and Darrell offers to accompany her back to her room. Either Joan is truly tired, or they are off on a secret rendezvous. This leaves me alone with Jean and we end up staying till closing time, engaging in small talk. I'm not nervous like I used to be in situations like this: going out on the town with a nice looking woman—single no less.

I accompany Jean back to her room. At the door she turns around with a look of anticipation, which is quickly followed by disappointment, for I politely give her a hug and say goodnight. I'm not ready for whatever going inside might entail.

Returning to my hotel, I climb the stairs to the second floor and reach the room where Darrell and I are staying, only to discover the door is locked. I search my pockets momentarily for a key, before remembering I don't have one. I pound on the door. No answer. I pound again and yell Darrell's name. Same result. Why doesn't he hear me? Is he even inside? Or is he in there with Joan? Or maybe, he's over at Jean and Joan's hotel. I never did actually go into their room, come to think of it.

I keep pounding and calling out Darrell's name, waking up everyone else on the floor except Darrell, it seems. Several guests poke their heads out of their room with looks of annoyance. I pound one last time before giving up.

I'm in a real dilemma. I could try to get a key from the night manager, but that would be awkward, for officially, I'm not supposed to be staying here. I'm left with two choices: either spend the night in my pickup, or go back to Jean's hotel and ask to stay the night. That last option is also awkward. She might take my request all wrong.

I step out of the hotel and into the night, closing my jacket tighter. The day had been pleasantly warm, almost hot in the high altitude sun. Now a chilly, penetrating air descends on the streets. I reach my pickup a few blocks away and climb in front. Regrettably, my sleeping bag is locked in the hotel room. All I have for warmth is a tattered down coat and a few towels. I cover myself as much as possible.

Sleeping up front proves uncomfortable. The steering wheel is in the way, and there's no place to lay my head. But that's better than trying to sleep on the hard floor of the truck bed. Then I remember there's a small foam rubber pad stowed back there—a pad Catherin had used in her massage business. I retrieve the pad, and after moving back up front, I roll it up as a makeshift pillow.

That foam pad isn't the only thing of Catherin's I have with me. Her water bottles and backpack also made the trip. So too the desert-camouflaged hip pack from our hike in the Superstitions. Tears well up as I remember that first hike together: the two of us sitting on a boulder, facing southwest, soaking up the timeless silence in view of haloed, backlit saguaros.

Having material things of Catherin's are no replacement for her. Instead of having a wonderful, romantic time, I have a cold and lonely night cramped in the front of a pickup. I sleep very little, waking up every fifteen minutes or so to get in another round of shivering.

There is no one to cry to.

Chapter 23.
A Time For Healing

My eyes open from the glare of sunlight reflecting off the dashboard of the pickup. The long cold night is finally over. I push aside the towels that served as blankets, and climb out into the crisp morning air, stretching my cramped legs and rambling down the street to a local bakery where the four of us had pre-arranged to meet for breakfast. None of the others had yet arrived. Hungry and cold to the core, I order hot chocolate and a breakfast burrito and shiver my way to an empty table. The hot meal goes a long ways in lifting my mood. I'm in much better spirits by the time the door bell jingles and Darrell walks in. He finds my table and pulls up a chair.

"Where were you last night?" he asks as he sits down.

"Camped out in my pickup, freezing my ass off."

I scowl at my cup of hot chocolate with fake anger. Earlier I had decided to read Darrell the riot act, just for fun. In truth, it no longer mattered I had been locked out the previous night. That was over and done with.

"You slept in your pickup?" asks Darrell.

"No thanks to you," I say, with a mocking pout.

"Why didn't you—of course! You didn't have a key!"

"And my sleeping bag and most of my warm clothes were in your room. I pounded on your door for what seemed like hours."

"I'm sorry. I didn't hear a thing. Honest!"

"It's okay," I say, my pretend anger dissipating with a smile. I raise my eyebrows and say in a teasing voice, "I just figured you had Joan in there with you."

"Don't I wish," says Darrell with a wistful sigh. "But no such luck. I must have been deep asleep."

"Well, some friend you are. The least you could have done is look out for me—especially after I picked up the two gals. You owe me, remember?"

"Believe me, I'm grateful," says Darrell.

"I'm glad you feel that way," I say, slurping the last of my drink, and then holding it out to him with a smile. "That means you won't mind getting me another cup."

Darrell rolls his eyes and laughs, then gets up to buy another hot chocolate and to order his own breakfast. Another jingle of the doorbell signals the arrival of Jean and Joan. They find their way to our table and pull off their coats and sit down. While waiting for Darrell to return, I repeat the story of being stuck in my pickup the night before, emphasizing how cold and lonely it was.

"You should have come back to our hotel," says Jean. "I'm sure we could have found room for you."

Darrell rejoins us in time to hear that last comment. "I'll bet you could have," he says to the girls, eyebrows rising.

The three of them share looks of amusement. I'm not sure how to respond, and simply smile too.

Jean had made her comments matter-of-factly, though I thought I heard a trace of surprising flirtatiousness in her voice—surprising because I'm sure I disappointed her the night before. Maybe she decided I had been acting a gentleman, and maybe there *was* something to her suggestive voice. Not that it matters, really, for I have no intention of starting anything.

After we finish breakfast, we hug goodbyes and go our separate ways. Darrell is going to spend a few more days camping, Jean and Joan are driving back to Fort Collins, and I am headed straight home to Phoenix. Jean and I exchange addresses and phone numbers and promise to keep in touch, but I know deep down it won't lead anywhere. There is too much distance between Fort Collins and Phoenix, and for me, there isn't yet enough distance from my days with Catherin.

I drive south out of Telluride, climbing up Lizard Head Pass, past rugged peaks, jeweled lakes, and large stands of white-barked, shimmering aspens that have spread up the staggering inclines. This is one of the prettiest areas of Colorado—at least my eyes tell me so—but my heart can feel none of it. Now that the festival is over, my only thoughts are that Catherin hadn't been able to share this great time with me. My spirits, which had lifted momentarily over breakfast, now sink to their newly customary low level. I find I have no tears. I'm numb inside.

Perhaps if I stayed longer, I could once more embrace the beauty of the mountains. I do have all my camping gear with me. I could even camp with Darrell. But no, I need to get back and take care of Bubba and Mrs. Bubba, and their new baby. He had fallen hard out of the nest a few weeks ago, hurting a leg. I had thus dubbed him Hopalong Cassidy. Even though they have enough food and water for a few more days, I'm sure the doves are getting lonely.

I take a different route back to Phoenix, traveling west through the Four Corners area instead of south to Gallup; driving through wild and lonesome Monument Valley country and on to Kayenta and Tuba City. Besides the squeaky speedometer cable, my only entertainment is the drone of pickup tires and a blizzard of fiddle tunes from the festival that swirl in my head. After many hours, I come to the Highway 89 junction and turn south towards Flagstaff. A sign announcing the turnoff to the Grand Canyon soon comes into view.

The Grand Canyon! Even though Zion now holds a special place in my heart, my favorite place of all is the Grand Canyon. A thunderstorm is brewing in the late afternoon sky—an ideal time to visit the canyon. From memories of previous trips, I imagine the sight of lightning flashing from above *and* below, the sound of thunder rolling across the vast network of side canyons, and afterwards, the juxtaposition of an elusive misty rainbow framing the glowing canyon sandstone. It seems like a detour is in order.

Decision made, I give up on my plan to drive straight to Phoenix, and head for the east rim of the Canyon instead, figuring to spend the night in the park's campground. I reach my favorite lookout, Lipan Point, and stop to watch the thunderstorms roll through the park, with the Colorado River coursing westward way down below.

Layers and layers of differing geological formations make up the Grand Canyon. They remind me of the layers of memories we each store in our minds. I have no memory of being at the canyon with Catherin, for we never came here together. And I'd just as soon not add the new layer that reality has provided. May floods of forgetfulness wash that layer away.

Nothing much happens with the afternoon storm—or at least, my dulled spirits can't appreciate it—and when darkness comes, I change my plans again and turn around to head out of the park.

It's over two hundred miles back to Phoenix, all of it night driving. But that's the way I like traveling—just rambling and changing directions on a whim, driving long distances even when it makes no sense. It's good to be able to do that again, but not so good given the reasons why. Though the thought makes me sad, I have no tears. I seem to be running out of them.

~ ~ ~

Robyn calls me the day after I return to Phoenix. "How was Telluride?" she asks.

"Absolutely incredible," I say. "The best live music I've ever heard. If that doesn't motivate me to keep playing, I don't know what will. And to think I'm going to attend another music festival next week."

"So you're still going with me?"

"Funny you should ask, but this morning I wasn't so sure."

"Oh, why not?"

"Well, taking two trips to Seattle was beginning to seem a little foolish. I wasn't sure I could afford to be flying off every other weekend. Not with my job situation still a bit shaky."

"Two trips?"

"Maybe I forgot to tell you; I'm attending a computer conference with friends the third week of July. The conference is in Seattle too."

"That's amazing! But why not stay in Seattle in between?"

"I have to start my new job the second week of July—at least I promised my new boss I would. Anyway, I started wondering how much sense it made to buy two roundtrip tickets to Seattle, not to mention all the other travel expenses. My bank account was starting to look a bit precarious. But guess what? I balanced my checkbook this morning, and discovered I had missed recording two paychecks, so now it's no problem at all."

"Talk about luck!" says Robyn. "It's almost like somebody is looking out for you."

"Sure seems that way. First, I'm given a job with barely any effort on my part, and then receive money in my bank account, just when I need it."

"Maybe you are doing just what you're supposed to."

"Maybe so."

"Bryan, the reason I called was to ask if you'd like to go to Victoria after the fiddle festival."

"Victoria?"

"You know, the capital of British Columbia? It's across the water from Port Townsend, on Vancouver Island. Victoria has great museums and wonderful flower gardens and beautiful scenery, at least, that's what I've been told. I've always wanted to go there. What do you think?"

"Would we have time?" I ask. "How would we get there?"

"We'll have two days before our flight back to Phoenix. There's a ferry ride to Victoria from Port Angeles, which is maybe forty miles west of Port Townsend. We could take the ferry on Sunday morning, stay in Victoria that night, and then take another ferry straight back to Seattle the following afternoon."

"I've never been on a ferry," I say. "Let alone multiple times on the same trip. It'll be a new adventure!"

"I'll take that as a yes," says Robyn. "Let's plan on it."

"I'm glad it's you who's doing the planning. I'll be happy to just tag along, and do whatever you'd like to do."

"Well, I'll be glad to have the company."

After the phone call, I reflect on my relationship with Robyn. She is attractive and creative, and here I am, gallivanting off to Seattle and other ports of call with her. Is something going to come of that? One never knows these things, but there is Scooter, missing though he is. And of course, there is Catherin. So close, yet so far away. So very far away.

~ ~ ~

On the first of July Alden drops me off at Sky Harbor Airport, and I search inside the terminal for Robyn. She's not hard to find, wearing a white cotton blouse and a patterned red skirt, fashioned in an old-timey, casual style that is popular with many contra dancers. I join her in the ticket line and say hello.

"It's good to see you," says Robyn, putting down her bags and giving me a hug. She stands back and surveys my belongings. Like her, I have a backpack, fiddle, and another carry-on bag. "Good idea bringing your backpack," she says. "I meant to suggest that to you earlier. It'll make it easier to get around."

"That's what I figured, with all the different kinds of traveling we're doing—bus, ferry, plane. Makes my head spin."

"So you're ready for an adventure?"

"My fiddle's ready," I say. "But the rest of me is still trying to catch up."

I can scarcely believe I'm going on this trip with Robyn. It's not every day I travel with a female companion. In fact, I can think of only one other time by plane, and that was with Catherin on our trip to San Diego. I never thought that a few months later I'd be flying off to Seattle with someone else. But Robyn is friendly and cheerful, and traveling with her is going to be a pleasant experience. I'm sure it will help soothe my shattered soul.

We board our red-eye flight to Seattle, which includes a layover in Las Vegas. Our plane lands in Las Vegas around eleven. The continuing flight to Seattle isn't scheduled for departure till two in the morning, implying a three hour wait at the airport.

Ordinarily, the late hour and the constant background noise from the concourse would have lulled me to sleep, but I am too psyched about the upcoming trip. Every so often, another jet takes off, the roar of engines announcing a departure to another exotic destination. Eventually I know we'll be on one of those planes. I just wish the time would hurry up. I'm restless, shifting from side to side in my chair, never getting comfortable. Robyn seems to notice.

"Let's get our fiddles out and play a few tunes," she suggests. "It'll help pass the time."

"I guess we could," I say, looking around. "I don't think I've ever played inside an airport before. Do you think people will mind?"

It's midnight, and the fact our flight doesn't leave for another two hours means there are few passengers at our gate. And they all appear to be sleeping. I suggest we find another spot. We gather our belongings and settle down at an empty gate nearby. From there, the noise from arriving and departing jets will surely provide enough cover for our playing.

We play a few standard tunes to warm up, one of which is *Arkansas Traveler*. A mother and daughter happen by and stop to listen. The little girl giggles and says, "Look mom, they're playing the *Bumble Bee* song."

I start another round of the tune while Robyn pauses to ask the girl, "Do you know the words?"

"Yes," she says proudly, dancing around in circles and breathlessly singing: "I'm bringing home a baby bumble bee, won't my mommy be so proud of me!"

When I finish playing we cheer and clap for the girl. She leaves with her mother and I comment to Robyn, "You know, *Arkansas Traveler* was one of the first fiddle tunes I ever learned. I remember picking up the notes right away, like I had always known the melody. Now I know why. I *had* always known it. I probably learned the *Bumble Bee* song when I was her age."

"You didn't know they were the same tune?" asks Robyn.

"I never realized it until now. I wonder, how many fiddle tunes did I hear growing up that I've forgotten about? Could it be when we learn something that comes to us naturally, we aren't so much learning, as remembering? And is it possible I know these tunes from a previous life?"

"Sometimes I think I was a potter in a past life," says Robyn. "And I get strong feelings that I lived long ago along the Arizona Strip, with a Native American tribe."

The *Arizona Strip* is the land that lies between the Grand Canyon to the south, and Zion and Bryce National Parks to the north. It's a wild, scenic country of red soil, buttes, and cliffs.

"I've always loved that country," I say. "Have since the first time I laid eyes on it. You know, we must have known each other before. Being around you feels so familiar and natural. Maybe I lived with that same tribe on the Arizona Strip."

"You think so?"

I shrug. "Makes a person wonder."

"Let's play one last tune," says Robyn. "Are there any waltzes you want to play?"

I think momentarily and say, "Yes, there is one. But I don't know how to play it and can't remember its name right now. Perhaps you do."

On my fiddle I scratch out the few notes I can remember, and fortunately it's enough for Robyn to recognize.

"That's *Midnight on the Water*," she says.

Robyn plays the tune for me and I am transported back to the first time I took Catherin to a contra dance. We had waltzed to this very tune. At the time, I had promised Catherin I would learn *Midnight on the Water* for her, but never did get around to it.

"You'll have to teach me that waltz," I say, stifling a yawn. "But not now. I think I'm sufficiently sleepy to zone out until our flight leaves."

~ ~ ~

The plane lifts off on schedule and we land in Seattle at four-thirty in the morning. We catch a city bus to downtown, then board a Greyhound that takes us to the ferry station. The ferry transports us across the Puget Sound, and after landing on Bainbridge Island, we catch yet another bus around the northeastern side of the Olympic Peninsula, through deep evergreen forests shrouded in drizzle. The forest occasionally opens to dramatic views of the Puget Sound.

I'm exhausted by the late-night traveling, my eyes engaged in constant struggle, wanting to close due to sleepiness, yet trying to stay open for all the new sights. Both of us are absorbed in our own groggy—and as it turns out—mutually gloomy thoughts. As the bus rounds a curve we hit a rough spot, and I bump and sway into Robyn, rubbing shoulders with her. I look over to apologize, and notice her moist eyes.

"You okay?" I ask.

"I'm alright," she says, though her brooding look says otherwise. "Scooter?"

Robyn nods. "He really should be here. And not knowing exactly what he's up to, or when I'll see him again, isn't helping matters."

"I can certainly empathize with your situation. But at least you know he can come back. He's still alive."

"I know," says Robyn. "But it doesn't make it any easier."

I instinctively reach over to give Robyn a sympathetic pat on the thigh. Being in such close proximity to her causes pleasant, yet unsettling stirrings. It seems wrong to entertain any such feelings, especially in light of our current discussion. I move my hands to my lap, acutely aware though, of Robyn's shoulder next to mine. It's a moment of private awkwardness and confusion for me.

We are both quiet as the rain intensifies, pattering against the windows of the bus. Rain, fog, and gloom. Will sunny skies return? Will love ever find me again?

A while later Robyn says to me, "I think it's remarkable how well you are coping. You always seem to be on an even keel."

"You've said that to me before," I say. "And maybe it looks that way from the outside. But to tell you the truth, I mostly feel numb. Well, that's not entirely true. I seem to have developed a strong sense of empathy. Whenever I encounter the scene of an accident, for example, I become overwhelmed with empathy for the victims. But that's for others. I have no tears left for myself."

"You are probably in shock, or in a state of depression," says Robyn. "Just give it time. You'll be fine, I'm sure."

"It would be nice to have the tears back," I say. "I don't feel normal without them—like I'm not human."

I settle back into my seat and in the process move away from Robyn. Our shoulders no longer touch. I wish they still did.

"They say there are five stages of grief," says Robyn, interrupting my mixed up thoughts and feelings. "Do you know them?"

I recount the stages of grief: denial, anger, bargaining, depression, and acceptance.

"I've had some of these," I say. "I think my denial stage lasted all of thirty minutes—the time it took to see the yellow police ribbons around Catherin's house. Or perhaps it was seeing them bring her body out on a stretcher, covered in red cloth. That certainly did the trick. But I don't understand the purpose of bargaining. It seems pointless. And the anger stage? I've had little of that."

"You haven't been angry about what happened?"

"Only once, for a short time."

I tell Robyn the story of knocking the photo of the killer to the floor.

"That's it, that's been the sum total of my anger. You know, before then it never occurred to me to even *be* angry. Is something wrong with me?"

Robyn shrugs. "Maybe it'll take a while for the anger to surface."

"I can't see that happening. Nothing's to be changed by it."

"That's a good attitude. Just make sure you aren't bottling up anything unknowingly," says Robyn.

The bus rounds another bend and enters the outskirts of Port Townsend, coming to a stop near the town center. We step off the bus and wait for a shuttle that will take us to our final destination, Fort Worden State Park, where the festival is being held. It's ten in the morning. Our journey from Phoenix has taken over twelve hours. By all rights, we should be totally fried, but that is masked by the excitement of finally arriving.

Fort Worden is a historic area just north of town that has been turned into a combination state park and conference center. The site is located at the tip of the peninsula, where you can walk a short distance either north or east and find the shores of Puget Sound. At least that's the theory. It's foggy when we arrive, and I have no idea which direction is which.

We find the camp headquarters and are handed information packets and directions to our dorm rooms. We are told lunch is about to be served, so after dropping off our belongings we find the cafeteria and eat lunch while perusing the festival schedules.

"Which workshops appeal to you?" I ask Robyn.

"I'm thinking of going to the Swedish fiddle workshop," she says. "And then maybe the old-timey workshop."

"I'm not sure what I want to do," I say, flipping through the schedule. "Maybe I'll go to this New England fiddle workshop by Rodney Miller, whoever he is. Do you suppose it's a problem we'll be attending these workshops after they've already been in progress for a few days?"

"I don't know," says Robyn. "To be honest, after looking at these schedules, I'm beginning to regret we came mid-week. Looks like we missed a lot already."

After lunch we go our respective ways, and I arrive at the New England workshop a few minutes late. The instructor, Rodney Miller, is teaching the students an original tune called *Contrazz*. As the name suggests, it's a cross between traditional contra dance music and jazz, with blues notes and syncopation. I join in best I can, but I'm soon frustrated by my lack of progress, especially when everyone else seems to be learning the tune quickly. It dawns on me later that they had worked on this piece since Monday. I'm definitely at a disadvantage.

I enjoy Rodney's class despite my frustrations, and am in awe of his fiddling prowess. It turns out I *should* be in awe, for later I learn he is one of the top New England style contra dance fiddlers.

Rodney uses a lively bowing style I haven't seen before: mostly straight saw strokes instead of the slurred bowing I am familiar with. There is a lot to be learned at this festival. Throughout the rest of the week, I have my fiddle in hand constantly, playing at every jam session I can find.

Being primarily a bluegrass player, I don't know many of the tunes being played, mainly New England, Southern, Cajun, Irish, and French Canadian dance tunes. I learn quickly that to play any of the standard bluegrass tunes risks getting dirty looks from others. This puzzles me. Isn't this the *American Fiddle Tunes* festival, as in *American*? And what could be more American than bluegrass? Puzzled though I am by this, I make the best of it, and use the opportunity to learn as many dance tunes as possible.

~ ~ ~

By Friday, my energy is running low. I take a break from the action to explore the surrounding area, rambling through the park grounds and eventually making my way up a bluff at the north end of the park. During the week the rainy weather had given way to clearing skies and pleasant temperatures. Between the clear weather and various breaks in the tall trees, I am able to get my bearings for the first time since arriving in Port Townsend. I'm surprised to discover sweeping views of Puget Sound, with numerous landforms lurking in the hazy distance.

I stretch out on a sunny patch of grass that has good views of the water. The hustle and bustle of the festival recedes far away and within a few minutes, memories of Catherin come swirling by, along with faint echoes of her singing that are ever-present—if I would just be still and listen.

The solitude envelops me, and I feel peace for the first time since that fateful day in May. The beauty of the open waters and surrounding evergreens brings to mind a song by Laurie Lewis:

Haven of Mercy

At the end of just another day
That's when I miss her most
When her memories gather 'round me
Like an old familiar ghost

Then high above this rocky coast
There's a place that I can go
To heal the wounds of a heartbreak
And soothe a lovesick soul

Chorus:

I can hear the angels singing
And I feel nearer my God to thee
As I watch the sun sinking
Below me, in the sea

The tall trees gather 'round me
Whispering pilgrim, welcome home
Sweet haven of mercy
Sweet peace for my soul

The hawk hangs above me
The raven glides below
The quail has found a hiding place
In the woods so dark and low

And I'm like a tiny sparrow
That's found a place to nest
At the very gates of heaven
My haven of rest

Chorus

— Laurie Lewis, 1985

I remember shivering with goose bumps upon hearing these haunting lyrics back in May, when Catherin and I were driving in the middle of night on our way to Zion. Little did I know then, how appropriate these lyrics would become. Was this another uncanny coincidence, like me coming up with the words "burning candles in the night"—only to have that come true?

~ ~ ~

On Friday night there is a big gathering in what was once the headquarters of the fort—a large two story building with many small rooms tucked away, and two ballrooms upstairs where simultaneous dances are held. From the first floor you can hear stomping through the ceiling, and an occasional whoop and holler. People are everywhere: on the stairs, in the hallways, and crammed into nooks and crannies. Fiddles are present in great numbers too, along with assorted accordions, mandolins, banjos, guitars, and flutes. The cacophony of sound is incredible.

I join a jam session in a small room with ten other fiddlers huddled around a talented swing piano player. They play a tune, *Dancing Bears*, which sounds like nothing I have heard before. Scored in a low, growling, minor key, the tune sounds just like a swarm of bees, especially when that many fiddlers play in unison. It's not hard to figure out where the name of the tune comes from. Just imagine bears dancing around the honeycombs.

I'm struck by the simple combination of fiddle and piano, and my eyes are opened to a new level of appreciation for this type of music. Playing tunes in that room becomes a defining moment for me. It's when I begin transitioning from bluegrass to contra dance music.

~ ~ ~

Saturday morning brings a concert where the students from each workshop give stage performances, playing the tunes they learned the past week. Robyn watches my performance with Rodney Miller's class, and I watch her play with the old-timey group. After her performance, Robyn comes down from the stage and introduces me to Doug, another musician from her class. With glasses, trim beard, and friendly manner, Doug seems familiar to me. I am beginning to realize that this is true of most old-time musicians I meet. It makes sense seeing how we share the common bond of music.

Doug turns out to be a fellow Arizonan from Tucson. He has family that lives in Seattle and offers us a place to stay the night before our flight back to Phoenix. Robyn returns the favor and invites him to travel with us for the next few days. Our destination, a tantalizingly short distance across the Strait of Juan de Fuca, is Vancouver Island, and the charming city of Victoria, British Columbia.

Chapter 24.
Crossing Over

July 5, 1987

Hunching my shoulders, I try unsuccessfully to shift my backpack to a more comfortable position before picking up the rest of my gear and trudging down the sidewalk, away from the Fort Worden dormitories and towards the shuttle stop. Weariness from marathon jam sessions the night before makes the gear heavy in my arms. As I join the throng of festival attendees reluctantly streaming out the park and back to the real world, farewells are given and car doors are slammed, breaking the morning stillness lingering in tall evergreens.

The morning breakfast—the last official activity of the festival—had been a sad occasion for all. No more *Dancing Bear* tunes in the nooks and crannies of the old commander's headquarters. No more whoops and hollers from the dancers, stomping their feet to music in the second floor ballrooms.

I catch up with Robyn and Doug at the shuttle waiting area just as a van pulls away.

"So much for that," I say, motioning towards the shuttle. "Sorry I'm late."

"I was wondering where you were," says Robyn.

"I'm such a space case," I say, shaking my head and putting down my gear to join them on a bench. "It took me three tries to make it out the dorm. First I forgot my carry-on bag, then my sunglasses, and the third time I didn't trust myself and went back to make sure I hadn't missed anything else."

"It's okay," says Robyn, waving it off. "Surely another shuttle will come soon."

I lean back, massaging sore hands and fingers. "Man I'm tired. I don't think I've ever played so many tunes in one night."

"Me neither," says Doug, massaging his hands too. "How long did you stay up? I think I played until two."

"That's about when I quit," I say.

"Dancing wore me out sooner than you guys," says Robyn. "I called it a night around twelve."

"It's hard to believe the festival is over," I say. "Seems like we just arrived."

"We sure made a mistake not coming for the whole week," says Robyn.

"How about you?" I ask Doug. "Were you here the whole time?"

"Yes," says Doug. "But I've been to this festival before. I knew better than to miss any part of it."

"Then you must know when the next shuttle will come," I say to Doug in a joking manner.

"Now *that* I don't know," he says, laughing.

We keep waiting. No shuttles appear. My foot wiggles.

"I suppose we could walk down to the bus station," says Robyn. "It's only a mile or so."

Doug scratches his beard and ponders the gear sitting in front of him. Like Robyn and me, he has a fiddle, backpack, and carry-on bag, but he's also burdened with a mandolin.

"I don't know about you guys, but I have no interest in carrying this stuff very far," says Doug.

"Me neither," I say. "Just coming from the dormitories was bad enough. Would we have time to walk downtown anyway? If we miss the bus to Port Angeles we can kiss the ferry to Victoria goodbye."

A man happens by that Robyn recognizes. "That's one of the festival directors," she says. Robyn calls out to him.

"Do you know if there will be any more shuttles?" she asks. "We need to make it to the bus station soon."

"I'm sure more are on their way," the man says. "But if you'd like, I can give you a lift into town." He points to his van.

We follow, thanking him profusely as we pile our belongings into the back and climb in. We make it to the station with time to spare before the Port Angeles bus pulls away.

An hour-long ride through lush evergreen forests, interspersed with glimpses of open water, brings us to the small downtown area of Port Angeles. We purchase tickets at the nearby ferry station, but the ferry isn't scheduled to depart for another hour. While we wait on a bench outside, I notice a coffee shop across the street that advertises healthy organic food and beverages. Suddenly, I'm hungry.

"How about we go over there for lunch?" I suggest, pointing towards the coffee shop.

"Good idea," says Robyn. "While grabbing lunch we can look at the brochures of Victoria I brought along."

We cross the street and settle into a corner table at the coffee shop, ordering tea and turkey sandwiches with bean sprouts and avocado. Robyn hands us brochures to read while we eat.

"I would like to find music to listen to while we're in Victoria," she says. "But we should also see the sights."

I scan one of the brochures. Listed are places like the British Columbia parliament buildings, the Empress Hotel, the Royal British Columbia Museum, and the famous Butchart Gardens.

"Looks like there are plenty of things for us to see and do," I say between bites of sandwich. "But can we get to these places by foot? According to this map Butchart Gardens is quite a ways from downtown. We'd have to rent a car, or go by bus."

"I haven't thought that far ahead," says Robyn.

"I'm game for anything you guys want to do," says Doug, sipping his coffee. "Just don't make me walk very far with all this gear."

"Any idea where you want to stay?" I ask Robyn.

"Beats me!" she says, shrugging.

I shake my head in mock disbelief and say, "So we don't know what to do, how to get around, or where to stay. We are such terrible planners—I like it!"

Robyn laughs. "Actually, I was thinking we could find a bed and breakfast—something close to the ferry."

A whistle blows from across the street.

"That must be the warning signal for departure," says Doug. "We better get moving."

We pay the bill and head back to the station. As we stand in line to board the ferry, a man just ahead of us, wearing a tweed jacket and jeans, turns around and sees our instruments.

"Have you come from the Port Townsend festival?" he asks.

"We sure have," Robyn replies.

"I suspected as much," he says. "I was there too. So where are you headed?"

"We thought we would go to Victoria for a day or two," Robyn says.

"You've made a good choice. I happen to live in Victoria."

"Really?" says Robyn. "Perhaps you can recommend things for us to do. We'd particularly like something musical."

"I'm sure I can help you in that regard. I'm a director at the Victoria Conservatory of Music."

"No kidding!" says Robyn. "Are there any good performances scheduled the next day or so?"

"I know of a coffeehouse that has live folk music. As a matter of fact, a French Canadian fiddler from the Port Townsend festival is having a special performance tonight."

"Was he the one that gave a concert on Thursday?"

"Yes."

Robyn turns to Doug and me. "I saw his performance. He's a wonderful player. We have to go."

The ferry whistle blows once again. The director proceeds ahead of us before we have a chance to gather up our gear.

"Wait, sir!" shouts Robyn as we rush to meet him. "You didn't tell us where to find this coffeehouse."

He pauses for a moment, and then reaches into his coat pocket and hands Robyn a business card. "Give me a call later today," he says. "I'll give you directions then."

"Thanks so much," says Robyn, slipping the card into her backpack. The man boards the ferry ahead of us.

"That was fortunate," I say to Robyn, as we follow behind.

"I'll say," replies Robyn. "But we forgot to ask about a place to stay in Victoria. Oh well, we'll figure it out."

Aboard the ferry, we search for enough empty seating to store our gear with us.

"How about the upper deck?" Robyn suggests. "That way we can take in all the sights."

The upper deck is exposed to sun and wind. Neither Doug nor I have any objections to this, but perhaps we should have. As the ferry glides out of port, a chilly wind follows, increasing in intensity as we move away from shore, causing me to bundle up my jacket tighter and to wonder how the seagulls soaring along with us manage to stay warm.

Robyn suggests we play music to pass the time, so we unpack our instruments and trade recently learned tunes, with Doug joining on mandolin. Chilly though it is, at least on the windy upper deck we can play and not bother others too much. Even so, a small crowd of appreciative listeners soon forms.

Later, my hands grow stiff with cold, and I repeatedly cup them over my mouth, blowing to keep them warm. My fingers feel mushy and sore from the jam sessions the night before. Doug says his are sore too. We call it quits and pack our instruments away, the impromptu audience clapping with applause and dispersing.

I settle back on the bench and close my eyes, thoughts of Catherin coming to the fore. How sad she isn't here. She would have loved Port Townsend: the music, the water, the mountains. What is it like for her now? Does she still exist in some form? I sure don't know the answer, but I'm becoming more convinced that something *does* exist beyond our ordinary reality. The odd coincidences surrounding Catherin's death serve as proof: The simultaneous hello and goodbye, the crossing jets, the peacocks with feathers raised, the burning candle premonition, the white dove flying by in the middle of the desert, and the oddest and spookiest of all, the wad of paper with the word "Proof."

My thoughts return to the past Friday, sitting in peaceful solitude on the grassy bluff overlooking Fort Worden Park. I wonder now if that bluff is visible from the boat. I open my eyes and turn my gaze across the water towards Port Angeles, and further southeast to where Port Townsend must lie. Fog blankets the coast, but to my amazement, a huge mountain range looms not far behind, high above the fog. I didn't realize how close the Olympic Mountains were to the coast.

Only the foothills are visible. The peaks are shrouded in ever-changing clouds that reveal, from time to time, tantalizing glimpses of scenic beauty.

Just like life, I say to myself. *We go through life with fog all around, knowing or suspecting there is something more, but only seeing what lies beyond in teasing glimpses.*

~ ~ ~

An hour after departing Port Angeles, the ferry glides into Victoria Harbor, with the Empress Hotel and the provincial parliament buildings close by. As the ferry pulls up to the docks, our seagull companions land with a flurry of fluttering and flapping, both in the water and on the ramp leading off the boat. Passengers disembark, disturbing the now-settled seagulls and causing them to once again rise up in whirring flight. Through all the commotion I spot someone familiar just up ahead.

"There's that music director again," I say to Robyn and Doug, pointing his direction. "Maybe we can ask where to spend the night."

When we catch up to him, Robyn taps his shoulder. He turns and greets us in recognition.

"Could you tell us any good places to stay?" asks Robyn.

"What kind of place are you looking for?"

"A bed and breakfast," says Robyn. "Preferably something close to the ferry, or close to downtown. It would be nice if we didn't have to do much walking."

"We're already close to downtown," the director says. "There are numerous bed and breakfasts in the area, though I can't think of any offhand. Maybe you can find information inside the ferry station."

Halfway down the ramp a small boy, perhaps ten years of age, hands out flyers. I ignore him at first, but after we pass by, he follows us down the ramp and waves flyers, insisting I take one. I give in and stop to put down my gear and take a flyer. Without reading it, I fold it in half, fully intending to discard it in the nearest trash can. On second thought I decide to open it. Inside is an advertisement for a bed and breakfast called *O'Ryan's*. The rates look reasonable, but how far away is it? Maybe the boy can tell me. I look for him, but he's gone. I pick up my gear and rush to catch up to the others, who are still walking beside the music director.

"Sir, could you tell me where this place is?" I ask the director, stopping to put down my bags again and pointing to the address on the flyer.

The director pauses to study the flyer. "Let's see, that would be only a few blocks from here. Just go up this street one block, turn right a couple more, and then left one block."

"What do you guys think?" I ask Robyn and Doug, showing them the flyer. They both say it looks good.

"Thanks again," I say to the director.

"No problem," he says. "Be sure to call me later about the coffeehouse. It opens at seven." He pauses for a second and says, "Tell you what. I was planning on going tonight. I could swing by the bed and breakfast and take you there."

"That would be wonderful," says Robyn. "We'll call later once we know where we are staying. We can't thank you enough."

The director walks on ahead and we find our way to the bed and breakfast, which turns out to be a blue pastel cottage fashioned appropriately in the Victorian style, with a white picket fence and a swinging sign out front saying *O'Ryan's*. We clamber up the porch and ring the door bell. A cheerful young lady with long reddish brown hair answers.

"May I help you?" she asks, with a thick Irish accent.

"We're looking for a room for the night," says Robyn.

"You're in luck. We do have vacancies, so come on in and I'll show you around. You can leave your instruments by the door for now." She leads us down a hallway elegantly decorated with pastoral-themed wallpaper behind photos and drawings mounted on ceramic plates. The place looks clean and well kept.

"So you are musicians?" she asks.

"Yes," says Robyn. "We just came from the Port Townsend Fiddle Tunes festival."

"Oh yes, Port Townsend," she says. "That's a great festival. I've been there with my husband. We're musicians too."

"Really?" replies Robyn. "What style of music do you do?"

"We play mostly Irish tunes. In fact, we moved here from Ireland a few years ago."

The three of us travelers look at each other with eyebrows raised in pleasant surprise.

"Then it sounds like we found the right place," says Robyn.

We round the corner and the lady opens the door to one of the guest rooms. She points inside.

"There are two beds in here right now," she says, "but we can move in another roll-away if necessary. The bath is down the hall to your left."

After seeing the elegance and cleanliness of the place, and learning the owners are Irish musicians, we don't need more than a quick glance in the room to know we are sold.

"We'll take it," says Robyn, after looking to Doug and me for confirmation.

"Great!" says the lady. "My name is Molly, by the way."

We make introductions and store our bags in the guest room and then Molly says, "You must join me for afternoon tea."

Molly offers us chairs at a table in a small dining area adjoining the kitchen while she serves tea and buttered scones. She asks lots of questions about Arizona and we ask lots of questions about Ireland and Victoria. Robyn and Doug do most of the talking as I am in my usual wall-flower mode: not saying much but listening intently. The conversation is so engrossing that nobody realizes how much time has passed until I glance up at the wall clock.

"Do you guys realize it's almost five?" I say. "We haven't even seen Victoria, other than from the harbor."

"I guess time flies when you're having fun," says Doug.

"That's for sure," says Robyn. "We better get a hold of the conservatory director and see about going to the coffeehouse."

She calls the director using the house phone and after hanging up, she says, "We're in luck! Not only is the director going to take us to the coffeehouse, he's going to take us out to supper beforehand. He'll be here in fifteen minutes."

Doug gets up to use the restroom, Robyn remains in the dining area to finish her tea, and I figure it might be chilly in the evening hours, so I rise and go to the guest room to retrieve my jacket, which is lying on a chair by the door. As I get ready to put on the jacket, I glance across the room. A familiar sight causes me to freeze.

"Well, would you look at that!" I say under my breath.

Chapter 25.
Sign of the White Dove

M y eyes are fixed on the framed picture hanging above the bed as I lower myself into the chair, jacket in hand. When the three of us rented this room, we had only glanced in, having been sold immediately on staying here. So I hadn't noticed the picture in front of me. But I have seen this picture before, many times in fact, hanging on the wall in Catherin's house. It's the picture of a white dove flying through the clouds.

In my last dream of Catherin, she had been trying to tell me something that I had confusingly interpreted as "Don't forget the perfume." Yet earlier in the dream she mentioned something about a picture. Maybe she was really saying "Don't forget the picture." Was this the picture she wanted me to make note of? Did she somehow know of my disappointment when her sister kept the picture for herself, back when we were sorting through Catherin's things?

I hear Robyn enter the room and say, "We should take our fiddles with us to the coffeehouse. Maybe they'll let us play a few tunes on stage."

But I ignore her, my gaze still locked on the picture. Questions are spinning through my head.

"You okay?" asks Robyn.

I break out of my reverie to find Robyn studying me.

"It's that picture," I say, pointing towards the wall. "Catherin had one just like it."

"Oh," says Robyn, moving over to place a sympathetic hand on my shoulder. "It must be hard being reminded of Catherin like that."

"On the contrary, I find it comforting somehow."

"Doves are a symbol of peace. Is that it?"

"It's more than that," I say. "Why would I happen to run across this exact image, twelve hundred miles from home? That's quite a coincidence—too much of one."

"What are you getting at?" asks Robyn, sitting down on the bed to listen more attentively.

"Well, here we are, at a bed and breakfast that's perfect for us. It's within walking distance of downtown and the ferry, and has a friendly owner who's a musician—Irish no less."

"So you are saying exactly what?"

"Maybe this is a signpost."

"A sign from Catherin?"

I shrug. "Could be. Or from God? The universe?"

"What's the sign supposed to be telling you?"

"That I'm right where I'm supposed to be?"

Something else occurs to me. I prop an elbow on an armrest and cradle my chin with the palm of my hand.

"Isn't it uncanny that we were practically guided to this very spot? This morning we had no idea what we were going to do or where we were going to stay. We happen to meet a man on the ferry who is highly connected to the music scene here in Victoria—a man who is going out of his way to show us around. And then as we leave the ferry, popping out of nowhere is a little boy who hands me a flyer to this very place. He's insistent that I take the flyer, and then he disappears."

"It does sound remarkable," says Robyn.

"And what about Catherin's doves? Do they figure in this? Also, I don't know if I told you about the white dove I saw in the New Mexico desert."

I relate to Robyn the story of the white dove flying by my pickup north of Gallup, on my way to Telluride, right when I had been thinking of Catherin and feeling especially down. I also relate the dream where Catherin may have been trying to tell me, "Don't forget the picture."

"All of these occurrences may be mere coincidences," I say. "But I have my doubts."

I rise from the chair and finish putting on my coat. "Now, what were you saying when you first came in?"

"Oh," says Robyn, "that we should take our fiddles in case we want to play at the coffeehouse."

Doug comes into the room at that moment and hears Robyn's comments about playing. He's amenable to the idea, so we gather up our instruments and store them in the living room while we wait for the music director to arrive.

The doorbell rings. Molly answers the door to another fiddler named Jerry, who has also just arrived from the Port Townsend festival and is looking for a place to stay. Jerry reminds me a lot of Scooter: an older fellow, tanned from many hours in the sun, with a salt and pepper beard and the discerning look of one who has traveled far and wide. I wonder if he reminds Robyn of Scooter as well, but if he does, Robyn never lets it show.

Once Jerry discovers that other musicians are staying at the bed and breakfast, he immediately rents the last room. Soon afterwards the doorbell rings again. It's the conservatory director, ready to take us to supper and then to the coffeehouse. There is room in the director's van for all of us, including Jerry, so he comes along as well.

We dine at a seafood restaurant in downtown Victoria and then go to the coffeehouse, located a few miles away. Housed in a small building, the setting is similar to the coffeehouse in Phoenix. One important difference, though, is that the Victoria coffeehouse has regularly-scheduled musicians who are not just locals. Some are regionally if not nationally known for their talents.

Before the scheduled musicians play there is an hour of 'open mike' performances. Robyn finds the owner and asks if we can play a short set, using the persuasive argument that we had come all the way from Arizona.

Too bad our playing doesn't measure up. Except for the ride on the ferry, the three of us hadn't practiced together, and we have to quickly cobble together a couple of tunes. On top of that, my hands are sore from the previous night's playing and I'm sure Doug's are too. The result is less than perfect. I'm embarrassed, even more so after hearing the subsequent performances by the much more accomplished artists. Oh well, at least we can say we are now international musicians!

The French Canadian fiddler from the Port Townsend festival puts on an inspiring show. Two local fiddlers join him towards the end of his set and they play a French waltz with exquisite triple harmonies. We are spellbound. I mention to Robyn that we have to learn the name of that waltz.

The next morning Molly fixes breakfast, and then invites us to play tunes with her and her husband. Of course we don't pass up this chance. We play Irish tunes at first, and then branch out to many different styles. Jerry, the other fiddler staying at the bed and breakfast, is there as well. It turns out he had indeed traveled far and wide, having attended many festivals and jam sessions over the years. He had collected a notebook full of tunes to prove it. I notice that many of the tunes in his notebook are on hand-written sheets.

"Jerry," I ask, "do you remember the French waltz they played last night at the coffeehouse, the one with triple harmonies?"

"Yes," says Jerry. "That was the *Waltz of the Little Girls.*"

"You don't happen to have that in your notebook do you?"

"I believe I do," he says, flipping through the pages to verify. "I'll try to make a copy and send it to you."

"I can help with that," interjects Molly. "We have a copier in the office."

Jerry finds the sheet and Molly makes a copy for us. This waltz later becomes part of our collection of dance tunes back in Phoenix.

~ ~ ~

The bed and breakfast could not have been more perfectly situated, for we are only blocks away from most of the attractions of Victoria, and it's time to explore. We plan on taking the last ferry back to Seattle in the evening, and Molly lets us store gear at her place until we are ready to leave.

We spend the rest of the day being ordinary tourists, walking the few blocks to the world class Royal British Columbia Museum. The collection of cultural artifacts of the Northwest is superb and we spend several hours perusing the displays. We stay downtown for lunch, browse through some of the shops, explore part of Beacon Hill Park, and even see the British Columbia Provincial Legislature in session, from a viewing gallery on the second floor of the parliament building. Unfortunately, we don't have time to make the trip to the famous Butchart Gardens, but vow to come back some day.

Around six o'clock we make our way back to the bed and breakfast, collect our gear, thank Molly for her hospitality, and head for the ferry station. We board the ferry at seven-thirty and settle in for the three hour journey to Seattle. As before, we sit on the upper deck, but this time it is enclosed. Unlike the ferry ride from Port Angeles, the weather has cleared off to the east and we can see many of the snowy, volcanic peaks in the state of Washington, including Mt. Rainier. The Olympic Mountains, however, are still enshrouded in clouds.

After watching the scenery drift by for an hour, we decide to play music, hoping the nearby passengers won't mind. They don't. At one point, Robyn and Doug leave to find something to drink while I stay behind and practice *Woodchopper's Reel*, a French Canadian tune that's becoming a favorite of mine. When I finish, a man that had been listening comes up to me.

"Don't you usually have it open?" he asks, pointing to my fiddle case.

"What are you talking about?"

"Your fiddle case. Don't you usually have it open?"

I can't figure out what he means, so I shrug and open the case. He throws in a quarter. Ah! He is giving me money for playing. Now I'm not just an international musician, but a professional one at that. I'm not sure how many ferry trips I can purchase on these wages though ...

Later I put the fiddle away and sit back to enjoy the scenery. We've crossed the Strait of Juan de Fuca, and are turning south down Puget Sound, just east of Port Townsend. Fort Worden State Park comes into view—the place where the fiddle festival had been held—along with the bluff at the edge of the park. It was there I had stretched out in the grass with memories of Catherin, the sounds of Laurie Lewis's *Haven of Mercy* reverberating in my head.

Floating by like this, reviewing scenes from the past, reminds me of the time I circled from above in Jeff's plane and saw the slowly rotating view of my childhood farm in Kansas. Was it this way for Catherin, I wonder? Did she come back to review her life? Floating from above, perhaps? What was her reaction to my part in her life? What was her reaction to her own death?

Robyn and Doug soon rejoin me with drinks. The ferry churns down the waters of Puget Sound, while skies darken and clouds gather, conspiring to obscure any colorful sunset we might have had. By the time the lights of Seattle come into view, the evening has grown quite dark. The setting reminds me of a particular song.

I turn to Robyn and say, "It's time for you to teach me that waltz."
"Which waltz?" she asks.

"*Midnight on the Water*. It was Catherin's favorite. I had promised her I would learn it and I guess I have plenty of time now."

We pull out our instruments and Robyn teaches me the tune phrase by phrase—it's not too hard—and we are still playing *Midnight on the Water* as the ferry glides into the port of Seattle, the lights of the city reflecting off the blackened waves.

~ ~ ~

It's Tuesday morning and I'm back in Phoenix, having just hugged Robyn goodbye at the airport. What a wonderful trip! Was it as wonderful as the trip with Catherin to Zion National Park? No, but that would be hard to top. And nothing romantic had happened between Robyn and me—not that I had expected it to. But I'm sure the memories of fiddle music, mountain scenery, and ferries gliding into the ports of Victoria and Seattle will be leaving lasting impressions.

And immediate ones too: A post-vacation letdown makes it hard to report for duty at my new job on Wednesday. I'm now part of a five man research and development team—actually four guys and one gal—whose mission is to take computer programs written in COBOL, (the language I said I would *never* work with), and translate them into a new form more amenable to analysis. My task is to write the section of code affectionately called *Grok* by my new boss.

The term *grok* comes from a science fiction novel by Robert Heinlein titled *Stranger in a Strange Land*. In this novel, the native Martians have the ability to grok others. As a Martian, you can come to know and understand fellow beings so completely that they in a sense become part of you. This ability extends to inanimate objects as well.

In the context of my team's software, to *grok* means to thoroughly analyze a program's step-by-step instructions and achieve a high level of understanding. My Grok component is supposed to automatically generate English-like descriptions of a program's intent, presenting the grand scheme of things. A big part of my job involves pattern-matching, something well suited to my current frame of mind. I am beginning to see patterns in my life, patterns I hope to someday *grok*.

As you might imagine, I'm not quite prepared for the mental switch back to working mode. It is quite a shock coming from almost two months off—gallivanting around the countryside, going to festival after festival, not having my logical, technical mind engaged much at all—and then being stuck in a sterile office full of computers.

But not to worry, for my first week on the job is a short one, and that weekend, as planned, I am traveling once again. I leave with my computer buddies—Alden, the keeper of Wacky the Robot, and Dr. Thomason, the master pontificator—to attend a conference on artificial intelligence in Seattle. The conference is held at the city center near the Space Needle, one of Seattle's most famous landmarks—the other being white-capped Mt. Rainer that looms in the distance. Fortunately for us, the weather is sunny, with temperatures in the 70s. The weather is so pleasant that it's hard to resist being outside. We frequently play hooky, exploring the surrounding areas of Seattle instead of attending lectures we paid good money for.

One day we play hooky big time and rent a car, crossing over to the Olympic Peninsula by ferry to tour the Olympic Mountains and the Olympic Rain Forest. It's strange to be traversing the same landscape I had seen just two weeks before with Robyn, but this time instead of drizzle and fog, the weather is clear. Finally, I am able to see the peaks of the Olympic Mountains that had beckoned me with only teasing glimpses before.

Our journey doesn't take us through Port Townsend, but we do stop in Port Angeles at the headquarters of Olympic National Park. After reviewing maps of the area, I suggest we take a short drive up to Hurricane Ridge, just south of Port Angeles. From there, we have sweeping views of the Olympic Range. But like my experience in Colorado, the mountains have lost much of their magic. My eyes keep telling me they are beautiful, but my heart feels little of it.

Our main destination is the Hoh Rain Forest, which is west, south, and then east around a half loop seventy-five miles from Port Angeles. We pass through several small towns and then head east along a narrow highway through the rain forest, with tall spruce and hemlock trees hundreds of feet high lining the road. Dr. Thomason drives a good portion of the way.

Since I tend to get car sick if sitting in the back, I'm up front on the passenger's side. I'm gazing out the windshield, intently watching Dr. Thomason drive, thinking about the artificial intelligence lectures from the conference—in particular, those on robot navigation. Alden is silent in the back, probably thinking along those lines too.

"Boy, you guys are a talkative bunch," says Dr. Thomason, as he steers the car around a curve.

"I'm just trying to detect any oscillation in your steering, by watching you drive," I say.

"Are you saying I'm a bad driver?" he asks, modulating his voice in mock offense.

"I'm not going to comment," I say, laughing. "I was just thinking how mechanical control systems always have oscillations inherent in their design. Our human control systems seem to waver more randomly."

"You mean like this?" replies Dr. Thomason, as he rapidly turns the steering wheel back and forth, causing the rental car to weave across the road.

"Yikes!" both Alden and I say at the same time, in feigned terror.

Dr. Thomason steadies the car, and I comment, "I *was* going to say our human control systems waver more randomly because we use intelligence. But now I'm not sure I can say that."

Alden and Dr. Thomason laugh at my remark.

"Seriously, what will it take for a robot to drive a car the way we do?" I ask. "Will that day ever come?"

"Ask Alden," says Dr. Thomason. "He's the one programming Wacky the Robot to navigate hallways."

"Actually, I went to a talk yesterday by Dr. Bartley from the Autonomous Robotics Institute," says Alden from the back. "He's an inspiration for me, for his research is all about creating mobile robots."

"So what's his spiel?" I ask.

"Using many processors with little brains," he says, "as opposed to a system with one giant brain and a highly complex program controlling it."

"So the idea is to use numerous small, parallel processors and sensors," I say, paraphrasing. "Each processor does something simple, but the complexity grows out of the system naturally?"

"Yes," says Alden. "And Dr. Bartley doesn't like the symbolic paradigm in vogue these days in the AI field."

Symbolic processing is the method of abstracting relationships using a set of symbols, and then manipulating those symbols mathematically. That's something I am intimately familiar with, for that's what my master's thesis had related to, and what I would be working on in my new job. In my analysis of COBOL programs, I would be using the computer language I used for my thesis: Prolog. In this language, you work with abstract symbols, and manipulate those symbols using the equivalent of mathematical logic theorems. In essence, you derive facts about the problem at hand, using Prolog to prove whether something is true, based on given assumptions treated as facts.

"Dr. Thomason, master pontificator," I say, "I'm going to turn the tables on you and say *you've* been awfully quiet. What's your take on all this?"

"Symbolic processing isn't the answer," says Dr. Thomason. "Getting a robot to drive a car is all about information theory."

The idea behind information theory is to transmit a message—to communicate—using the minimum amount of data. You only need to transmit what the receiver on the other end doesn't already know. Ideally, you transmit only what's changed, what's new.

Dr. Thomason continues, "I've done the calculations, and I think I could get by with just eight bits of information per second to keep this car on the road."

A *bit* in computer programming is a single on/off switch, the basis of all computer data.

"Just eight bits per second?" I ask. "How did you derive that? On second thought, never mind. Your answer would probably take the rest of the trip, you being Mr. Pontificator."

Dr. Thomason laughs, his beard going up and down with his chuckles. "Yes, just eight bits per second. To prove it, I'm going to close my eyes while steering this car."

This elicits a second round of "Yikes!" from Alden and me. But Dr. Thomason is just kidding—I think.

Fortunately, we safely reach the Hoh Rain Forest Visitor Center and go inside to study the displays, and then go hiking along a dark, heavily forested trail, with giant moss-covered trees serving as canopy. The trail is soft and damp, something we aren't used to, coming from the dusty climes of Arizona.

As we clop along I'm still thinking about robots, control systems, and information theory.

"Dr. Bartley is right about using lots of parallel sensor processing at the low level," I say, "doing simple calculations, comparisons, and so on. But I think he's falling into the same trap as everyone else. He's still avoiding the more important question, the harder question. How do you make sense of all that data? Who or what makes overall plans and determines how to accomplish those plans?

"You have to start somewhere," says Alden.

"True, but I think he's missing the forest for the trees," I say, as we climb over a mossy log blocking the trail, my friends in the lead.

Both Alden and Dr. Thomason turn back to roll their eyes at me as I finish clearing the log.

"What?" I ask, with pretend innocence.

My friends just shake their heads slowly.

"I'm serious," I continue. "If robots are going to drive down the road, they have to deduce what's in front of them. They have to be aware of their surroundings and then formulate the next move. How will this be accomplished? Maybe that's where symbolic, logical processing comes in."

"Dr. Bartley thinks having layers of processors operating in parallel will do this automatically," says Alden.

"Based on what—magical thinking?" I ask.

"So what's your solution, Mr. Flamig?" asks Dr. Thomason, with a light hearted jeer. "Just use Prolog, like you do at your new job, and do theorem proving by manipulating symbols? Like *that's* going to work."

I pause for a moment to untangle my thoughts, and shrug, saying, "I don't know."

We come upon a huge rotting log, the remains of what was once a hundred foot Sitka spruce, according to a sign placed nearby. The log is in an advanced state of decay, so advanced that another tree, twenty or thirty feet high, is growing out of the remains.

Life rising out of death, my thoughts say, *a perpetual cycle—like reincarnation. A metaphor*. It's at this point that I have a moment of clarity. I try to communicate this to my friends.

"About this notion of symbolic processing," I say, "I wasn't trying to say I'm for or against it. For what I do at my new job, it's a good tool, but that's for analyzing computer programs, something already abstract. Intelligence in real life is another matter. I do think, however, that symbols play an important role."

"How so?" asks Dr. Thomason.

"Take this rotting log with a new tree growing out of it," I say, pointing to said log. "We might look at this log and say, 'Gee, this represents the cycle of life and death.' That is, we can use the rotting log as a metaphor, as a way of showing how life and death relate."

"I'm not sure I follow," says Dr. Thomason.

"Me neither," says Alden.

"Well then, maybe I shouldn't either," I say, laughing. "Seriously though, it seems to me that thinking in metaphors—in symbols—is a major way we relate to the world and to each other. Indeed, isn't that what language itself is based on, symbols and metaphors?"

I finish my mini-lecture to let my friends ponder this question, while I ponder it myself, wondering if I'm just babbling nonsense. We turn around and hike back to the car, and this time, *I* drive as we make our way back to Seattle. I don't trust Dr. Thomason's eight bits per second.

~ ~ ~

All this traveling leaves me exhausted. When I return from Seattle for the second time, I want nothing more than to stay put in Phoenix and rest. But that is not to be. A week later I find myself flying, all expenses paid, to yet another computer conference—this time in Santa Cruz, California—at an event hosted by a software company famous for writing fast programming tools. They have a new Prolog product to show off, and I'm offered the opportunity to go as a representative of a fledgling AI magazine I had written a few articles for.

I no more than get back from Santa Cruz when my boss informs me that I'll be attending a Prolog training seminar with my co-workers the following week, in Mountain View. So back to California I go.

After class one evening I discover a record store near our hotel. I step inside and receive a surprise. Featured front and center is the current folk music selection—an album I know well: It's Laurie Lewis's *Restless Rambling Heart*. I can't believe my luck. I had been searching all over Phoenix for this record, to no avail. My taped copy was worn out from being played so many times during the summer; the songs *Here We Go Again*, *Green Fields*, and *Haven of Mercy* having been completely fused with my memories of Catherin. I buy the record without hesitation.

Located next to the record shop is a bookstore and I venture inside to peruse the New Age and Self Help sections. During the summer I had been reading numerous books on death and grieving, and welcomed new perspectives. A particular book, just published, catches my eye. It's titled *Synchronicity: The Bridge Between Matter and Mind*, by F. David Peat.

Synchronicity—where have I heard that term before? Then I remember. It was in connection with the *I-Ching* discussions I had with Catherin back in the spring—discussions I had forgotten. Portions come back now.

Synchronicity, a term coined by Carl Jung, can be defined as two or more coincidental events having significant meaning for an observer, but without identifiable causal connections. Suppose you go for walk, reminiscing about your father who just passed away. You recall how you loved playing baseball with him as a child, and then, just a few steps down the street, a baseball drops in front of you. Though imbued with deep meaning for you, the two events—the thought of playing baseball, and the baseball suddenly appearing— have no identifiable cause and effect. You wouldn't say the thought of baseball *caused* the ball to appear, would you? That type of coincidence is a synchronicity.

Thinking back through the summer, I realize I've had my share of synchronicities: The burning candles premonition in connection with the Magic Farm; the strange connection between a particular *Riders in the Sky* tape and tragic events in my life; the peacocks showing their feathers right after Catherin's death; the crossing jets when they brought her body out of the house; the recurring image of a white dove; and last but not least, the wad of paper dropping out of my dresser, with the word "Proof" printed on it, after I had asked Catherin for proof of her continued existence.

I buy the book on synchronicity and study it that night in my hotel room. I flip randomly through the pages—my usual way of reading non-fiction, never quite following the front to back order— and land on a section discussing how synchronicities often occur in greater frequencies during times of crisis, such as the death of a loved one. That certainly fits my case—in spades.

The book suggests that synchronicities are tied with our perception of the universe—very apropos to my current interests professionally, emotionally, and spiritually. And I am intrigued by the subtitle, *The Bridge Between Matter and Mind*. What does that have to do with synchronicity?

I stay awake most of the night, reading and pondering.

~ ~ ~

By mid-August the travels of summer finally come to an end, and I settle into a routine of working during the day, and reading books or practicing music in the evenings. Sometimes I work on software projects at home, one of which is the astrology program I had promised to write for Catherin. I don't know why I spend time on it anymore—it's something to amuse myself with I guess. The program is taking shape. I can type in a person's date, time, and place of birth, and a full color astrological chart is displayed, with small symbols representing the position of planets and other astrological objects.

One nifty feature is that I can press keys on the computer to easily move backward and forward through time on the chart, and I can watch symbols spin around. That feature intrigues me more than any other. While spinning symbols around a chart one day, I have a flash of insight: Astrology could be treated abstractly, solely in terms of symbols and patterns. And what are symbols, but one of the keys to intelligence, as I had suggested to my friends. And what about another key to intelligence—the ability to perceive patterns?

From having watched Catherin analyze astrological charts, I know that great emphasis is placed on the angular relationships— the patterns—between symbols on a chart. These relationships indicate the quality, 'color', and strength of the energies, events, and associated personality traits. Could it be these patterns of astrology are more than meet the eye? Perhaps they really do represent some underlying order of the universe. I see now, for the first time, their relationship to synchronicity.

Astrology is often dismissed with arguments such as: "How can a planet or star so far away have any effect on an individual? The earth's gravity is many orders magnitude greater, and any feeble rays coming from planets and stars are overwhelmed by rays from the sun."

Such arguments miss the point. It's not about gravitational forces, magical rays, or other physical properties we don't yet know how to detect. It's about patterns and symbols, and how these tend to represent and coincide with certain events and personality traits.

The key words here are *tend* and *coincide*. Synchronicity has its roots in the idea that certain events, objects, and other aspects of our daily world have affinities for each other. They *tend* to *coincide* at auspicious moments. These synchronicities, these affinities, are possible markers to hidden connections in the universe.

Reading the book on synchronicity leads to other insights. A skeptic might say, "Okay, so there are traits, events, and the appearance of objects in the world that tend to occur together. But no one has explained where these tendencies come from."

To counter this criticism, one could reply: "Newton's first law of motion, which describes inertia, states that objects at rest *tend* to stay at rest; objects in motion *tend* to stay in motion. But nowhere does this law explain *why* this occurs. The principle of synchronicity is like this too. It describes the tendencies of certain events to coincide, without explaining why that happens."

Where does inertia come from? Scientists have been trying to answer this question—along with others from the realm of physics—by delving deep into matter, all the way to sub-atomic particles, and still no one knows the answer. So if one criticizes synchronicity, astrology, *I-Ching*, or any other metaphysical system, based on the lack of explanation as to how they work, then one must also criticize physics. It would only be fair.

There *are* fair criticisms of astrology. Do the connections it describes actually exist? How about the *I-Ching*, which is also related to synchronicities? Do these systems stand up to statistical analysis? There have been experiments run over the years to test these claims—with mostly negative results.

But there's a catch. What's being tested? In the case of astrology and the *I-Ching*, how are subjective entities like *traits* and *tendencies* identified and quantified? Can they be quantified? And are the experimenters really being objective in their tests, without hidden agendas?

Astrology and the *I-Ching* have their flaws, I'm sure. But what about synchronicities in general? That synchronicities are often strange and uncanny is due in part to the lack of identifiable causes for the coincidences. This is especially true the more improbable a coincidence seems to be. Without the explanation of random chance, or any known causal connection, you are left with non-ordinary, metaphysical interpretations.

Skeptics argue that the coincidences aren't as uncommon as they might seem, and that they are indeed just random chance. They argue that since we experience events every second of our lives, sooner or later we are going to experience strange coincidences. There's even a law for this, attributed to a Cambridge University professor, J.E. Littlewood.

Littlewood's Law goes something like this: Assume we experience at least one 'event' every second of our lives. Assume we are awake eight hours a day to observe and interact with these events. Assume a 'miracle' is defined to be an event that has a one in a million chance of occurring. Using these assumptions, Littlewood concluded that a miracle would occur for us roughly every 35 days.

Who knew?

But hold on a moment. How often have miraculous events occurred in *your* life? Every 35 days? Really? I would say such events aren't miracles at all. A miracle should be an improbable, momentous, once in a life-time event. (Though you could argue that life itself is one long series of miracles and I wouldn't disagree.)

Other issues arise: What's an event? Who gets to decide? And below what probability do you say an event is a miracle? One in a million, as Littlewood suggests? One in a trillion? One in ten raised to the hundredth power? How about near impossible? Isn't that the attribute we often give miracles?

Synchronicities shouldn't be confused with miracles. Not all synchronicities are of the miraculous nature, and not all miracles are synchronicities. Furthermore, a miracle might be just a single event, whereas a synchronicity requires at least two coinciding events.

What's the probability of two or more coinciding events? Since in synchronicities the events are acausal (having no known causal connections), the events are independent by definition, and the laws of statistics tell us to multiply the individual probabilities together to get a combined result. This joint probability may be very low. And in some cases, we may have to account for the timing and positioning constraints placed on the coincidental events, driving each individual probability even lower. Suppose our events each have one in a million odds. Multiply them together and you are talking serious odds: one in a trillion. It would take an average of 35 million days (roughly 100,000 years) for a coincidence involving such events to occur, using Littlewood's criteria.

Of course, not all events have such low probabilities. I don't mean to imply they do; and to be part of synchronicities, they don't have to. All that's required is that they be acausal, and that they have significant meaning to the observer. It is duly noted that if you experience coincidences having low enough probabilities, you are more likely to take notice, and this can lead to a sense of significance all on its own.

How are probabilities determined? In order to know the odds, you have to know the population from which samples are drawn. To determine the odds of pulling a particular ball out of a box, you have to know how many balls are in the box. That's easy since we can look inside and count them. But if you are considering events, the problem is more difficult, especially for certain kinds of events.

It's not uncommon for a *thought* to be one of the events of a synchronicity, as in the baseball example earlier. How do you determine the total number of thoughts a person thinks, and how do you determine the percentage that are about baseball? And won't that person's frequency of thoughts about baseball change over time, as circumstances and interests shift? It's hard to come up with the numbers, and those who say they can are not being forthright. They can't possibly know what others are thinking at all times. They are pulling numbers out of thin air.

Skeptics often invoke another related law to help explain synchronicity—the Law of Truly Large Numbers, which states that with a large enough sample, any outrageous thing can happen. This law allows skeptics to have it both ways. They can say, well, if a coincidence is actually common, then it's just chance, and not very interesting. If it's *not* common, the skeptics conveniently assume a large enough number of events to draw from, and this large number counteracts the low probability, so they can argue the coincidence has a greater possibility than it might seem. See, it's mere chance after all. No metaphysical explanations are needed.

Let's take this logic to its fullest conclusion and use it to explain the law of inertia. There is a chance that a spaceship can keep moving in a straight line because all the particles of the ship *just happen* to move together in a straight line, and just happen to *continue* to move together. What are the chances of this? Well, the universe is very old and very large, infinite even. I can make it as old and large as I want. (I can pull numbers out of thin air too.) And I can have multiple universes, an infinite number of them. By the Law of Truly Large Numbers, any strange thing can occur, including having spaceships in some universe (perhaps our universe) moving as they do by pure chance. Who needs the laws of physics when random chance will do?

Sound absurd? Yes. And not very useful either. It doesn't help us understand or predict things in life. It leaves little appreciation for the beauty and wonder of life and the universe we live in. Yet similar logic is being employed to 'explain' synchronistic events.

Skeptics are fond of bringing up logical fallacy claims when attempting to debunk metaphysical ideas. They like to point out fallacies such as *confirmation bias*, (if you believe in something then you tend to ignore evidence to the contrary; and vice versa, if you don't believe in something, you'll ignore supporting evidence), and *sweeping generalization*, (applying a statement too broadly). The irony is, some skeptics are guilty of using these fallacies themselves.

For example, since certain coincidences are common, (like having the same birthday as someone else at a party), some skeptics immediately latch onto them and use them as evidence to dismiss all synchronicities. That's a sweeping generalization. Not all synchronicities are common, and not all are trivial.

Synchronicities come in many flavors, from the merely curious or amusing, to the truly profound. Of the synchronicities I experienced during the summer, two were of the latter category. The burning candles premonition was quite striking; the wad of paper with the word "Proof" even more so. These cannot be easily explained away. Dismissing the appearance of the wad of paper as merely a random coincidence is, to me, an act of denial. It's a perfect example of confirmation bias: The skeptic is ignoring the evidence—or dare I say it, ignoring the proof.

As mentioned earlier, the probability of a coincidence being high or low is moot anyway. More important is the meaning attached to the coincidence, and whether we take notice. If the coincidences I experienced had occurred at some other time in my life, would they have had such impact? Would I have even noticed? Why were *those* particular coincidences meaningful to me? Why notice them, and not others? That certain coincidences are noticeable and meaningful implies that our perception—our awareness—is involved, and this implies that synchronicities are in part a product of the mind.

In light of this analysis, the bridge between mind and matter begins taking shape. Our minds notice certain tendencies in the patterns of coincidental events, and these are described by the principle of synchronicity. Likewise, matter has certain tendencies that are described by the laws of physics. Neither of these descriptions— that of mind or that of matter—attempt to explain why mind and matter behave the way they do. But the book on synchronicity suggested that mind and matter are part of the same phenomenon— an underlying order to the universe, perhaps similar to the way the particle and wave aspects of light are related in modern physics. A far-fetched idea, to be sure, but an intriguing one.

I spend many hours pondering these topics. I come to no certain conclusions, but my mind is fascinated and engaged. I keep feeling I am close to … well … *grokking* the problem, but the answers always seem out of reach. I have a suspicion the insights I desire will remain partially hidden, and that, like the fog-enshrouded peaks of the Olympic Mountains, I will have to settle for teasing glimpses into the mysteries of life that come my way, and hope for further glimpses in the future.

~ ~ ~

One day I arrive home from work, feeling particularly down. I miss Catherin's delightful yet lonely and sad smile. I miss her warm embrace, her kisses, her caresses, her shining brown eyes. All I have left are the memories—which I've been diligently writing down in a journal—and a few of her things in my possession.

I begin rummaging through those possessions and discover a tape that's a recording of a visit she made to her astrologer, Michael. I recall she had mentioned him once. I play a few minutes of the tape, listening to the conversation between Catherin and this Michael. It's spooky, yet somehow comforting, to hear Catherin's clear, pure, radio-quality voice again. After a while though, I feel uneasy about listening any further—it seems like I'm invading their privacy.

Given my recent insight into astrology, symbols, patterns, and synchronicities, I decide to contact Michael. I want him to do my horoscope and Catherin's as well, particularly for the time period surrounding her death. I find his phone number on the outer case of the tape and call to make an appointment. All I tell him is that I had been Catherin's boyfriend, and I provide my birth particulars. He already knew of Catherin's death.

I go to see Michael a few days later. He first discusses Catherin's chart, generated for the time of her passing:

"I can clearly see indicators of her death," says Michael. "There are a couple of planetary alignments in her transits that definitely point to it."

Transits have to do with the current positions of the planets in relation to their positions on the birth chart. They supposedly indicate tendencies or energies for the time period the transits are computed.

"What are these indicators?" I ask.

"They have to do with the positions of Mars and Uranus," he says. "In simplistic terms, Mars is the symbol of violence, Uranus, our subconscious. Uranus is also associated with death. So we have the indicators of a violent death."

Like Arielle's psychic pronouncements, it's hard to know what to make of these comments. Had Michael constructed a rationale based on knowledge of Catherin's actual death? Did he make it up after the fact? I then remember Catherin mentioning that Michael had said 'major changes' were in store for her that summer. Had he noticed these ominous transits back then? And if so, had he communicated them in detail to her? Is that what her 'Breaking Crayons' story was really about? It would certainly explain her sadness, and her fears that we would soon be apart.

I decide not to ask Michael about this. That there might have been such foreknowledge is too disquieting to dwell on.

Michael continues: "The position of Saturn in Catherin's transit chart is significant. Saturn is associated with karma. She was clearly entering a new karmic cycle in her life."

Michael's mention of karma triggers a memory of jokes that had been made during band practice way back in the spring.

"It's strange you should mention karma," I say. "Members of our band were making tasteless jokes about Ethiopians last spring. Catherin's killer was Ethiopian, and the jokes were made in jest, long before he became her roommate. I had mentioned this to Catherin after he moved in, and she had remarked, 'I guess he's my karma.'"

"That's spooky," says Michael.

"And very unpleasant to think about," I reply.

This strange and morbid coincidence makes us both quiet for a while, and then Michael continues: "You should know that at some level, Catherin knew about her impending death. At some level, she even picked the time of her own passing. I should point out that there are aspects in her chart that were favorable for this. She had reached certain milestones in her life, and had learned important lessons, so it wasn't a bad time for her to leave this earthly plane."

I'm taken aback by these words. "I'm not sure I understand," I say. "And I'm not sure I want to—but proceed."

Michael elaborates further: "The philosophy is that we are here to complete certain tasks, to learn certain lessons, the details of which are unique to each soul. We may not complete these tasks or lessons in a given lifetime, and the soul, along with its spirit guides—or God, if you will—determine the opportune time to transition out of this life."

"So Catherin consciously chose to die the way she did?"

"Not like you are thinking," says Michael. "For each of us, this decision takes place at a subconscious level, and the actual details depend on those around us and the current circumstances of our life. For instance, Catherin's killer was acting under the influence of his own karma."

What Michael is saying is disturbing. It must be showing on my face.

"I know this is a lot to absorb, and it's probably painful," says Michael. "Just be comforted that Catherin is where she needs to be, for her own soul's journey. And so are you."

"How do I figure in all of this?" I ask.

"Your own karma put you in the position of being her boyfriend, of having to go through the hard lessons of losing her. The way to think of it is this: All three of you were at certain points in your own life journeys, with energies, tendencies, and lessons to be learned—karma that is. All of these things combined to trigger the event."

That is indeed a lot to think about, and it puts much strain on me emotionally, but my well of tears is still dry. I wonder if that well will ever fill up again.

"That's all I can handle right now about Catherin," I say. "Maybe you could go over my chart."

Michael pulls my chart out of a folder, and reviews notes he had made prior to the interview. He makes comments that are similar to ones Catherin had made: That a strong Virgo coupled with a strong Mercury means talent in the areas of communication, computers, music, and anything analytical that involves attention to detail and focus. I have an eye for art and beauty, and a tendency to be self-centered, secretive, and a loner. The influence of my sun sign in Leo is there, but perhaps is not expressed directly.

Michael continues with his assessment: "The thing that really strikes me about your chart is that you are here to learn mind over matter. In fact, there are certain angles in your chart that indicate it's something you are supposed to master in this lifetime."

I catch my breath.

"It's funny you should bring that up," I say. "I've been reading a book on synchronicity, sub-titled 'A Bridge Between Matter and Mind.'"

"What a coincidence!" he says.

"I've been experiencing a lot of those lately, it seems."

I tell Michael about the strange coincidences surrounding Catherin's death.

"The wad of paper printed with the word 'Proof' was the most uncanny," I say. "And the picture of a white dove flying through the clouds, the most comforting."

"That's interesting," Michael replies. "What do you suppose it all means?"

"I don't know," I say, swiveling in the chair, glancing across the room to an adjoining hallway.

Hanging on the wall is that picture of a white dove, flying through the clouds.

Chapter 26.

Frozen in Time

September, 1987

Round and round the empty lot I go, forming a path of trampled weeds. If I were to stop a little short each time around, before turning and starting a new circuit, I could cover the whole lot, spiraling inwards like a tractor in a field of Nebraska summer fallow. I muse about this, while also dreaming a daydream—the same daydream I've had all summer: those few sweet months with Catherin.

It's hot out, already 100 degrees, even though it's only lunch time. Ah, yes, the dog days of an Arizona summer. Who doesn't relish them? And speaking of lunch time, I really ought to get back to work. My air-conditioned office is only a few blocks away, across several empty lots like this one, all destined to become yet another Scottsdale office park. I decide to make one more loop before heading back.

Air-conditioning sounds good—but sitting in front of the computer? Not so much. Even though I now have a dream job, and even though I'm still working only part-time, my heart is not into it. More often than not, instead of looking at the computer screen, paying attention to the code displayed there, I'm staring out the window, reminiscing about the days with Catherin. Those days were the best of my life, and made all others seem dull, drab, and mundane.

As I make that last loop around the empty lot, a song from the Laurie Lewis album comes to me, written by one of my favorite bluegrass artists, Tim O'Brien. The song is titled *Hold to a Dream*, and talks about being "frozen in time."

Hold to a dream. Frozen in time. That's exactly how I feel. I'm not in the present at all, let alone planning for the future. My mind is frozen in the past, back when Catherin was alive. With frozen thoughts like these, I have no room for new ones, and since my job involves mostly thinking, there's a problem. My job performance has been pathetic. Deep down I know this, but such is the state I'm in that I pay little heed.

Though I work in north Scottsdale, I still live in Tempe. It makes for a long commute. The twenty-five unsynchronized stoplights I encounter each way (I counted them once) are driving me crazy. I need to move closer to work, and moving might also break me out of the stupor I'm in, nudging me into the present, where I belong. So I begin searching for an apartment closer to work. By the middle of September I find one. Since moving involves signing another lease, I want to make sure my job is secure—that I can start working full-time. I go to see my boss Ray about it the next day.

I knock on his door and hear him yell to come in. Ray likes to keep the lights off, and the shades of his office window to the outside are partially drawn. As I open the door, I see him swivel around in his chair. His long, straight, silvery hair is backlit by the large computer monitor off to the side, the glow framing his dark silhouette. A peace-pipe, complete with feathers and totems, lies next to his keyboard.

"Could I interrupt you for a second?" I ask, as I stand in his doorway.

Ray gives me a confused but amused look.

"Well, what am I to say to that?" he asks. "You've already interrupted me by knocking on my door and asking the question."

He gives me a wry, ironic smile that's his trademark, and motions me to sit down across the desk from him.

Ray is very intelligent and just as crazy. That makes him a great guy to work for and we get along well. Being a Karuk Indian, his viewpoints and problem solving methods are very different from those I am used to. He works on "Indian time" he likes to say, sometimes leaving problems alone because, as he says, "It's not yet time" to solve them—a striking contrast to Catherin's "Don't waste time" mindset.

"So what did you want to see me about?" asks Ray, as he props up his bare feet on the desk. "I'm hoping it's because you've made a breakthrough with Grok."

"Grok is still very much a work in progress," I say, hesitating. "Okay, I admit, I haven't gotten very far with it."

"I'm only too aware of that."

"I could start working full-time," I say. "I found an apartment nearby, and I'm thinking of moving there."

Ray stares across the darkness, the glint in his eyes reflecting the light of the computer screen—and his eyes are uncomfortably penetrating.

"We-ee-ll," he says, slowly drawing out the word as he likes to do, "the problem is, I'm not sure I want you to."

"You don't want me to … what … work full-time?"

There is a long pause as Ray picks up and fiddles with his peace pipe. "I'm not sure I want you working here at all."

"Oh, I see," I say, slumping back in the chair. "Have I done something wrong?"

I say this innocently, but I'm not fooling anybody, least of all myself. I know exactly what the problem is.

"Well, you haven't produced much work since you started here," Ray says. "I know you have extenuating circumstances, but we can't afford to keep paying you to get over them."

He's right, of course. And the darkness I feel isn't entirely due to the lights being off in his office. I'm in danger of losing my job. How will I survive? I could end up homeless and all alone.

Is this the whack of the cosmic two-by-four my former boss had warned me about? But why now? Why this way? First I lose Catherin, and then I find a new job—a job that had been handed to me on a silver platter, it seems. Am I to be given this job miraculously, only to have it taken away a few months later? What sort of convoluted purpose is behind that?

Maybe I should become a hermit and go live in the mountains somewhere. That has always had some appeal. Yes, out in the wilderness, where I wouldn't have to deal with people, and wouldn't have to worry about losing another companion, or losing a job, and—

"It's not yet time to panic," says Ray, interrupting my fevered thinking, almost as if he knew my thoughts.

"If you finish certain tasks by October," he continues, "we can talk again about your working full-time. Otherwise, I'll have to let you go."

Ray outlines the tasks. I accept his challenge and leave for the day.

Back home, I pace back and forth from room to room, worrying about my fate. Needing some solace—and some good advice, I call up a friend I once worked for as a software contractor. He knew me well enough to make an objective assessment of my predicament.

"It's like I was handed this job on a silver platter, only to have it taken away," I say to my friend, after explaining the situation to him. "What do you suppose it means?"

"You're just being tested," he says.

That has to be it. I had been given a free gift in the form of this job, and now I have to show that I am worthy of it.

The situation I found myself in reminded me of one I had back in my undergraduate days at the University of Nebraska:

I was studying engineering, and was taking a course in electronics. The instructor, though well intentioned, was a lousy teacher, and I learned practically nothing during the semester. His tests didn't seem to have anything to do with his lectures. I found myself, a straight A student otherwise, in the situation of having only a forty percent average going into the finals. In other words, I was flunking the course.

I went to see the instructor a week before finals.

"What are my chances for passing this course?" I asked the professor, wondering if he thought my question some sort of twisted humor.

He told me his surprising policy: "Whatever you get on the final will be your grade for the course."

"Even if I'm flunking right now?"

"Regardless of your grade coming in, unless it's higher, then the final will be thrown out."

"Let me see if I have this straight. You mean to tell me if I get a hundred on the final then I get an A in the course?"

"If you get a ninety percent or higher, you get an A," the professor corrected.

I knew immediately what I had to do. I went home and crammed like never before. I wasn't used to having to cram, because usually I was on top of my courses. I did know how to study for tests, though, which had pulled me out of scrapes before. I learned more in one week than I had the whole semester. I took the final, and when the results came back, I had scored a ninety-eight, missing two points on a stupid arithmetic error.

Well, here I am, in Scottsdale, Arizona, ten years later, in much the same situation. It is finals week—put up or shut up time. I put aside all thoughts of Catherin and buckle down to work. I go ahead and sign a lease on the new apartment, even though I'm still not guaranteed a full-time job. But I am confident I will pass this new test. And surely, the universe will continue to look after me like it had all summer, won't it?

Chapter 27.
The Green Fields of Earth

October, 1987

A pleasant breeze filters through the museum grounds as I pace nervously, fiddle in hand, behind the gazebo being used as a stage. The audience on the lawn claps after a band finishes the last tune in their set. They clamber down the steps behind the stage and pass by.

"It's your turn," says the stage manager to the three of us. "You guys ready?"

I look over to Robyn and Scooter. They give confirming nods.

"As ready as we'll ever be," I say.

We climb onto stage. Robyn props her guitar on the back railing and finishes unpacking her fiddle. Scooter rosins his handmade bow, and I pluck the strings of my fiddle like a mandolin, surveying the medium-sized audience relaxing in lawn chairs under the mixed shade of pine and cottonwood trees.

It's a beautiful fall afternoon in Prescott, Arizona, at the Sharlot Hall Museum, during the *Sharlot Hall Folk Music Festival*; just a few blocks away from Whiskey Row, the section of downtown where Prescott gained notoriety in its earlier years. Prescott is now a peaceful town filled with Victorian-style houses and a cooler, more relaxed lifestyle than the hot, sprawling suburbs of Phoenix that lie ninety miles away and some four thousand feet lower.

While stage hands adjust our microphones, I play a few double stops on the fiddle as a final tuning check. The three of us line up well behind the microphones. I take a deep breath and let out a sigh.

"You're not nervous are you?" asks Robyn.

"You think I'd be used to performing on stage," I say, "but it's been awhile."

"You'll be fine," interjects Scooter. "Besides, the old-timey tunes we're doing don't have more than three or four notes to worry about anyway."

Sporting his salt and pepper beard and wild, graying, curly hair, Scooter laughs at his own joke, and I laugh with him.

A month earlier, Robyn had called to invite me over to play tunes and to inform me—with relief evident in her voice—that Scooter had returned from his summer wanderings. He was fresh back from the *Old Time Fiddler's Convention* in Galax, Virginia, with a bevy of new tunes to spring on us. The particular old-timey style that Scooter likes is characterized by driving, rhythmic bowing and the use of double stops, often played using resonance-enhancing, open cross-tunings, with less emphasis placed on individual notes, which are pared down to just an outline of the melody—hence the joke about tunes having only three or four notes to worry about.

During the course of September, I had gone over to Robyn's house to learn some of these tunes from Scooter. On one visit, Robyn asked if I would like to join them for a performance at the Sharlot Hall festival. I said yes, hoping it would break me out of the spell that Catherin's death had cast over the summer. I felt frozen in time, not quite able to break free and move on with my life. And I hadn't performed on stage since *Dusty River's* last performance—well, other than a few tunes at the festival-ending concert in Port Townsend, and the coffeehouse in Victoria.

The emcee announces our band, and we step up to the microphones. I look over to the others to see if they are ready to begin. With a relaxed smile on her face, Robyn seems happier now than on our trip to Port Townsend, when she had lamented the absence of Scooter—who had left for the summer without making a promise he would return. As I had noted to her then, Robyn's loss was possibly only temporary. Scooter being on stage now serves as confirmation of that.

I have no such luck. My friend, my soul mate, is gone permanently—at least from ordinary view. She may still exist in some form; a wad of paper printed with the word "Proof" provides haunting evidence of that. Is her spirit on stage with me now? A wave of emotion sweeps over me and my eyes moisten. It figures my tears would wait all summer to return, only to come back now, on stage.

Wiping away the tears, I try to regain my composure and focus on the task at hand. Robyn nods for me to begin. I tap my foot to calibrate an appropriate tempo and start the 'four potatoes' to kick things off. For our first number, we choose one of the old-timey tunes Scooter had brought back from Galax. I play fiddle with Scooter while Robyn backs us on guitar.

Many of the old-timey tunes are like hypnotic mantras. With their driving rhythms, it's easy to get lost in the music and lose track of time. Fortunately that doesn't happen now. After a few rounds Scooter raises his foot off the ground—the universal band signal to end a tune.

We perform a few more old-timey tunes and then switch gears completely, with just Robyn and me on fiddles. We play a Swedish 'walking tune' that Robyn had learned during a workshop in Port Townsend, and for our finale, we play as a duet the *Waltz of the Little Girls*. In my head I still hear this tune in three-part harmony, as we had first heard it at the coffeehouse in Victoria. We can't duplicate those triple harmonies, but I try my best to invent a harmony line, on the fly. I'm not sure about my success.

"Oot-oooo-weee-hooo!" I can hear Bubba and Mrs. Bubba say to me in my memories. "So you think you can play music!"

To a scattering of applause, we bow to the audience and step off stage.

"I'm glad you decided to play with us," says Robyn, as we pack our instruments away. "Your harmonies sounded good on that last waltz."

"Thanks," I say. "I wasn't sure how I'd do. You know, it was hard playing on stage without Catherin."

"I thought I saw a tear or two," says Robyn.

"It's alright," I say. "At least I feel human again."

Robyn and Scooter go off on their own to attend a workshop. I find an available spot on the lawn near the gazebo and lie down, using my fiddle case as a pillow of sorts, content to close my eyes and listen to a few other bands. A Cajun band is playing when someone taps me on the leg. I look up to see the familiar face of Jessie, her long, straight, black hair swishing in the breeze. A fiddle case dangles from her shoulder.

"Well I'll be damned," I say, rising up to give her a hug. "I haven't seen you in a while. What are you doing here in Prescott?"

"Visiting my family," she says, "and escaping jail for an afternoon."

I give her a puzzled look. Jessie laughs.

"This is as good an excuse as any to get away from the loud, smoky bars I have to play in all the time," she says.

"I see. The dues you pay to become a star."

"You got that right."

"Are you still playing at the *Salt River Saloon?*"

"Yes," says Jessie, slowly sighing. "It gets kind of old." Her eyes brighten. "But hey, we did have fun yesterday. We played at a country music festival in Phoenix."

"Really? I hadn't heard about it."

"It was downtown."

"Wish I could have been there to see you play."

"You missed quite an event. And not just local bands were playing, either. Waylon Jennings was there." Jessie beams. "It was thrilling to be on the same stage."

"Wow," I say with an approving nod. "I'm impressed."

"I suppose I should add we weren't on stage at the same time," Jessie says, laughing. She adjusts the strap of her fiddle case and motions with her arm.

"Come with me while I look for one of the bands playing today. Do you remember the *Tempe Ramblers?*"

"Of course I do."

The *Tempe Ramblers* were comprised mainly of two brothers, plus a few other members. Jessie once rented a room in their family house and that's where my early lessons were held.

"I remember the first time I heard you play a fiddle tune on your cello with those guys," I say to Jessie. "Until then, I didn't know bluegrass on cello was possible. And you know, it was great inspiration when you all would invite me to jam, even though I only knew about two tunes at the time."

Jessie laughs and says, "That seems so long ago."

"It seems like a lifetime to me," I say.

Indeed it does seem like a lifetime. Catherin's passing had divided my life in half: before Catherin, after Catherin.

As we search the museum grounds for Jessie's friends, she says, "Someone else was at the country music festival that you would have enjoyed seeing."

"Oh? Who was that?"

"Laurie Lewis. Didn't you mention her music to me once?"

I freeze in my tracks.

Laurie Lewis. The songs on her album had been my theme music throughout the summer. They would transport me back in time, back to when Catherin was alive, and back to our camping trip in Zion National Park. It was then we had come to appreciate Laurie's music. Indeed, we had played a tape of her music virtually the whole time. After having worn out that tape, I was sure glad to have found a copy of the album while in California during the summer.

I relate all this to Jessie, and she holds my arm as we continue along.

"It's really something that Laurie Lewis was in Phoenix," I say. "I can't believe I missed a chance to see her in person."

"I'm sure there will be other opportunities," says Jessie.

We round a corner and see a crowd gathered on the porch of one of the historic buildings dotting the museum grounds. The *Tempe Ramblers* are in the midst of that crowd, tuning their instruments.

"There they are," says Jessie as she spots her friends. "Let's go jam with them. I want to hear you play—see if you've improved any." She laughs and punches my shoulder in jest.

We cross over to the porch and say hello. It turns out the *Tempe Ramblers* are warming up for their turn on stage, but they let us join their practice anyway. We pull out instruments and wouldn't you know, they pick the very tune that is my nemesis: *Blackberry Blossom*. I never could play it the way I wanted. I wondered if I ever would. As I fumble through the notes, Jessie plays in the style unique to her: standing up, but with her fiddle propped on a knee, playing the instrument like a cello.

Other than at a few jam sessions at the *Telluride Bluegrass Festival*, I hadn't played bluegrass much during the summer, now mostly focusing on contra dance music. My appreciation for the dance music is growing, and my abilities are more suited to its style, but the old familiar bluegrass tunes sound good to my ears. I miss hearing and playing the mix of blues, jazz, and old-time folk music that makes up bluegrass.

Soon it's time for the *Tempe Ramblers* to play their set on stage, and they pack up and head for the gazebo.

"Gosh, Bry, I'd like to stay longer," says Jessie as we put our fiddles away. "But I've got to get back to Phoenix for a gig tonight."

"I guess that's the problem with being a *star*," I say, emphasizing the word *star* for humorous effect. "You don't own your own weekends, do you? Well, I'm sorry to see you go. I'll try to catch your band playing some time."

"Please do. And take care, Bry." Jessie gives me a hug, slings her fiddle over her shoulder, and walks away, leaving me standing there all alone.

The *Tempe Ramblers* start their set. I haven't seen Robyn or Scooter for a while and don't know where they are, so I scan the crowd for anyone else I might know, without success. I spy an empty patch of grass on the main lawn not far from the gazebo, near the south end, where a grassy berm rises into a natural backrest. Claiming the spot, I lean back and close my eyes, soaking up the bluegrass music; the sounds of which take me back to the days of Catherin, and leave me feeling nostalgic and blue.

After the *Tempe Ramblers* finish, the emcee steps on stage and makes an announcement.

"Folks, I've got a little surprise for you," he tells the audience. "The band just leaving was supposed to be the last for the day, but I've been informed there will be one more performance."

Hmm, I say to myself. *I wonder who this could be.*

"This group has just come up from Phoenix and was on their way to Flagstaff when they decided to swing by our lovely little town. They have agreed to play a few minutes. So friends, please welcome *Laurie Lewis* and the *Grant Street String Band!*"

My jaw drops open. Popping out of nowhere and stepping on stage is Laurie Lewis, the rest of her band not far behind. Amazed, I search the crowd, looking unsuccessfully for anyone I can share this incredible moment with. I give up and quickly claim an empty chair near the front row, as close as possible to the gazebo. No way am I going to miss any part of this show.

The *Grant Street String Band* plays their brand of bluegrass for half an hour. I know most of their songs by heart, and sing along in a whisper, rocking my head up and down and side to side, like some people do when singing to the radio in their car. I also tap a syncopated rhythm on my knees, as any drummer would.

After the band finishes and leaves the stage, I am momentarily frozen in my chair, trying to summon up the courage to go and find Laurie Lewis—to thank her for her music, and to tell her what it means to me.

"Don't waste time!" I can hear Catherin say in my memories. This prompts me out of the chair and around the back of the gazebo. I join a small line that has formed in front of a table where Laurie is selling records and tapes.

When my turn comes, I put my fiddle case down and say to Laurie, "I'm glad you decided to swing by Prescott and play here today. I'm a big fan."

She looks at me for a moment and says, "Oh yes, you were the one I saw out there singing words to all my songs."

My face flushes at the thought of standing out so much. "I know those songs by heart," I say. "I have your *Restless Rambling Heart* album, and listen to it all the time."

"I'm glad you like it," she says.

I want to say more, but how can I put all the things I am thinking and feeling into a few words? I look up through the trees and see the clear blue sky. There are no roaming thunderheads ready to pounce and call me a "fool" should I flounder. The monsoon season is long over. But I don't need the thunderstorms prodding me anymore. The events of the past year have made me less shy, or at least, I like to think so.

"I'm sure you hear this all the time," I finally say to Laurie, "but you have no idea what your music has meant to me, and what it means to see you here today."

I briefly tell her the story of Catherin, and how the music on her album is somehow intertwined in it all. Laurie seems moved by this and gives me a consoling hug.

I make way for the next person in line, but linger close by while Laurie sells records and tapes. She glances at me from time to time, acting as though she isn't quite sure what to do with me. I'm not quite sure what to do with me either.

The line dwindles down, giving Laurie more time for me. She notices the fiddle case on the ground by my side.

"You play the fiddle?" she asks.

"Well, I try," I say, eyes lowering momentarily. "I played in a bluegrass band with my late girlfriend. Your music was an inspiration to both of us."

I stand frozen, my shyness taking hold again. I try to think of a way to keep the conversation going. A gust of wind helps, blowing through the shimmering leaves of the cottonwood tree overhead. That's it. That's my cue.

"I really like your song about the tree," I say to Laurie. "The one where you play the hardingfele, the Norwegian fiddle?"

"Oh, you mean *Maple's Lament.*"

"Yes. What a haunting song. It gave me and my girlfriend goose bumps whenever we listened to it."

Maple's Lament is indeed a haunting song, for it tells the story of a maple tree that is ultimately cut down, its wood transformed into stringed instruments—"bound so tight in wired strings" as the song goes. The dead tree mourns over its inability to feel the wind and rain, and takes solace in memories of sunlight dancing on its leaves. For me, during the course of the summer and early fall, the symbolism of death and transformation portrayed in the song had transmuted from that of a maple's lament, to Catherin's lament, on her loss of life.

Laurie becomes busy selling records and tapes again, so I move out of her way. I overhear her telling someone that she is playing in Flagstaff the following Wednesday. I find and grab one of the concert flyers from the table. I make up my mind to go to that concert no matter what.

On the drive back to Phoenix, the melody and lyrics of *Maple's Lament* reverberate through me, sending me back in time to that magical drive with Catherin through the plateaus of southern Utah, under endless starry skies; a waxing moon setting on the western horizon. Contrasting these bittersweet memories is the excitement and amazement of the chance meeting with Laurie Lewis, author of that melody and those lyrics.

~ ~ ~

It's Wednesday. I'm on my way to Flagstaff and the Laurie Lewis concert. I hadn't wanted to drive up alone, but ultimately I didn't bother to ask anyone else. I didn't think I'd find anyone crazy enough to drive to Flagstaff with me after work, mid-week, and then come right back afterwards in the middle of the night.

I reach the streets of Flagstaff by eight-thirty, and make my way downtown to where Laurie Lewis is playing, at a pub located on the ground floor of the historic *Hotel Weatherford*. I park on a nearby side street, and walk over to the hotel and peer through the windows. Not many people have arrived yet. I don't feel like waiting inside—bars aren't my scene, so back to the pickup I go. There, I wait in silence, the windshield separating me from the real world and all the people strolling by on the sidewalk. It seems I'm always doing this: looking through the windows of life, just like at the Christmas party nearly a year ago—longing to participate, but being held back by my own inhibitions.

I resolve to break free of these old habits once and for all. I climb out of the pickup again and cross the street to the pub. I've almost waited too long—the place has quickly filled. Fortunately, I find the last empty table and promptly claim it.

Within minutes I feel isolated once more. There's no one here I know, and I see everyone paired off into couples—everyone except me. *It isn't supposed to be this way anymore*, I say to myself. Similar thoughts had occurred at the Telluride festival, right before Jean and Joan had sat down in front of me. But no such luck this time.

The band strikes up their first number. Laurie has a strong voice and plays a fast and powerful fiddle. Even so, her performance is almost lost in the sea of chatter that makes up this typical, crowded bar. Not many people seem to notice she is playing. It's just an ordinary night on the town, to them.

Pay attention! I want to say to the crowd. *This is not ordinary. This is important!*

Well, at least it is to me.

At intermission I pick my way through the maze of tables and head towards the stage. I find Laurie sitting at a table nearby with the rest of her band.

"Oh yes, I remember you," she says, after I introduce myself. "Why don't you sit with us?" She motions towards an empty chair at her table.

Laurie introduces me to the members of her band. I feel honored to be sitting at the table as an invited guest. She makes out a song list for her next set and looks up to ask, "Do you have any requests?"

I know my answer immediately.

"Could you play the one about the green fields?"

"That's a good one," she says, adding the song to her list.

Midway through the next set, Laurie plays my request. As soon as I hear the sweet strains of *Green Fields*, shivers course down my spine. I have a hard time believing all this is happening. Here I am, sitting at the table of the very author of *Green Fields*, at her invitation, listening to her sing it live, at my request.

The lyrics of *Green Fields* will always remind me of Catherin and her dissatisfaction with living in the sprawling desert city called Phoenix; a long way—in both time and space—from the green fields of her youth on a farm in western Pennsylvania. She had expressed a desire to live in a smaller, more peaceful place, with a close circle of friends—the way life should be. Even so, she had found her peace, her patch of green, right in the midst of a vast desert metropolis, at a place she called the Magic Farm. Alas, the green fields surrounding the Magic Farm are being devoured by the so-called march of progress. And now that Catherin has passed from this earthly plane, where are her green fields now?

~ ~ ~

After the concert I make my way up front, where Laurie is selling records and tapes. I pick a copy of *Restless Rambling Heart* off the table.

"I already have this," I say to Laurie, handing her the album. "But I want to buy another so you can autograph it."

Laurie looks at me for a moment and then signs the cover. She hands back the album, saying, "Here, I'll just give it to you."

"You don't have to do that," I say. "But thanks."

I read her autograph: "Many thanks for listening."

I look up and nod appreciatively. "And many thanks for your music. This will always be special to me."

It's past midnight when I drive south along the freeway back to Phoenix. On both sides of the road mysterious canyons beckon. I can almost appreciate them again, though not with the ease and worry-free simplicity of more innocent times. But I'm okay with that. I know someday my heart will once again embrace the beauty of the mountains and canyons, in deeper and more meaningful ways. I know someday my heart will know peace and contentment. I'm already starting to feel it.

~ ~ ~

During the next few days I'm distracted, not able to focus at work. I can't get the surprising events of the past week out of my mind. One evening, with Catherin very much in my thoughts, I make a pilgrimage to the Magic Farm. In the darkening twilight, I crunch alongside the graveled canal, eastward below the hi-tech power lines that stand as counterpoint to the low-tech cluster of dilapidated buildings that make up the farm.

"I can feel the vibrations of your spirit," Catherin had once said to me under these power lines.

"I can feel your spirit with me now," I say to her, whispering.

I turn south along the intersecting canal, and partway down I stop to face the west. A cacophony of chirps, hoots, and whistles come from the trees and tall bushes that line the eastern edge of the property. Numerous peacocks perch atop the water tower, in silhouette against the twilight sky—the way I will always see them in my mind.

Memories swirl by: hope, joy, sorrow—a jumble of thoughts and feelings, music and song, interlaced with teasing glimpses into the unknown, as made manifest by a remarkable series of synchronicities. The surprise appearance of Laurie Lewis at the Sharlot Hall festival was the culmination of this extraordinary set: The burning candles premonition involving the Magic Farm; the dizzying sensation of simultaneously saying hello and goodbye to Catherin on the last day of her life; the *Riders in the Sky* tape and its strange relationship to recent dramatic events in my life; the crossing of two jets in the sky as they bring Catherin's body out on a stretcher; the peacocks with their feathers raised right after her death; the picture of a white dove flying through the clouds that seems to appear at auspicious moments; the white dove that flies by my pickup on the way to Telluride when I am feeling especially down; and the extremely odd coincidence of a wad of paper that falls out of my dresser with the word "Proof" printed on it, after I had asked Catherin for proof of her continued existence.

Gazing westward towards the water tower, I blink my eyes and capture the scene, adding it to my chain of recursive memories. I really hadn't expected the Magic Farm to last this long, thinking it would have been torn down by now, but somehow, it is still here. Maybe it truly is a magical place. Alas, many of the green fields are gone, and the big cottonwood tree we used to sit under is no more, having been cut down sometime during the summer.

Crossing the bridge at the intersection of the two canals, I say goodbye to the farm and stroll westward along the dry canal. The last time I had walked this way, I had been carrying a torch and had set it down at the west end, as final witness and guard to the Magic Farm. I have no such torch tonight, but I know the Magic Farm does not need guarding anymore. It will always be with me.

The streets of Catherin's neighborhood are only a little further, and I end my pilgrimage on the dark sidewalk in front of her house. The candles of my memories cause a flickering of light and shadow across the front door, which no longer opens to her cheerful presence and warm embrace.

I look up into the night sky, recalling the two jets that had crossed when they brought out Catherin's body. At the time, I knew somehow it was her jet, her spirit, flying west into the clouds, and that mine was the jet heading northwest, away from the clouds, still bound to this life. And now I imagine Catherin, the dark-haired, white mountain bike woman, looking down past the muttering thunderheads to the green fields of Earth, her spirit singing:

> *Where are my green fields now?*
> *No, nowhere around*
> *So I'll steal away, with my memories*
> *And in green fields, I'll lay me down.*

~ ~ ~ — ~ ~ ~

Epilogue

A summer's eve, 1988

It's been a year since Catherin's passing, and memories of our time together grow distant. But tonight, she's on my mind. Hearing excellent fiddle music at a house concert—featuring Kevin Burke, a world-class Irish fiddler—has left me feeling nostalgic and blue, a feeling not unfamiliar, but not as frequent these days.

Too bad you couldn't be at the concert, I say to Catherin in my thoughts, as I wind my way up Tatum Boulevard, heading home through scenic Paradise Valley. *Oh, how I wish we were still together ...*

An intersection comes into view. Since the light is green I hold a steady speed. Then I see something out the corner of my eye. Another white dove? Nope. It's a Chevy Blazer coming from the left—and on an immediate collision course.

There's no way to avoid hitting the Blazer. I don't apply my brakes very hard. At forty-five miles per hour, there's little point. Right before T-boning the Blazer, time slows down, and I see my life flash before my eyes. Is this it? Has my number come up?

That's not exactly what I meant about us being together! I say in my thoughts, just before impact.

Though the front of my truck gets demolished, I come out unscathed, other than having a sore neck. The other driver is charged with a DUI—and for running a red light.

In some respects, this accident wasn't unexpected. I had a dream about it, a premonition of sorts, just a week before. In the dream, *I* was the one at fault, and it was I who was charged with a DUI. Witnesses kept asking why I hadn't used my brakes. In the days following the dream, I was nervous about driving, sensing an impact waiting to happen, flinching any time a car got too close.

Did I really have a premonition? Sure seems that way, though some of the facts were backwards. But I guess I should pay more attention to my dreams, and be more careful of any requests made to the universe.

Afterword

Many years have passed since the events of this story took place. In this memoir I have tried to faithfully record the circumstances, thoughts, and feelings of that time, and to remain true to the memories of conversations with Catherin. A journal started after her death helped tremendously in this effort.

I've also faithfully portrayed the insights into metaphysics and spirituality I had back then. These views aren't necessarily ones I hold today, though they are not that different. Today's are more refined—at I least I like to think so. These days, my main focus has been on the practice of yoga. It's the most sober-minded approach I've found in sorting out the puzzle of how our mind relates to this mysterious world filled with matter and spirit. Indeed, yoga is often called the "science of the mind."

I still carry a healthy amount of skepticism about things, but it's also in my nature to keep an open mind, to always be questioning, to always be searching. Sometimes, as Catherin suggested to me in song, I let my heart decide and not my mind. Decisions still don't come easy for me, though. Dang moon in Gemini. Even today, it's hard to rule out various explanations for the synchronistic events I experienced that fateful summer.

Writing this memoir was a great catharsis for me, lessening significantly the emotional impact of Catherin's death. That doesn't mean I'll ever forget her—she will always hold a special place in my heart. But other than the innumerable hours spent working on this manuscript, the shock, sadness, and grief of her passing have faded into the background of my current life.

I'm now happily married and live in the Phoenix valley. I still make the trek to the Magic Farm from time to time. Amazingly, it is still there, after all these years.

Notes

References

Books that contributed to the viewpoints I had back in the day:

Gödel, Escher, Bach: an Eternal Golden Braid, Douglas R. Hofstadter, 1979.
Metamagical Themas: Questing for the Essence of Mind and Pattern, Douglas R. Hofstadter, 1985.
The Teachings of Don Juan: A Yaqui Way of Knowledge, Carlos Castaneda, 1974.
The Fire from Within, Carlos Castaneda, 1984.
The Mists of Avalon, Marion Zimmer Bradley, 1983.
The Road Less Traveled, M. Scott Peck, M.D., 1978.
Synchronicity: The Bridge Between Matter and Mind, F. David Peat, 1987.

Recordings that shaped the tone of this story, ranging from blue-grass to western to new-age to jazz to southern rock:

Restless Rambling Heart, Laurie Lewis, 1986.
Hot Rize/Red Knuckles and the Trailblazers Live — In Concert, Hot Rize, 1982.
Riders in the Sky, Live, Riders in the Sky, 1984.
Timeless Motion, Daniel Kobialka, 1982.
Summer Suite, Teja Bell and Jon Bernoff, Marc Allen, Robert Powell, 1983.
Natural Light, Steven Halpern and Dallas Smith, 1984.
As Falls Wichita, so Falls Wichita Falls, Pat Metheny and Lyle Mays, 1981.
Carolina Dreams, Marshall Tucker Band, 1977.

You too can write a memoir

This project started as a journal, slowly evolving into a memoir over a span of some twenty-plus years. At one point, I realized I had enough material for a full-length book, and began wondering if I was capable of finishing the effort. I looked for any 'how-to-write' books that might help in this regard. That search proved frustrating, for time and again the books would recommend staying away from publishing anything about yourself.

"Unless you are a celebrity," these supposedly helpful books would say, "nobody wants to hear about your life." They suggested writing fiction instead. Apparently, a story about fictional events and characters is deemed more interesting and more important than a story about true events and real people. Dismayed by this attitude, I made it a point not to buy any of these particular 'how-to' books.

They say truth is stranger than fiction, and that certainly fits this story. Had I written it as pure fiction, it would not have been believable. Coincidences don't work in fiction. So I made an effort to keep the story as true as possible, only changing names and other details to protect the privacy of others.

But this led to confusion. I wanted to write about true events, dramatized with narrative and dialogue. Like fiction, yet not. None of the 'how-to' books addressed this scenario, so I was left to my own devices. After numerous drafts of questionable quality, I eventually found help in my endeavors, in a book tailored specifically towards writing memoirs: *Writing Life Stories*, by Bill Roorbach.

Rather than give the 'helpful' advice of "Don't bother," Roorbach's book *encourages* you to write your life story, and explores numerous ways to make your writing be its best. This book gave the style I was striving for a name: *creative non-fiction*. With this knowledge I was able to proceed, confident I now had the tools to take on the monumental task of writing 110,000 coherent words. I was able to employ all the standard methods for creating a good story: carefully crafting scenes, balancing exposition with narrative and believable dialogue, and giving the story a cohesive overall structure that keeps the reader engaged.

Along with Roorbach's helpful book, here's a list of others I can whole-heartedly recommend:

Writing Life Stories, Bill Roorbach, 1998.
The Creative Writer's Style Guide, Christopher T. Leland, 2002.
Scene & Structure, Jack M. Bickham, 1993.
Writing Dialogue, Tom Chiarella, 1998.
Beginnings, Middles & Ends, Nancy Kress, 1993.

These days, with a wealth of information available on the Internet, there are plenty of other places to find help in writing your life story, and in getting your story published. And it's not about vanity. We all have life experiences to share that can be of help and interest to others. There's nothing wrong with that. So what are you waiting for?

About the Author

Bryan Flamig is an engineer and computer scientist, having graduated from the University of Nebraska and Arizona State University. He's also a writer, and besides this first novel, has written numerous books on C++ programming. He plays fiddle and percussion in a local contra dance band, and also enjoys cycling, photography, and yoga. Bryan is married and lives in the Phoenix valley with his wife Leslie and Goldendoodle named Ki Jai.

CPSIA information can be obtained at www.ICGtesting.com
Printed in the USA
BVOW021742020212

281920BV00012B/1/P